# GOD, MIND AND KNOWLEDGE

# The British Society for the Philosophy of Religion Series

*Series Editor:*
Harriet A. Harris, University of Edinburgh, UK

*Series Advisory Board:*
Robin Le Poidevin; Andrew Moore; Yujin Nagasawa; Christopher Hamilton;
Oliver Crisp; John Taylor; John Cottingham; Brian Leftow;
Richard Swinburne; Roger Trigg

Philosophy of religion is undergoing a fascinating period of development and transformation. Public interest is growing as the power of religion for both good and ill is becoming ever more apparent, as energetic forms of atheism open up the public imagination to many philosophical questions about God, and as fresh perspectives and questions arise due to the unprecedented level of interaction between different religious faiths. The British Society for the Philosophy of Religion harnesses, reflects and further promotes these interests, within the UK and internationally. The BSPR is the UK's main forum for the interchange of ideas in the philosophy of religion. This series, in association with the BSPR, presents books devoted to themes of major concern within the field of philosophy of religion – books which will significantly shape contemporary debate around key themes both nationally and internationally.

*Other titles in the series*

***God, Goodness and Philosophy***
Edited by Harriet A. Harris

# God, Mind and Knowledge

ANDREW MOORE

*Regent's Park College, University of Oxford, UK*

ASHGATE

Published by
Ashgate Publishing Limited
Wey Court East
Union Road
Farnham
Surrey, GU9 7PT
England

Ashgate Publishing Company
110 Cherry Street
Suite 3-1
Burlington, VT 05401-3818
USA

www.ashgate.com

**British Library Cataloguing in Publication Data**
A catalogue record for this book is available from the British Library

**The Library of Congress has cataloged the printed edition as follows:**
God, mind and knowledge / edited by Andrew Moore.
  pages cm. – (The British Society for the Philosophy of Religion series)
  Includes index.
  ISBN 978-1-4094-6208-8 (hardcover) – ISBN 978-1-4094-6210-1 (pbk) – ISBN 978-1-4094-6209-5 (ebook) – ISBN 978-1-4724-0756-6 (epub)  1. Religion–Philosophy.  I. Moore, Andrew.
  BL51.G6835 2014
  210–dc23

2013031410

ISBN 9781409462088 (hbk)
ISBN 9781409462101 (pbk)
ISBN 9781409462095 (ebk – PDF)
ISBN 9781472407566 (ePUB – PDF)

Printed in the United Kingdom by Henry Ling Limited, at the Dorset Press, Dorchester, DT1 1HD

# Contents

# Acknowledgements

This book has its origins in a conference organized by the British Society for the Philosophy of Religion, and most of the chapters it contains are descended from papers given at it. I am grateful to the contributors for their help in the preparation of the book, and to Harriet Harris – the BSPR Series Editor – and Robin Le Poidevin for their help and advice at various stages in its gestation. It has been a pleasure to work with Sarah Lloyd and David Shervington of Ashgate, and thanks are owing to them for their encouragement, patience and unfailing helpfulness.

AJM

# Contributors

**Ben Arbour** is a PhD candidate at the University of Bristol. He teaches courses in philosophy and ethics at Weatherford College, and he currently lives in Fort Worth, Texas.

**Anthony Bolos** is a Postdoctoral Research Fellow at the Institute for Advanced Study at the Shalem Center in Jerusalem where he is currently working on a Templeton funded project in Philosophy and Analytic Theology.

**Gabriel Citron** is a Postdoctoral Fellow in Jewish Philosophy, at Yale University. He has published articles on the philosophy of religion and on Wittgenstein, and is currently co-editing *Wittgenstein's Lectures: Cambridge 1930–33*, from the notes of G.E. Moore.

**Stephen R. L. Clark** is Emeritus Professor of Philosophy at Liverpool, and an Honorary Research Fellow in Theology at Bristol University. His most recent book is *Ancient Mediterranean Philosophy* (Continuum, 2012).

**John Cottingham** is Professorial Research Fellow at Heythrop College, University of London, Professor Emeritus of Philosophy at Reading University and an Honorary Fellow of St John's College, Oxford. His recent books include *Why Believe?* and *Cartesian Reflections*.

**James K. Dew, Jr** is the Dean of the College and Associate Professor of the History of Ideas and Philosophy at Southeastern Baptist Theological Seminary.

**Anthony Kenny** was Fellow and Tutor in Philosophy at Balliol College Oxford, of which he then became Master from 1978–89. Later he was President of the British Academy and Chairman of the British Library. He is the author of some 40 books, mainly on Philosophy.

**Robin Le Poidevin** is Professor of Metaphysics at the University of Leeds and Editor of *Religious Studies*. His publications include *The Images of Time: an essay on temporal representation* (Oxford, 2007) and *Agnosticism: A Very Short Introduction* (Oxford, 2010).

**Andrew Moore** is a Fellow of the Oxford Centre for Christianity and Culture, Regent's Park College, University of Oxford. He has published widely on topics on the borderlands of theology and philosophy.

**Yujin Nagasawa** is Professor of Philosophy at the University of Birmingham. He is the author of *God and Phenomenal Consciousness* (Cambridge University Press, 2008) and *The Existence of God* (Routledge, 2011).

**Charles Taliaferro** is Professor of Philosophy, and Chair of the Philosophy Department at St Olaf College, USA.

**Olli-Pekka Vainio** is a Research Fellow of the Philosophical Psychology, Morality and Politics Research Unit of the Academy of Finland at the University of Helsinki. His most recent publications include *Beyond Fideism: Negotiable Religious Identities* (Ashgate, 2011).

**Aku Visala** is a Postdoctoral Research Fellow at the University of Notre Dame and a Research Fellow of the Finnish Academy.

# Foreword

In *The Family Reunion* T.S. Eliot had his Chorus declare that 'the circle of our understanding is a very restricted area. Except for a limited number of strictly practical purposes we do not know what we are doing; and even, when you think of it, we do not know much about thinking'. This acknowledgement of our own ignorance of 'what is happening outside the circle, and what is the meaning of happening' lies at the core of much traditional philosophy – and also much traditional religion. Philosophy begins in Wonder – in puzzlement, and amazement. The philosophically inclined find even familiar things very puzzling: why is there anything at all, and why does it seem to change so quickly; how do we tell how others feel and think, and why do we suppose that there is a world beyond our own brief life (whether that world is the one described by astronomers and palaeontologists, or the one imagined into being by poets and priests)? Should we, could we, manage to remember that much larger world even when dealing with everyday affairs (our health and wealth and reputation)? Maybe, like Eliot's Chorus, we could be content to 'understand the ordinary business of living' if only those other matters did not keep intruding: 'we can usually avoid accidents, we are insured against fire, against larceny and illness, against defective plumbing, but not against the act of God', the moment when we don't know what to think or do.

The wonder in which Philosophy begins is not just *puzzlement*: it is also Awe. Whether or not we find that Awe itself a puzzle, we can acknowledge that it is a fact: we can be awed by natural beauties, far distances and long ages, really bizarre occurrences, as well as by unusual courage, self-sacrificial generosity, delicate engineering and the sound of trumpets. Wonder, amazement, worship is the root both of Religion and of Science: the impulse to fall silent and admire as well as the impulse to interrogate and comprehend. How much *more* marvellous things seem when we have begun at least to wish to understand them rather than letting them slip by unnoticed. We seek to understand not merely to get rid of a nagging puzzlement that things are the way they are (whatever way that is), but to draw closer to reality. Athenians were wrong to think that Socrates and his *elenchus* were destructive of proper piety, of reverence, of the love of beauty. On the contrary, by revealing our own ignorance and confusion Socrates was showing the right way: 'where both the truth and our human teacher (whether that is Parmenides or Plato) are our friends, true piety is to prefer the truth', even if the truth is that we are at a loss.

Any gathering of philosophers, like any gathering of believers, will be filled with disagreements, mutual confusions, even fierce attacks on error. Only so, it seems, are we ever likely to get clearer even about our own beliefs, let alone about the world made up of truths (whether those truths are only our mortal opinions or an eternal vision). A gathering of philosophers (of many different traditions) that is also a gathering of believers (of many different sects, including the atheistical) will be yet more argumentative. No single collection of papers will ever fully reflect the lived reality of such a meeting, but it may still serve to amuse, instruct, provoke and even perhaps enlighten. Long may the Society – a gathering of philosophers and theologians, believers and unbelievers – flourish.

Stephen R. L. Clark
*President, British Society for the Philosophy of Religion, 2011–13*

Chapter 1

# God, Mind and Knowledge in Contemporary Philosophy of Religion

Andrew Moore

Philosophy of religion was once a backwater of analytic philosophy but in recent decades it has undergone a revival of interest and has gained institutional strength, particularly in North America. One reason for this is recognition of the intrinsic philosophical interest of the questions it discusses; another is a greater willingness to acknowledge the importance of the topics it covers, not only for philosophy but for the general public.[1] Though the public value of philosophy of religion may at times be done a disservice by the superficial treatments its themes receive in more popular contributions to debates about the place of religion in contemporary society, undergraduate courses in philosophy of religion in universities are popular and often serve as ways into philosophy for those whose principal course of study is, for example, theology or the study of religion.

This collection of chapters aims to capture some of the vibrancy of current work in the discipline and to offer something to the newcomer as well as to the professional. Its origins lie in a conference of the British Society for the Philosophy of Religion (BSPR) with the same title as this book, the aim of which was to take soundings on the state of the discipline across a broad range of topics. The BSPR has its origins in the Christian Philosophers' Group, founded in the early 1960s by Ian Ramsey, and it has grown not only numerically but also in religious diversity. The Society's membership includes Jews, Christians, Muslims, atheists and agnostics, and some of that sometimes overlapping diversity is represented amongst the contributors to this collection. The book does not claim to represent all contemporary strands of what may be broadly referred to as philosophy of religion: it does not represent the Continental tradition of philosophizing, though some of the chapters in it share interests with that tradition. However, it does show the way in which contemporary philosophy has much to gain from (and perhaps to contribute to) other areas of philosophy – whether these be epistemology, the history of philosophy, the philosophy of perception, the philosophy of language, metaphysics or the philosophy of mind.

---

[1]  See, for example, the essays by the atheist philosopher Thomas Nagel in his *Secular Philosophy and the Religious Temperament* (Oxford: Oxford University Press, 2010).

## The Epistemology of Religious Belief

Twenty years ago it would have been virtually inconceivable that major funding for research in religious epistemology would have been offered to, let alone accepted by, any leading university. But as at least one major British example illustrates, things are different now and this change of climate is reflected in the range of topics covered by the first section of the book. John Cottingham proposes 'a new kind of religious epistemology' that is based on a fresh understanding of what kinds of experience are religiously relevant, and in arguing for it he takes up some arguments of Pascal.[2] Cottingham's argument differs from the two widely canvassed approaches of reliabilist (or externalist) and internalist epistemologies. Whereas reliabilist epistemologies hold that for a belief to be warranted it must have been formed in a reliable way, internalists argue that for a person to be justified in holding a belief he or she needs to be aware that that belief is justified. Taking the former route, Reformed epistemology was developed by a group of philosophers who are in the Reformed tradition of the Christian church – that is, those Protestant churches particularly influenced by John Calvin.[3] It is based upon human experience but the kind of experiences which ground Reformed epistemology are clearly identifiable as 'religious': a sense of guilt before God, an awareness that God is speaking to me when I read the Bible, a spontaneous outburst of praise to God for the beauty of creation. By contrast, Cottingham argues for a religious epistemology based on experiences that are less clearly identifiable as obviously or specifically religious.

Reliabilist accounts of religious belief such as Plantinga's face several well-known problems (and some new ones developed in this book), not the least of which is the question, pressed by Richard Swinburne, as to 'whether [religious belief] is probably true, given our evidence'.[4] Swinburne rejects reliabilist religious epistemology in favour of internalism because he believes that only its arguments can meet our epistemic obligations to provide objective evidence which shows that the belief that God exists *is* probably true. Given our background knowledge and the available evidence, the hypothesis that God exists has greater probability than the hypothesis that he doesn't. So the existence of God is the best explanation of the data of human experience.

This is where Cottingham's distinctive understanding of God comes in. He does not think that human beings are capable of speculating about the cause of the cosmos so as to arrive at a quasi-scientific explanation of it. And, he observes, the Bible sees God's identity as the Creator as inseparable from a reciprocal moral obligation under which creatures are placed. So knowledge of God will require

---

[2]    Below, p. 21.

[3]    The key work is Alvin Plantinga and Nicholas Wolterstorff (eds), *Faith and Rationality: Reason and Belief in God* (Notre Dame, Indiana: Notre Dame University Press, 1983).

[4]    Richard Swinburne, 'Plantinga on Warrant' in *Religious Studies* 37 (2001), p. 207.

paying attention to our sense that life has, or ought to have, meaning and moral purpose: 'the divine call is chiefly heard as a moral and practical as opposed to a theoretical or purely cognitive one'.[5] To consider religious epistemology as a matter of 'objective evidence' – as Cottingham's title puts it – is too restrictive.

Instead, Cottingham argues that signs of God's existence are be related to God's saving purposes – though we should not expect these signs to be too evident, otherwise they might restrict human freedom. Such signs occur, Cottingham argues, where we have an experience in which we seem to have gained epistemic access to something ourselves and yet which also seems to depend on some 'gracious bestowal'.[6] These are moments where our ordinary experience is intensified and where we glimpse a pattern to life that transcends us and is not of our own making. Such experiences may occur through natural beauty, music or awareness of a moral demand upon us. They may be taken by the believer to be revelations of God but they are not non-natural, and their occurrence does not entail our having any special religious faculty or sense apparatus – such as Plantinga's *sensus divinitatis*. These are 'natural intimations of the transcendent', 'natural glimpses of the divine'.[7]

These experiences have common features with some other kinds of knowledge – the knowledge that arises from being in love, from participating in psychoanalysis, or from the appreciation of poetry: they have a self-involving character. It distorts these kinds of experience to see them primarily as evidential for they require a vulnerability and a receptiveness on the part of the one who has them – a willingness to be changed, even. And this means that despite their natural character, it belongs to these experiences that 'relevant evidence [of God's existence] is available only to insiders in the form of the personal transformation they themselves experience'.[8] Such experiences as these convey a knowledge that is only available to insiders, but the 'insider information' they carry is not the exclusive possession of a privileged club for it is available in principle to all as 'part of our ordinary natural human heritage'.[9]

One objection that it would be hard to lodge against Cottingham's argument is that it struggles to give an account of the value of knowledge. Although questions could be asked about whether the value that we find in such experiences as Cottingham discusses is inferred, or whether their value lies on the face (as it were) of the experiences (as it seems to in the cases Taliaferro discusses in his chapter), since his argument and the experiences he discusses are clearly based on a Christian conception of God as the one who gives meaning and value to life, and since the experiences themselves are of life's having meaning and value, the knowledge that results from these experiences clearly has value.

---

[5]   Below, p. 20.

[6]   Below, p. 27.

[7]   Below, p. 29.

[8]   Below, p. 25.

[9]   See below, p. 31.

As noted above, Reformed epistemology has been criticized from a number of angles, but Tony Bolos brings a debate from mainstream epistemology to bear on it in his argument that Reformed epistemology fails adequately to account for the final value of knowledge. Reformed epistemology was developed partly out of dissatisfaction with foundationalist epistemologies out of which had developed the evidentialist objection to religious belief. This states that religious belief lacks evidence and good argument, so it is irrational. An obvious reply would be to use – as many theists have – the arguments of natural theology to show that there is good evidence for belief in a God, and hence that belief is validly inferred. However, Reformed epistemologists reject this strategy because they have theological suspicions of natural theology. In any case, they argue, classical foundationalism is, as Plantinga puts it, 'self-referentially incoherent' and leads to scepticism about beliefs that we normally take to be rational even though they are not formed inferentially, such as perceptual beliefs, memory beliefs and beliefs about other minds. Reformed epistemologists extend the range of reliable sources of belief by arguing that belief in God can be formed without inference via (what Calvin called) the *sensus divinitatis* and the internal instigation of the Holy Spirit. If belief in other minds is not irrational, nor is belief in God.[10]

Reformed epistemology is a reliabilist epistemology: a sufficient condition for being in the epistemically superior state of possessing *knowledge* is that the relevant belief forming faculty was functioning reliably. But why, Bolos asks, is knowledge to be valued more than true belief by Reformed epistemologists? After all, so long as we have a true belief, it doesn't really matter whether the belief was formed reliably or unreliably and if that doesn't matter, then there seems to be no good reason for valuing knowledge more than true belief. What we value is the true belief that, say, God exists, rather than the whether it was formed reliably or unreliably. So the Reformed epistemologist seems to have a problem accounting for the distinctive value of knowledge, of reliably formed true belief, in contrast to the value of true belief *simpliciter*.

However, Bolos argues, unlike the value of true belief, the value of knowledge is not just epistemic; it is general and it has to do with cognitive achievement on the part of an agent. Bolos wants to strengthen the case for Reformed epistemology, but those familiar with Reformed theology will immediately spot a problem here, for this theological perspective puts particular emphasis on the fact that human knowledge of God is God's free gift rather than a human achievement. So in the final section of his chapter, Bolos explores the relationship between divine and human agency in the operation of the *sensus divinitatis* and argues for a solution to the theological problem for his account of the value of knowledge.

It is widely held by atheists and some believers that, rather than being taken to be veridical, religious experiences should be presumed guilty until proved innocent: the burden of proof is on the shoulders of the person who would accept

---

[10]   See Alvin Plantinga, 'Reason and Belief in God' in Alvin Plantinga and Nicholas Wolterstorff (eds), *Faith and Rationality*, pp. 16–93.

them as being genuinely of God. But Charles Taliaferro presents some fresh arguments for an attitude of 'critical trust' towards such experiences. They should not be accepted uncritically but neither should they be rejected; rather, we should be – like the Cambridge Platonists – open to the possibility of experience of the divine as being 'natural and good'. Also, Taliaferro argues, a priori concepts of what God can or cannot do, or of what it is fitting for God to do or refrain from doing, seem to beg the question. But perhaps the one who is disposed to accept religious experiences as veridical is mistaken to do so, not because the experiences are, like miracles, a priori massively unlikely or because they entail implausible concepts of deity, but because the knowledge (or true belief) the one who has the experience claims to possess is exclusive to him or her and to other believers. For this reason, Anthony Kenny has argued that a proper intellectual humility requires us to be agnostic about religious experience, but in his final section, Taliaferro argues against this view. And even if the believer is warranted in not adopting the agnostic stance Kenny commends, it does not follow that he or she is constrained to take pride in the experience or to see it as a personal achievement.

Taliaferro argues that there is good reason to adopt a stance of 'critical trust' towards religious experience, and in doing so he provides an example of the influence wielded in contemporary philosophy of religion by the evidentialist objection to religious belief. One – perhaps *the* – classic version of this objection in twentieth-century philosophy of religion is posed by Antony Flew in his contribution to a famous symposium on 'Theology and Falsification' that was published in an anthology which laid the foundation for much subsequent debate. Influenced by Logical Positivism and Karl Popper, Flew thought that if the content of a belief is meaningful it must be possible to show what could falsify it – what would count as evidence against the belief. So he challenges the believer to come up with some evidence which could falsify religious belief (and hence show that religious language is meaningful):

> Just what would have to happen not merely (morally and wrongly) to tempt but also (logically and rightly) to entitle us to say 'God does not love us' or even 'God does not exist'? I … put to the succeeding symposiasts the simple central questions, 'What would have to occur or to have occurred to constitute for you a disproof of the love of, or of the existence of, God?'[11]

Taking this question and the responses offered to it at the symposium as his starting point, Gabriel Citron challenges a consensus that underlies both Reformed epistemology and the epistemology of those who accept that religious belief must meet the evidentialist challenge. That consensus has assumed that 'religious belief' is a logically monolithic category, that it is characterised by a

---

[11]    Antony Flew in Antony Flew and Alasdair Macintyre (eds), *New Essays in Philosophical Theology* (London: SCM Press, 1955), p. 99.

single underlying logic. In fact, Citron argues, although some religious belief is an ontological hypothesis grounded in evidence and is empirically falsifiable, other forms of religious belief may be more like the expression of an attitude that is 'non-groundable and non-falsifiable' and so not conform to the logic of evidence, hypothesis and verification or falsification.[12] There seems to be more variety to the logical forms that religious belief can take than is usually thought. The difficulty is that this variety usually escapes our notice because all the varieties of belief are expressed using much the same language.

Using Wittgenstein's method of laying out a range of simple examples, Citron sets out different forms of religious belief so as to enable recognition that religious belief really does come in multiple forms. To assume that all religious belief is of the same logical variety may be to distort the belief the philosopher is examining and lead to its being misunderstood and misevaluated. If philosophy of religion is correctly to understand and evaluate what a belief in a good and loving God (for example) amounts to – the role it plays in people's lives – it will need to ensure that it has paid proper heed to the particular logical variety of belief, understanding of which is being sought in any particular instance. Perhaps religious belief is not uniform; perhaps it does not have a single 'essence' about which philosophers may generalise. People can often hold religious beliefs in a way that is indeterminate, mixed or fluid between the different logical varieties of belief. Recognizing that given religious beliefs come in different logical forms is the first step to recognizing that religious beliefs as people actually hold them are often more complicated and messy than philosophers of religion usually take them to be.


## Divine and Human Minds

What kind of an activity is philosophy of religion; what, if anything, does it accomplish? It is sometimes thought that disagreements between believers are evidence of the falsehood, or at least the implausibility or irrationality, of religious belief. Yet if long-standing, unresolved arguments amongst believing philosophers of religion is an example of the implausibility of belief in God, perhaps we shouldn't be too quick to draw too strong a conclusion from their disagreements: does disagreement about which arguments for the existence of other minds, or of the external world, are to be preferred warrant our concluding that belief in them is implausible? Nevertheless, it doesn't take a particularly close or sophisticated reading of the Bible to see that it contains or alludes to many arguments and disagreements – even about quite fundamental matters such as the nature of God. On the other hand, there seems also to be consensus: in the Hebrew Bible, about God's gift of the Torah to his elect people. And despite its containing or alluding to arguments about many matters, the New Testament contains no argument

---

[12]    Below, p. 69.

(and doesn't offer evidence that there was argument) about what was probably the most controversial innovation made by the earliest 'followers of the Way', as Christians were then known – the worship of Jesus as (co-)divine. These core beliefs and practices of Jews and of Christians provide the conceptual, social, cultural and political context in which other disputes within those communities find their home. They sustain argument and disagreement amongst believers about matters internal, as well as external, to the community and in doing just that, these beliefs and practices sustain humane community. (For example, Paul argues that since God has reconciled humans to himself in Jesus' death and resurrection, Christians ought to be reconciled to each other, and they ought also to manifest that reconciliation to a divided and wounded world. Similarly, in the Torah, exclusive worship of Yahweh is symmetrically related to the prohibition of covetousness.) One of the roles of philosophy of religion may be to clarify what is at stake philosophically in these disputes, and perhaps even to indicate ways in which they may be settled.

Believing communities are embedded in broader social, cultural and political contexts, and they usually extend across great periods of time. When the Christian gospel reached the pagan Latin- and Greek-speaking world, it encountered ideas, beliefs and patterns of thought that stimulated further debate and controversy on matters that were as much philosophical as they were narrowly theological. This has occurred throughout the history of the church. Sometimes these debates have been about matters internal to understanding the Bible, and sometimes about how the Bible is to be interpreted in relation to other patterns of belief. For example, the doctrine of the Trinity came into being as a result of questions about the meaning of biblical passages about 'the Word of God' and about how those passages were to be interpreted in the context of pagan cosmology. So the arguments that produced the doctrine of the Trinity were arguments both about what the Bible meant, and how that meaning was to be appropriated in the Greek and Latin worlds beyond the Holy Land. Doctrinal arguments similar to these continue, in different terms, in the present, and the second section of this book principally concerns contested topics that are fundamental to Christian belief.

Charles Taliaferro concludes his chapter with a suggestion, drawn from Augustine, that philosophical debates between opposing viewpoints should take the character more of a 'non-polemical' dialogue among friends than that of a competition. But it takes little familiarity with philosophy and theology to know that this is often not the reality of the matter. Disagreements run deep and the stakes can be very high when those engaged believe that matters of fundamental truth or falsehood are in play. In the chapter that opens this section, Vainio and Visala discuss research on 'cognitive bias' in psychology and the cognitive science of religion which offer ways of understanding how, quite apart from intrinsic logical or conceptual factors, philosophical disagreement can arise and why different people tend to find different proposed solutions to philosophical problems attractive.

Entrenched disagreement doesn't make philosophical enquiry less valuable, not even in the philosophy of religion where the clash between naturalist and non-naturalist outlooks seems to make the possibility of deep progress particularly unlikely. Our minds may be such that we are unlikely to reach agreement, but this does not make philosophy (of religion) any less worthwhile than, say, engaging in political debate. And the communal nature of the enterprise may help in overcoming the psychological factors that can distort individual perspectives on philosophical questions. Research in the cognitive science of religion appears to suggest that humans have a natural propensity towards forming religious beliefs. If this is correct, then the kind of reasoned reflection practised by philosophers may be able to make an important contribution by moderating instinctual processes. And even if the tendency to form religious beliefs is more an instinctive than a reflective process, this, Vainio and Visala argue, does not remove the need for philosophy, and especially natural theology, in evaluating one's beliefs rationally and perhaps reformulating them.

Instinct and reflection are certainly not the only components of religious belief. For Judaism and Christianity narrative is central, and in her recent, magisterial book on the problem of suffering, Eleonore Stump has recovered for the tradition of analytic philosophy of religion the importance of narrative. Biblical 'narrative', she claims, 'makes a contribution to philosophical reflection that cannot be gotten as well, or at all, without the narrative'.[13] Israel identifies God (or, perhaps better, Israel's God identifies himself) by means of a narrative – as occurs, for example, in the giving of the Torah; in the Shema, Israel identifies herself in relation to God by narrative.[14] At the heart of Christian faith is Jesus Christ whose unique, 'unsubstitutable identity' (as the theologian Hans Frei described it) is given narrative shape in the gospels, and the central tenets of Christianity receive capsule summary in the form of a narrative. As the Nicene Creed puts it: 'For our sake he was crucified under Pontius Pilate; he suffered death and was buried. On the third day he rose again …' Unlike the philosophical traditions of Aristotle, Plato and the Stoics on which they have at various times drawn, Judaism and Christianity both appear to be committed to a strong account of God's involvement with human beings in time and history, which helps explain the centrality of narrative in these traditions. So it is not surprising that one of the deep questions lying in the background of many of the chapters in this book, and in this section in particular, concerns the degree to which it is possible or desirable to abstract from narrative in philosophizing about a religious tradition.

One of the most intractable problems for any religious tradition that holds that God providentially guides his creation to accomplish his purpose, and that he may be petitioned in prayer, is that of the relationship between God's knowledge and

---

[13]    Eleonore Stump, *Wandering in Darkness: Narrative and the Problem of Suffering* (Oxford: Oxford University Press, 2010), p. xviii. For an introduction to Stump's views on the role of narrative in philosophy of religion, see her 'The Problem of Evil: Analytic Philosophy and Narrative' in Oliver Crisp and Michael Rea (eds), *Analytic Theology: New Essays in the Philosophy of Theology* (Oxford: Oxford University Press, 2009), pp. 251–64.

[14]    Exod. 20.2ff; Dt. 6, especially v. 20ff.

action, and human willing. If God guides history and *fore*knows what will happen, then can any significant content be given to the idea that human beings are free agents? And if they are not free, can they be considered morally responsible – as typically members of those traditions believe humans to be? On the other hand, if human beings are genuinely free, can God be said to know what they will do, and if he can't then is he genuinely omniscient? And perhaps he isn't omnipotent either: can genuinely free humans thwart God's purposes?

Debate about these matters in the philosophy of religion in recent years has received new impetus from a position, or cluster of positions, known as Open Theism, which contests classical theism on the grounds that it is inadequate to the Bible. Open theists typically seek to be (as they see it) more closely faithful to what Scripture says about God's relationship with humans, his knowledge of human action, the way in which humans are presented as being able to act freely and the way in which God is presented as guiding history. One of the key philosophical texts in the debate about open theism is *The Openness of God: A Biblical Challenge to the Traditional Understanding of God* and in introducing its themes, the Preface summarises the contributors' understanding of the biblical view of the relationship between God and God's creatures:

> God, in grace, grants humans significant freedom to cooperate with or work against God's will for their lives, and he enters into dynamic, give-and-take relationships with us. The Christian life involves a genuine interaction between God and human beings. We respond to God's gracious initiatives and God responds to our responses ... and on it goes. God takes risks in this give-and-take relationship, yet he is endlessly resourceful and competent in working toward his ultimate goals. Sometimes God alone decides how to accomplish these goals. On other occasions, God works with human decisions, adapting his own plans to fit the changing situation. God does not control everything that happens. Rather, he is open to receiving input from creatures. In loving dialogue, God invites us to participate with him to bring the future into being.[15]

Open theists are so termed because they hold that God is open to influence from human beings and what will happen in the future is therefore genuinely open. This, they argue, is the full, biblical picture: God is in time, and humans have libertarian free will. God changes in relationship with his creatures, accumulates knowledge, takes risks and becomes more perfect as his purposes are accomplished. Classical theists contend, however, that the Bible presents God as unchanging and omniscient, and, they argue, such ideas as those of open theists amount to an unworthily anthropocentric conception of the transcendent fullness and self-sufficiency of God.

---

[15]   Clark Pinnock, Richard Rice, John Sanders, William Hasker and David Basinger, *The Openness of God: A Biblical Challenge to the Traditional Understanding of God* (Downers Grove: InterVarsity Press, 1994), p. 7.

The issues between open and classical theists are complex, both theologically and philosophically, and they go to the heart of our understandings of God and of the nature of time. Any theistic account of God holds that God is omniscient, but in his chapter, Ben Arbour argues that on open theists' arguments, given their commitments about the nature of time and to a libertarian account of free will, God not only does not have foreknowledge, he also has no knowledge of any present truths involving free will. Hence we should reject open theism.

Another area where there has been debate between different metaphysical approaches to Christianity concerns the account of human nature that is affirmed by the Bible, especially in relation to the doctrine of the resurrection. Since the early twentieth century, scholars of both the Hebrew Bible and of the New Testament have been in virtual unanimity that both biblical Judaism and early Christianity held that humans are a psychosomatic unity. Scripture, so it is argued, provides no warrant for (Cartesian) substance dualism; the seed of that was the influence of pagan Greek thought on Christian teaching.[16] Likewise, orthodox Christians have generally agreed that scriptural teaching about the resurrection of Christ and the goodness of God's material creation require belief that Christ was raised bodily – though Paul, for example, is careful not to imply the Christ's risen body is composed of the same 'stuff' as, or is reconstituted from, his pre-resurrection body. Creedal Christianity affirms not the immortality of the soul but 'the resurrection of the dead'.

Yet what the creed affirms may be read in a way that is consistent with dualism, and this is why what has become the consensus amongst contemporary biblical scholars and doctrine specialists has, under the influence of pagan philosophy, not been the majority view in Christian history. That view has favoured dualism of various kinds, and in his chapter James Dew defends this traditional view against Kevin Corcoran's revisionist position. A particular problem for non-dualists is to offer a philosophically plausible account of personal identity before and after bodily resurrection. Appeal to an immortal soul would make the task a lot easier but, obviously, it is not admissible by a Christian materialist such as Corcoran. Dew focuses his attack on Corcoran on the difficulty he has in giving a persuasive, non-dualist account of the resurrection of the dead, and he argues that, in fact, Corcoran's argument collapses back into a version of dualism.

'My thoughts are not your thoughts' says the Lord, through the prophet Isaiah.[17] It follows from the transcendence of God that God is beyond our comprehension. Theologians have sometimes been too quick to appeal to mystery, but if what the prophet says is true, it is unsurprising that there should be features of (belief about) God that strain the limits of human understanding. The debate between classical and open theists may represent an instance of this,

---

[16]   The classic theological statement of this position is Oscar Cullmann, *Immortality of the Soul or Resurrection of the Dead?: The Witness of the New Testament* (London: Epworth Press, 1958).

[17]   Is. 55.8.

as may how we are to understand bodily resurrection. Another instance is the doctrine of the Trinity, which is not so much a human attempt to explain God or to develop an abstract, logically coherent account of the divine nature as to state what has to be said in order to read the Bible for maximal internal coherence.[18] Neither the doctrine of the Trinity, nor the Chalcedonian definition of the nature of Jesus Christ as fully divine and fully human, is explicitly stated in Scripture. Since Scripture is the principal authority for Christians, if creedal statements based on Scripture present logical problems, they are of a different order from the logical problems posed by the text of Scripture itself, especially where the passage forms a discrete whole.

In his chapter on the paradox of Eden, Yujin Nagasawa analyses the story of the Garden of Eden which, it has been argued, entails that, contrary to what Jews and Christians believe on the basis of other biblical passages, justice is not one of God's essential properties. The entailment arises because the story presents a paradox: if Adam and Eve knew that eating the forbidden fruit would be to disobey God, then God is unjust in having set them the test; if, on the other hand, they did not know that eating the fruit would be to disobey God, then God is unjust in having set them the test. On either reading of the story, God is unjust in setting the test, so it is concluded that justice is not an essential property of God – which, as Nagasawa observes, is effectively an argument against the existence of God. Nagasawa puts this paradox in its strongest possible form and goes on to identify a structural parallel between it and the well-known black-and-white Mary thought experiment against physicalism in the philosophy of mind. He then shows that arguments that the thought experiment prompts against physicalism may be used to refute the supposed paradox of Eden.


**The Status of God**


If God's thoughts are not our thoughts, is it possible for humans to express any truths about God? One may be grateful for the injunction of the Preacher of the book of Ecclesiastes who said, 'God is in heaven and you are on earth, so let your words be few'![19] But philosophers of religion, like most theologians, have tended not to heed this advice. As the example of the Preacher shows, one topic

---

[18]   The great commentator on Thomas Aquinas, Gilles Emery, OP, expresses a view of Thomas that is representative not only of him but of the great bulk of the preceding Christian tradition: 'The most speculative reflection on personal properties and Trinitarian relations is not superimposed on biblical teaching, but is included in biblical exegesis, because it has as its aim to extract the profound sense of the text by the means of intellectual resources, in faith … Trinitarian theology … starts from Scripture to return to Scripture' (Gilles Emery, OP, *Trinity in Aquinas* (Naples, Florida: Sapientia Press, 2006), pp. 318, 317).

[19]   Eccles. 5.2.

which has preoccupied reflective thought since the earliest days of the Judaeo-Christian tradition, and especially since the gospel entered the pagan world, has been precisely that of how we can talk about God. Is religious language to be interpreted literally or figuratively: consider, for example, 'God is my rock' on the one hand, and, on the other, 'God is love'. And does such talk genuinely refer to God, and if so, how?[20]

In his chapter, Anthony Kenny analyses language used to talk about God and argues that it is not possible for us to say anything that is literally true about God's nature. But does it follow from this that it is not possible to speak of God? One possibility that has been widely canvassed is that talk of God uses language analogically. Whilst some have seen analogy as a distinct trope, others have understood it to be a special instance of literal discourse. Kenny belongs to the latter group but he does not think that it follows from this that we must give up on talk of God, for a case remains for arguing that we can speak of God by means of metaphor. However, if religious language is (irreducibly) metaphorical can truth-values be given to religious statements? Everyday use of metaphorical expressions suggests they can but at the expense of their not being 'straightforwardly subject to the principle of non-contradiction'.[21] For precisely this reason, religious statements should foster toleration amongst believers: religious creeds which, if taken literally, would contradict each other, may, when taken metaphorically, not do so. And, unlike the Logical Positivists who argued that because religious language is meaningless, atheism is the only option, Kenny's argument permits agnosticism to be debated as a philosophically respectable position. His argument also has some interesting consequences when applied to texts central to Christian worship, not the least of which is that the belief that 'on the third day' after being crucified under Pontius Pilate, Christ was raised from the dead, may be interpreted literally and has clear truth conditions. It therefore occupies 'a unique position in the structure of Christian belief'.[22]

Whilst the status of religious language continues to be a focus of debate in philosophy of religion, a related topic has relatively recently come onto its agenda – partly as a result of arguments about religious language – and that is the question of religious realism. Is God real; does a transcendent divine being exist, entirely independently of our minds and our language? The religions of the West have traditionally understood themselves, and been interpreted by philosophers, in a realist way. However, some members of religious communities have argued that although religious explanations fail and sound arguments for God's existence are unavailable, we shouldn't move to atheist secularism: God may not exist as an objectively real entity but religion is not worthless. Religious community life and ethics have a social utility, so religious belief should be reinterpreted in a non-realist

---

[20]   The classic discussion is that of Thomas Aquinas, *Summa Theologiae*, 1a. 13.

[21]   Below, p. 151.

[22]   Below, p. 155.

way.[23] Another reason some have abandoned religious realism has been suspicion of the veracity of religious experience. As is noted elsewhere in this book, since at least Hume's day, philosophers and theologians have been particularly occupied by the possibility that (some) religious experience has its origin not in anything divine that exists independently of human beings but in our desire to make sense of and to feel at home in the world. If these critics are right, we should abandon the attitude of 'critical trust' towards religious experience and be suspicious of 'natural intimations of the transcendent': so-called 'religious experience' is merely the result of our projecting our own emotional states onto the world.

So the question as to whether God is a projection is an important one, but in his chapter, Robin Le Poidevin examines the question of what threat if any projectivism poses to realism about God. In fact, he argues, the two may be combined in ways which make a strong case for a representative realist account of religious experience according to which, whilst we do project images of the divine, there is a divine reality that plays a causal role in our projections. There are other areas of human experience where realism and projectivism are not inconsistent, such as in perception of what, since Locke, have been called the secondary qualities of objects – colour, taste, sound, heat and cold. As the example of depth perception illustrates, humans engage in projection when there is good reason to do so. Projection has a teleological explanation: we project our experience of the secondary quality of heat onto the fire so as to avoid injuring ourselves, but we don't project our experience of pain onto it.

But, Le Poidevin argues, religious experience is different from other experiences that may seem analogous – such as the experience of pain – for in the religious case we project a feeling outside ourselves which we present to ourselves as a perception of something external to us. Yet if the reason we project when we do is teleological, then in the case of religious projections, Le Poidevin thinks it is hard to come up with an explanation that doesn't make reference to a mind-independent being, so it is not obvious that the occurrence of projection makes realism redundant. But this doesn't amount to a positive argument for orthodox realism, for if we are to think about God in a realist way, then we need to think about God himself – we need to be able to engage in 'singular thought' about God. But it is not easy to see how this can be possible given the extent to which projection is involved in our conception of God: the conceptions we have of God as God *is* are muddled with our projections in such a way that we seem unable to think of God himself. Again, comparison with other forms of experience may come to the rescue, for although there are problems with engaging in singular thought about objects in everyday life, we can still be involved with them and think about them in ways that are at least approximately true.

---

[23]     The most widely influential statement of Christian non-realism (as the position has become known) has been that of Don Cupitt; see his *Taking Leave of God* (London: SCM, 1980). See also the chapters by Gordon Kaufman and Peter Lipton in Andrew Moore and Michael Scott (eds), *Realism and Religion: Philosophical and Theological Essays* (Aldershot: Ashgate, 2007).

Moving from the realm of our human experience to things that lie beyond it but which are nevertheless creatures of a divine creator, Stephen Clark pursues themes from Classical writers, science fiction and other forms of speculation to ask whether our finding alien creatures, radically different from humans, elsewhere in the universe would tend to support atheism. If we found aliens who were like humans, this might support theism, but what if they were not like us? On earth, humans are made in God's image and likeness, but why should we suppose that any extraterrestrials we discovered, also made in God's image and likeness, would be like us? May not they – with their alien moralities and social structures – be as good an image of God as we are? We should not have too high a view of our place in the cosmic scheme of things. Clark invites us to consider our view that rationality, as we understand it, is a sure guide to how it 'really is' with the universe; may there not be extraterrestrials so different from us and, living as their creator meant them to do, that our view would come to seem to be a matter of faith? 'The God of Gods, or whatever principle it is that governs things and is the good of all, may allow for human personality or personhood, but It is not confined by that. God's ways are not our ways'.[24]

---

[24]    Below, p. 186.

# PART I
# The Epistemology of Religious Belief

Chapter 2

# Knowledge of God:
# Insider Information or Objective Evidence?†

John Cottingham

## Natural Knowledge of God and the Neutrality of the Cosmos

A notable passage in Paul's letter to the Romans declares that 'ever since the creation of the world God's eternal power and divine nature, invisible though they are, have been understood and seen through the things he has made'.[1] The idea seems to be that we can all infer God's existence from observable features of the natural world. And not just that we can do so, but that that we *ought* to – for Paul goes on to declare that those who fail to recognize the divine authorship of the world and in consequence fail to give God thanks are 'inexcusable'.[2] Following this lead, there is a long tradition in Christian philosophical thought that maintains that natural inferential knowledge of God is readily available to humans. Aquinas' approach in the Five Ways provides a conspicuous example. And the First Vatican Council reaffirmed this tradition in 1870, when, explicitly invoking the passage from Paul, it laid it down that 'God, the beginning and end of all things, can be known, from created things, by the light of natural human reason'.[3]

It seems as unambiguous a position as anyone could wish. But actually, things are not quite as simple as may at first appear. The Pauline passage, though

---

†   This paper, under the title 'Confronting the Cosmos: Scientific Rationality and Human Understanding', first appeared in the *Proceedings of the American Catholic Philosophical Association* in August 2012. I am grateful to the Editor and the Philosophy Documentation Centre for permission to reproduce it here.

[1]   *Ta gar aorata autou apo ktiseôs kosmou tois poêmasin nooumena kathoratai, hê te aidios autou dunamis kai theiotês* (Rom. 1:20). The thought is a recapitulation of earlier ideas, found for example in the Wisdom of Solomon, 13:1, 'Surely vain are all men by nature who are ignorant of God, and could not out of the good things that are seen know him that is; neither by considering the works did they acknowledge the workmaster'.

[2]   *anapologêtos* (Rom. 1:20). Compare Wisdom, 18:8: 'Neither are they to be pardoned'.

[3]   *Sancta mater Ecclesia tenet et docet, Deum, rerum omnium principium et finem, naturali humanae rationis lumine e rebus creatis certo cognosci posse: 'invisibilia enim ipsius a creatura mundi, per ea quae facta sunt, intellecta, conspiciuntur'* [Rom. 1:20]. First Vatican Council, Dogmatic Constitution on the Catholic Faith (Dei Filius) [1870], Ch. 2.

affirming our knowledge of God on the basis of his works, makes it clear that the divine attributes themselves, God's power and divine nature, are *not* known: they are beyond our ken, or as Paul puts it, *invisible*. This is in line with the frequent warnings in the New Testament, prefigured in the Hebrew Bible, that God is not to be seen by human eyes: he dwells (as the first letter to Timothy expresses it) 'in light inaccessible, whom no man hath seen or can see'; or, as the book of Exodus puts it, rather more dramatically, no man can see God and live.[4] Consistently with this, when we come to Aquinas, although the Five Ways patently aim to demonstrate God from his effects, the conception of God so arrived at is, in the words of one distinguished commentator, Brian Davies, a very 'minimalist' one[5] – the proofs don't disclose the nature of the invisible God, but simply allow us to infer the existence of an original, uncaused, unmoved *something*, an ultimate X, to which, as Aquinas puts it, we apply the label 'God'.[6] And finally, to come to the passage from the First Vatican Council document, although a place for natural reason is clearly affirmed, this affirmation occurs in a concessive clause, which immediately leads on to an emphasis on the role *not* of natural inference but of special divine revelation and faith – the main subject of the document in question. So the sense of the relevant passage is somewhat as follows: although the mysterious and invisible God *can* certainly be inferred by the natural light via created things, nevertheless the truths on which our salvation depends are those revealed to the eyes of faith. The text goes on to say 'this faith, which is the beginning of man's salvation, is a supernatural virtue, whereby ... we believe that the things which he has revealed are true ... *not* because of the intrinsic truth of the things, viewed by the natural light of reason ...' And it concludes by quoting the definition of faith in the letter to the Hebrews (11:1): faith is 'the substance of things hoped for, the conviction of things *that appear not*'.[7]

---

4    God dwells in 'light inaccessible, whom no man hath seen nor can see' (*phôs oikôn aprositon, hon eiden oudeis anthrôpôn oude idein dunatai*) (1 Tim. 6:16). Cf. Col. 1:15: Christ, who has 'delivered us from the power of darkness' is 'the image of the invisible God' (*eikôn tou theou tou aoratou*). See also 1 John 4:12 ('No man hath seen God at any time'). For the Hebrew Bible, see Exod. 33:17, 20 (Moses) and 1 Kgs 19:13 (Elijah): no human can see God and live.

5    B. Davies, *Aquinas* (London: Continuum, 2002), p. 27.

6    See Thomas Aquinas, *Summa Theologiae* [1266–73], Ia 2.3 ('and this we call "God"', or some such phrase, is found at the end of each of the Five Ways).

7    *Dei Filius*, Ch. 3. The Greek word here translated as 'substance' is *hypostasis*. But this rendering (found for example in the King James Version) makes things sound, to my ear, far too settled and solid. *Hypostasis*, rather, is a prop or support. I have argued elsewhere that a willed act of trust can be epistemically facilitating – it opens us to seeing what, if all goes well, will confirm the appropriateness of the trust – and also psychologically and morally facilitating (it supports or reinforces the hopeful pursuit of something that is not yet in our grasp). It's worth adding that in the second half of the phrase, 'the certainty of things unseen', the Greek term is *elenchus*. But *elenchus* in Greek is a demanding, open-ended process – like the *elenchus* Socrates made famous – a probing inquiry, a reaching forward,

So despite Paul's thundering about those who fail to infer God being 'inexcusable', and despite Vatican I's insistence that there can be natural knowledge of God, the emerging picture from a closer reading of these texts is that the natural light won't actually get us very far when it comes to knowing God. So even in what may be called mainstream Catholic Christianity, the results achievable by natural reason alone are somewhat limited; and I take it that the Protestant tradition is for the most part even more sceptical about what reason alone can tell us of God (think of Kierkegaard, for example; or, in the twentieth century, Karl Barth, who actually urged people to 'turn their back on natural theology as a great temptation and source of error').[8]

I don't, however, want to become embroiled in denominational controversies in this chapter, but to try to get clear, from a philosophical perspective, on what it makes sense to say about natural knowledge of God – that is, the kind of knowledge that might be available to any human being, without the aid of special divine grace or revelation. Let me start by saying outright that it's hard to accept Paul's stern insistence that those who fail to acknowledge God in this way are blameworthy, or 'without excuse', as he puts it. For it seems abundantly clear, at any rate speaking in our own contemporary context, that there are many sincere atheists and agnostics: people who have honestly scrutinized the arguments and the evidence available from a purely rational perspective, and have found them wanting. It's very hard to believe that such people have just omitted to draw obvious inferences or that they have culpably failed to notice something they ought to have noticed. On the contrary, it's much more plausible, I think, to regard the universe as contemplated from an impartial and open-minded perspective as *poker-faced*, to coin a phrase once used by the existentialist writer Colin Wilson: 'the world', he said, 'appears to have "no grain", to be poker-faced when interrogated about its relation to human aspirations and destiny'.[9]

The processes giving rise to our planet and its biological systems can often appear to be at best *blank* or *neutral* with regard to us and our human concerns. The vision of the poet A. E. Housman of a 'heartless, witless Nature' that 'neither cares nor knows'[10] about us and our activities seems entirely consistent with a physical and biological system which allows entire species to be swept away, and

---

which might lead to impasse or aporia. So, to transfer this to the religious context, faith is a reaching forward – not, to be sure in the Socratic spirit of critical inquiry, but still as a kind of risk, a test, like thrusting a piece of iron into the fire that will test it and either destroy it or temper and refine it so as to make it stronger.

[8]   Karl Barth, *Nein!* [1934] in Emil Brunner and Karl Barth (trans. P. Fraenkel), *Natural Theology* (Eugene, OR: Wipf and Stock, 2002), p. 75; cited in B. Davies, 'Is God Beyond Reason?', *Philosophical Investigations* 32/4 (2009), p. 342.

[9]   Colin Wilson, *Beyond the Outsider* (London: Houghton Mifflin, 1965), p. 27.

[10]   'For Nature, heartless, witless nature,/Will neither care nor know/What stranger's feet may find the meadow/And trespass there, and go/Nor ask, amid the dews of morning/If they be mine or no.' Final stanza of 'Tell me not here, it needs not saying', A.E. Housman,

countless individuals to perish in the struggle to gain enough nutrition even to survive and reproduce. By 'heartless', of course, Housman does not mean that nature is cruel or callous, merely that it is not the sort of thing to have emotional concerns or awareness of any kind – it just *is*. Or as Tennyson so graphically put it in *In Memoriam*, imagining Nature speaking: 'Thou makest thine appeal to *me*: I bring to life, I bring to death/The spirit does but mean the breath/I know no more'.[11] Yet on the other side, the following vision, recently articulated by Jonathan Sacks, is arguably also consistent with the observed facts:

> The story told by modern cosmology and Darwinian biology is wondrous almost beyond belief. It tells of a universe astonishingly precisely calibrated for the emergence, first of stars, then of second-, third- and fourth-generation stars, then of the formation of planets, one of which met exactly the conditions for the possibility of life. Then, in a way that still remains utterly mysterious, life emerged and evolved, through billions of years, yielding self-organizing systems of ever-increasing complexity, until finally one life form appears capable of standing outside its biological drives for long enough to become self-conscious … and sensing in all of this a vast intelligence that set it in motion and a caring presence that brought it into being in love.[12]

Which is more plausible – the view of Housman or the view of Sacks? Over half the world's population appear to believe that something like the second view is more plausible; but it is not my purpose to decide that question here. My point is that either view appears, in a certain light, to be quite tenable on rational grounds, and it does not seem remotely plausible to think that either side has made a simple inferential error, or blame-worthily failed to advert to certain manifest observational facts. You may, or course, say that the second, religious, picture, in speaking of a loving creator, wantonly fails to acknowledge the appalling facts of biological waste and individual suffering; or you may say that the first, purely naturalist picture, with its stress on a blind impersonal process, wantonly ignores the overwhelming improbability of complex conscious life emerging from a random series of contingencies. Both these adversarial strategies have been tried, but neither obviously succeeds; and it seems most reasonable to conclude that on present evidence the honours are even. The universe, as scrutinized by an impartial and rational spectator, is indeed poker-faced; and, *pace* Paul's strictures, those who do not see it as the work of a divine creator are, at the very least, not guilty of any obvious error of logic or observation.

---

*Last Poems* [1922], XL, reprinted in *Collected Poems* (Harmondsworth: Penguin, 1956), pp. 152–3.

[11]   Alfred Lord Tennyson, *In Memoriam* [1850], lvi.

[12]   J. Sacks, *The Great Partnership: God, Science and the Search for Meaning* (London: Hodder & Stoughton, 2011), p. 232.

## The Epistemic Context for Human Awareness of God

One might conclude from the discussion so far that rational inquiry about God leads to a standoff, or an *impasse*, at least on the basis of evidence available to the natural light of rational inquiry. But before we rush to a Scottish verdict of 'not proven', the idea of something's being *obvious to the natural light* may need further scrutiny. Our original Pauline text says that since the creation God's invisible attributes, his eternal power and divinity, being grasped or understood [*noumena*] through his works, have been seen since the creation of the world. The King James translation, instead of just 'seen', says '*clearly* seen', an emphasis followed in many subsequent English versions; but the original Greek verb *kathorao* lacks any such implication of obviousness – it simply means to see or observe or discern.[13] This prompts the thought that the divine authorship of the world might be something that is not supposed to be just clear or obvious to anyone who looks at it, but which might require a certain discernment or understanding to grasp.[14]

One analogy here might be that of scientific truths, such as some of the truths of modern nuclear physics, for example: these may be clear enough, once the scientific work has been done to make the structure of the relevant phenomena intelligible, but they first require diligent and complex investigation to enable them to be uncovered and grasped. If knowledge of God is like this, then it could hardly be inexcusable not to attain to it, since many people might not be in a position to analyse the relevant evidence, or to follow the complicated arguments needed to make the divine origins of our world discernible.

Of course there are a number of very distinguished philosophers of religion who do indeed think that knowledge of God is to be established on the basis of more or less complex probabilistic reasoning.[15] Although I greatly respect the high philosophical quality of much of this work, I do not happen to favour such an approach myself, partly because (as already indicated) I am impressed by the 'poker-faced' nature of the universe when it is impartially and dispassionately scrutinized, and partly because I think that we are not really in a position to speculate about what might have caused the cosmos, or what its observable features might reveal about its authorship, since when we are dealing with something *ex hypothesi* utterly unique, the mysterious singularity that is the existing universe, all normal probabilistic and inferential reasoning must break down. So I agree here with the Dominican thinker Herbert McCabe, that invoking God does not have genuine explanatory power in anything like the scientific sense – it does not dissolve the mystery of existence.[16]

---

[13] Luther's German version has simply *ersehen*.

[14] This would be consistent with Paul's typically intense way of expressing himself: the phrase *ta aorata kathoratai* ('things invisible are seen') is evidently a kind of paradox or oxymoron deliberately used for rhetorical effect.

[15] Most notably and most impressively by Richard Swinburne, in a series of distinguished studies; see especially *The Existence of God* (Oxford: Clarendon, 2005, 2nd edn).

[16] Compare Herbert McCabe, *Faith Within Reason* (London: Continuum, 2007).

That, however, is a debate which I shan't pursue here, since I want in this paper to shift the focus to a *different kind of knowledge*, one that seems more relevant to Paul's wider purposes in his letter to the Romans, but more important – since my concern here is not with scriptural exegesis but with the epistemic status of religious belief – one that illuminates something crucial about how knowledge of God might reasonably be expected to become available to human beings.

When one reflects on traditional religious understandings of the nature and purposes of God, at any rate in the Judaeo-Christian tradition, I think it becomes clear that the scientific analogy for knowledge of God is curiously beside the point. To read the canonical texts of the great Abrahamic faiths is to realise that the principal focus of religious belief is not on explanatory hypotheses about the world or the workings of nature, but rather on the meaning of human existence, and about how we should live our lives. The collective evidence of Scripture, which is a rich source for our grasp of what is involved in religious belief and allegiance, is pretty clear on this point: the divine call is chiefly heard as a moral and practical as opposed to a theoretical or purely cognitive one. God is, to be sure, often described as 'the maker of heaven and earth'; but his exalted role as creator is *always linked to what he requires of humans morally*. The reality which the patriarchs and prophets of the Hebrew Bible and the key protagonists of the New Testament are made aware of is one that calls them to change their lives, to follow a certain path of righteousness, to hear the cry of the oppressed, to love one another, to forgive those who have wronged them and so on through a long catalogue of luminous moral insights that form the living core of the Judaeo-Christian tradition.[17]

The primary domain of religious thought and language, in short, is the *practical domain of meaning and morality, not the theoretical domain of science or explanatory theory*. Jonathan Sacks, from whom I quoted earlier, draws attention to the fact that three of the most seminal thinkers of our modern intellectual culture, Einstein, Freud and Wittgenstein, all concur on this point. 'To know an answer to the question "What is the meaning of life?" means to be religious', said Einstein; 'the idea of life having a meaning stands or falls with the religious system', said Freud; 'to believe in God means to see that life has a meaning' says Wittgenstein.[18] You may think that a triple *argumentum ad verecundiam*, appealing to three authorities in one sentence, is a bit much. But the agreement of the three

---

[17]   Similar calls, for compassion and self-purification, for example, are found in the Islamic scriptures. For an expansion of the point developed in this paragraph, see J. Cottingham, 'Conversion, Self-discovery and Moral Change' in I. Dalferth (ed.), *Conversion* (Claremont Studies in Philosophy of Religion, Mohr Siebeck: Tübingen, forthcoming).

[18]   Albert Einstein, *Ideas and Opinions* (New York: Dell, 1954), p. 11; Sigmund Freud, *Civilization and its Discontents* [*Das Unbehagen in der Kultur*,1929], Ch. 2 (PFL, Vol. 12, p. 263); Ludwig Wittgenstein, *Notebooks 1914–1916*, 2nd edn, trans. G.E.M. Anscombe (Chicago: University of Chicago Press, 1979), p. 74e, 8.7.16. All cited in Sacks, *Great Partnership*, pp. 204, 318.

intellectual giants in espousing a moral and hermeneutic rather than a theoretical and explanatory conception of God is nonetheless striking. Such a conception, moreover, has some interesting motivational implications. If the primary motivation for believing in God is that one finds the God hypothesis plausible, then a major factor in one's religious allegiance will be the thought that one is in possession of an intellectually satisfying explanatory theory. Should the God hypothesis lose its appeal in this respect, should one be able to say with Laplace, *je n'ai pas besoin de cette hypothèse*, then the allegiance will be significantly undermined. By contrast, if the allegiance to God is based on my seeing that commitment to God gives my life meaning and value, then the stakes are rather different. My allegiance will be bound up with questions about salvation, transformation of life, the ability to live with affirmation and hope – the questions that have always been at the heart of the religious life as traditionally conceived. It is in this context, I am suggesting, that we can most fruitfully approach the question of how knowledge of God might be available to human beings.

Such a perspective points us towards a new kind of religious epistemology – one that, rather than trying to make religious knowledge conform to a neutral, secular-style epistemic template, takes account of the special conditions under which God, if he exists, might be expected to manifest himself. The primary focus will be on the moral and practical context in which awareness of God can be expected to be generated, rather than on the context of abstract speculative or theoretical belief. Now the God of the Judaeo-Christian tradition has often been conceived as Blaise Pascal underlined, as *Deus absconditus*, the hidden God: his purpose of entering into a free and loving relationship with his creatures would be thwarted were he to coerce their allegiance, so he can be expected (in Pascal's words) 'to appear openly to those who seek him with all their heart, and hidden from those who shun him'. It is entirely consistent with this that God should provide signs that offer, in Pascal's words, 'enough light for those who desire to see, and enough darkness for those of a contrary disposition'.[19] This crucially alters the epistemic rules that govern what we can expect by way of evidence in the case of God. Instead of evidence of the kind that is available to any objective and detached observer, one might expect the signs of God's existence to more closely related to God's salvific purposes.

This last point gives us a further reason for rejecting the idea that knowledge of God might be like technical or scientific knowledge, needing complicated and diligent investigational techniques in order to be disclosed. If the call to turn to God is primarily a moral and spiritual call, then given the basic premise of Abrahamic monotheism about a universally loving and compassionate God, one would *prima facie* expect the call to be able to be heard without special training or expertise or intellectual prowess. To put it in the Christian terms famously

---

[19] *Il y a assez de lumière pour ceux qui ne désirent que de voir, et assez d'obscurité pour ceux qui ont une disposition contraire.* Pascal, *Pensées* [c. 1660], ed. L. Lafuma (Paris: Seuil, 1962), no. 149.

rehearsed by René Descartes in Part One of his *Discourse on the Method*, the kingdom of heaven must be 'no less open to the most ignorant than to the most learned'.[20] So one might conclude from this that knowledge of God cannot in principle be something complicated for humans to attain: rather, it seems one ought to expect that, like the divine mercy of which Portia spoke, it must drop 'as the gentle rain from heaven upon the place beneath'.[21]

However, though not requiring complex inferential processes or other learned investigations, such knowledge need not be supposed to be quite as universal and freely available as the drops of rain which fall on all alike whether they like it or not. The Pascalian phrase just mentioned ('enough light for those who desire to see, and enough darkness for those of a contrary disposition') suggests that, instead of an unavoidable rain shower, a rather more apt simile for how awareness of God comes about might be the fleeting appearance of morning dew – certainly not something that needs complicated techniques to experience, but something that requires you to be interested enough to get up early in the morning and go out into the fields. A somewhat similar point has recently been put by Stephen Evans, who argues that we ought to expect knowledge of God to be (i) 'widely accessible' (given the deity's benign purposes), but also (ii) 'easily resistible' (as it ought to be if human freedom is to be respected).[22] What kind of knowledge might fit these conditions?

---

[20]    *Le chemin [au ciel] n'en est pas moins ouvert au plus ignorants qu'aux plus doctes.* René Descartes, *Discours de la Méthode* [1637], part i (AT VI 8: CSM I 114). René Descartes, *Meditations* [1641], Second Replies (AT VIII 148: CSM II 105–6). In this essay, 'AT' refers to the standard Franco-Latin edition of Descartes by C. Adam and P. Tannery, *Œuvres de Descartes* (12 vols, rev. edn, Paris: Vrin/CNRS, 1964–76); 'CSM' refers to the English translation by J. Cottingham, R. Stoothoff and D. Murdoch, *The Philosophical Writings of Descartes*, vols I and II (Cambridge: Cambridge University Press, 1985).

[21]    'The quality of mercy is not strained./It droppeth, as the gentle rain from heaven,/ upon the place beneath', William Shakespeare, *The Merchant of Venice* [c. 1597], IV, i.

[22]    'One thing we might expect, given God's intentions for humans, is that the knowledge of God would be widely available, not difficult to gain. If we assume God cares about all humans, and that all of them are intended by God to enjoy a relationship with God, then it seems reasonable to believe that God would make it possible at least for very many humans to come to know his existence … I shall call this the "Wide Accessibility Principle" … According to [the "Easy Resistibility Principle"] … knowledge of God is not forced on humans. Those who would not wish to love and serve God if they were aware of God's reality [should] find it relatively easy to reject the idea that there is a God. To allow such people this option, it is necessary for God to make the evidence he provide for himself to be less than fully compelling. It might for instance, be the kind of evidence that requires interpretation, and include enough ambiguity that it can be interpreted in more than one way' (C. Stephen Evans, *Natural Signs and Knowledge of God* (Oxford: Oxford University Press, 2010), pp. 13, 15).

## 'Kardiatheology' and Personal Transformation

One answer to this question has been proposed by Paul Moser, in his two recent books *The Elusive God* and *The Evidence for God*, both of which display a marked scepticism about the value and appropriateness of traditional arguments for God offered by natural theology.[23] Moser rails against the demand made by 'skeptics and philosophers' that God should provide us with what he calls 'spectator evidence' of divine reality – the kind of evidence that can be gathered and evaluated by a detached impartial observer. Such a demand, argues Moser, misses what would be the main redemptive aim of the Jewish and Christian God, by allowing the topic of divine reality to become a matter for 'casual speculative discussion', and thereby in a certain sense trivializing it.[24] Moser offers instead a quite different model of theology, a *kardiatheology*, as he calls it, which is aimed 'primarily at one's motivational heart, including one's will ...'[25] And this connects crucially with the question of evidence. Moser maintains that on any plausible understanding of the nature of a God worthy of worship, 'divine self-revelation and its corresponding evidence ... would seek to transform humans *motivationally*, and not just intellectually, towards perfect love and its required volitional cooperation with God'. It follows from this, Moser argues, that the traditional methods and arguments of natural theology suffer from a 'debilitating flaw': they offer 'no evidence whatever' of a living personal God who is worthy of worship and seeks fellowship with humans'.[26]

But what does 'kardiatheology' yield in the way of evidence? Moser's answer is that the evidence will take the form of *individual experience of divine transformative power*. That might suggest a very personal and subjective approach, bordering on fideism – an appeal to the need to trust oneself to the salvific power of God either without rational support, or even in the face of reason. But Moser is adamant that faith needs the support of reason – it needs to be 'cognitively commendable';

---

[23]    Paul Moser, *The Elusive God* (Cambridge: Cambridge University Press, 2008), and *The Evidence for God* (Cambridge: Cambridge University Press, 2010).

[24]    'For purposes of cognitively rational belief that God exists, skeptics and philosophers generally demand that God provide us with *spectator evidence* of divine reality. In doing so, they miss what would be the main redemptive ... aim of the Jewish and Christian God ... Spectator evidence from God would allow God to be ... domesticated and taken for granted by us in our selfish ways, because it would lack corrective judgement toward us and our selfishness. Given spectator evidence, the topic of divine reality would readily become a matter for casual, speculative discussion, and would thereby be trivialized ... Opposing selfish human pride, authoritative divine evidence would work by *cognitive grace*, a free, unmerited gift from God, rather than by any human earning that supposedly obligated God to redeem a person or to give divine self-revelation to a person ... The God of perfectly authoritative evidence would therefore not fit well with the docile gods of the philosophers and natural theologians' (Moser, *Elusive God*, pp. 47–9; cf. p. 10).

[25]    Moser, *Evidence for God*, p. 26; cf. p. 253.

[26]    Moser, *Evidence for God*, p. 158.

and this in turn requires that there be a rational basis for commendation. Such a rational basis, according to Moser, can be found in the radical change *I myself* find myself undergoing as I open myself to the transforming Spirit of God. We are now a million miles from neutral, secular epistemology, both because the evidence invoked makes irreducible reference to the transforming Spirit of God, and also because it involves not some impersonally accessible body of data, but something that becomes, as Moser puts it, 'salient to me, as I, myself, am increasingly willing to become such evidence – that is, evidence of God's reality'.[27]

The epistemology implied here raises some interesting philosophical questions. Moser himself calls it a 'grace-based' epistemology,[28] and this may lead some secular critics to dismiss the whole idea as question-begging, nothing more than an appeal to the unsubstantiated theistic claims of a cosy club of insiders. Certainly, such humanly experienced acquaintance with God's call will hardly be accepted by all as a coercive argument for God's existence, but it is not meant to be: Moser's case, and it seems hard to gainsay, is that it can still validly function as evidence for a given person of God's existence. Admittedly we are dealing here with what might be called 'insider information' – reports in favour of a certain outlook coming from individuals caught up in a process that already implies being committed to that outlook, or at least being deeply receptive to the possibility of its truth. But so far from this being an unusual situation in human life, there are many parallels. Sigmund Freud, in citing the evidence supporting his psychoanalytic outlook, readily acknowledged that his evidence was not of a kind to satisfy normal scientific rules of procedure. The processes involved, he admitted, are not susceptible of public investigation under normal observer conditions, since the psychotherapeutic process takes place in a 'private consulting room' and 'only under the conditions of a special affective relationship to the physician'.[29] His underlying point is that the kinds of insight gained in therapy are not achieved via objective and detached scrutiny; on the contrary, the patient who maintains a sceptical and detached stance is already in a condition that tends to block the healing effects of the process, or even prevent it getting off the ground in the first place. Only by allowing oneself to be vulnerable and open to the images dredged up from the depths of the unconscious – a process which itself requires a certain openness to the terms of the 'affective relationship' with the therapist – will the work of healing be able to make itself felt. The affective dimension, including the painfulness and the vulnerability, is quite simply part of the process; and the subject's entering into such a state is a precondition for the confirmatory evidence to be manifested.

Some sceptics may be inclined to respond: 'so much the worse for the epistemic status of the claims of psychoanalysis'. But whatever one feels about this particular example, it seems hard to deny that there are phenomena which

---

[27]   Moser, *Evidence for God*, p. 172.

[28]   Moser, *Evidence for God*, p. 172.

[29]   Sigmund Freud, *A General Introduction to Psychoanalysis* [1920], Lecture I, trans. J. Riviere (New York: Washington Square Press, 1952), pp. 22–4.

are not such as to be apprehended under the standard scientific conditions for what counts as objective evidence, but which require receptivity by the subject, and possibly even internal transformation, in order to make themselves manifest. If one does not like the psychoanalytic example, there are other more familiar instances. People speak of the transformative power of love, or of great music or poetry, yet the relevant evidence for such power is available only to *insiders*, those who find themselves undergoing radical change as the result of what they allow themselves to be exposed to.

There are, to be sure, some caveats to be entered here, before we give a blank cheque to the claims of this kind of 'insider evidence'. In the first place, we need to be clear what the evidence is supposed to be evidence *for*. Roger Scruton, describing the experience of a great work of music, speaks of 'sacred' moment, moments 'outside time, in which the deep loneliness and anxiety of the human condition is overcome', and 'the human world is suddenly irradiated from a point beyond it'.[30] Evidently one might accept his claim about the power of great music to produce the changes he describes without conceding that this is evidence for a transcendent source of change – something that irradiates the world 'from a point beyond it'. So similarly, the personal and moral changes undergone by someone who believes they are opening themselves to God do not automatically guarantee that the source of those changes is the external transcendent source that the believer takes it to be. In the second place, evidence need not be *conclusive* evidence: there may be 'defeaters'. So if I take certain spiritual transformations I myself undergo to be evidence for God ('personifying' evidence', as Moser puts it), this does not remove the need to consider possible counter-evidence for God's existence (for instance, evidence arising from the problem of evil). Nevertheless, and notwithstanding these caveats, it seems reasonable to conclude from this part of our argument that there are certain areas or dimensions of reality where the relevant evidence is available only to insiders in the form of the personal transformation they themselves experience.


**Natural Intimations of the Transcendent**


How do our conclusions so far bear on the traditional theological claims concerning natural knowledge of God? Moser's 'grace-based epistemology', stressing the gracious action of the Holy Spirit in transforming human lives towards cooperation with God, might seem to belong in the domain of faith and revelation rather than natural reason; but as we have seen, things are not a simple as that, since Moser is at pains to point out that the relevant motivational changes do function as genuine evidence for God. Rather than spending more time unpicking Moser's position, however, I want to broaden the argument by considering the more general

---

[30]   Roger Scruton, 'The Sacred and the Human' [2010] http://www.st-andrews.ac.uk/ gifford/2010/the-sacred-and-the-human/ (accessed 30 March 2010).

approach to religious epistemology that it exemplifies – what might be called the 'Pascalian' approach. By this I mean an approach which emphasises evidence for God that arises not in the context of theoretical theological argument, but in the context of interior change and personal transformation – evidence, in short, of the kind that is by its very nature available only to insiders, in the sense of those who have undergone the relevant interior changes.

How, then, does this 'Pascalian' epistemology bear on the question of natural knowledge of God? The Vatican Council document of 1870, quoted at the start of this chapter, follows a long-standing distinction between, on the one hand, the 'natural light' of human reason, and, on the other, supernatural revelation (for example the revelations reported in Scripture, or handed down via apostolic authority), which must be believed on faith. But if we start to think in terms of Pascalian epistemology, it seems clear that the kinds of phenomena it invokes don't fit very well into the traditional dichotomy between faith and reason.

The stark dichotomy between 'two sources of illumination', as René Descartes put it (following a long Christian philosophical tradition) – the *lumen naturale*, or light of reason, and the lumen *supernaturale*, or light of faith,[31] suffers from the following problem: it suggests that *either* evidence has to be such as to be accessible by purely natural human secular reason, *or else* it has to be revelatory, and/or perceptible only to the eyes of faith. Aquinas' idea of faith 'making up' for the deficiencies of the ordinary natural senses encapsulates this idea.[32] However, there is surely a *tertium quid*. Let us suppose, for example, that someone is not satisfied with the logic of the Five Ways; or let us suppose they find contemporary arguments for the 'fine-tuning' of the universe insufficient to licence the inference of a cosmic intelligence at work; and suppose they have similar dissatisfactions with the other weapons of standard natural theology. Does it follow that to come to knowledge of God they are now dependent on the supernatural light, on faith and revelation?

The answer, I suggest, is no; and I want to close by drawing attention to some crucial aspects of our human experience that function, if you will, as a kind of bridge between what we can access through our natural human endowments, and

---

[31]     'The clarity or transparency which can induce our will to give its assent is *of two kinds* (*duplex*): the first comes from the natural light (*lumen naturale*), while the second comes from divine grace … Those who read my books will not be able to suppose that I did not recognize this supernatural light (*lumen supernaturale*), since I expressly stated in the Fourth Meditation that it produces in our inmost thought a deposition to will, without lessening our freedom'. René Descartes, *Meditations* [1641], Second Replies (AT VIII 148: CSM II 105–6).

[32]     From the hymn *Pange lingua* [1260]. Aquinas' position on the relation between faith and reason is not what is sometimes called a 'fideist' one, that faith *substitutes* for reason; the two, rather, are complementary. Thomas elsewhere describes an 'ascent' via natural reason, coupled with a 'descent' from God via revealed truth: *Summa contra Gentiles* [1259–65], trans. A.C. Pegis (Notre Dame, Ill.: Notre Dame University Press, 1975), IV. 1, and see Introduction to Vol. I, p. 39.

what seems to depend on the gracious bestowal of something more extraordinary and special. Consider the 'transcendent' moments that very many people will from time to time have experienced, the times when the drab, mundane pattern of our ordinary routines gives way to something vivid and radiant, and we seem to glimpse something of the beauty and significance of the world we inhabit. Wordsworth expressed it as follows, in a famous passage in *The Prelude*:

> There are in our existence spots of time,
> That with distinct pre-eminence retain
> A renovating virtue, whence – depressed
> By false opinion and contentious thought,
> Or aught of heavier or more deadly weight,
> In trivial occupations, and the round
> Of ordinary intercourse – our minds
> Are nourished and invisibly repaired;
> A virtue, by which pleasure is enhanced,
> That penetrates, enables us to mount,
> When high, more high, and lifts us up when fallen.[33]

What 'lifts us up' is the sense that our lives are not just a disorganized concatenation of contingent episodes, but that they are capable of fitting into a pattern of meaning, where responses of joy and thankfulness and compassion and love for our fellow creatures are intertwined; and where they make sense because they reflect a splendour and a richness that is not of our own making. Notice that this kind of 'transfiguration' is not a 'religious experience', if that latter term is understood in the rather narrow way that has become common in our culture, when philosophers speak, for example, of the 'argument from religious experience'. What is often meant under this latter heading is some kind of revelation which is taken to be evidence for, or to validate, the supposed truths of some particular creed or cult – a vision of the Virgin Mary, for example, or the sense (reported by one of William James' correspondents) of 'the close presence of a sort of mighty person'.[34] This kind of notion is I think uppermost in many people's minds when they insist that they have never had a 'religious experience'. By contrast, the kinds of 'transcendent' experience described by Wordsworth and many other writers involve not so much a revelation of supernatural entities, but rather a heightening, an intensification that transforms the way in which we experience the world. The term 'transcendent' seems appropriate not in the sense of that there is necessarily an explicit invocation of metaphysical objects that transcend ordinary experience, but rather because the categories of our mundane life undergo a radical shift: there

---

[33]   William Wordsworth, *The Prelude* 12, 208–18 [1805 edition].

[34]   William James, *Varieties of Religious Experience* [1902] (London: Fontana, 1960), Ch. 3, p. 75.

is a sudden irradiation that discloses a beauty and goodness, a meaning that was before occluded.

Other examples could be drawn from the world of music, for instance as described in the work of Roger Scruton which I mentioned earlier. Yet another example presents itself in the exercise of our human moral faculties. The Danish philosopher Knud Løgstrup speaks of the 'ethical demand' in terms of trust and self-surrender that are a basic part of human life.[35] His particular focus is the openness and responsiveness to another person which is morally required in any human encounter or relationship. But a phenomenologically somewhat similar process occurs, it seems to me, in our responsiveness to central moral values. What philosophers have come to call 'normativity' is one way of referring to a remarkable feature of moral values like the wrongness of cruelty, for example, or the goodness of compassion: such values exert a demand upon us, they call forth our allegiance, irrespective of our inclinations and desires. When we contemplate such properties, with the required combination of attentiveness yet receptivity, we transcend ourselves, as Pascal might have put it (I am thinking of his dictum *l'homme passe l'homme* – humanity transcends itself)[36]: we are taken beyond our own inclinations or endogenous attitudes to something higher and more authoritative. No matter what you or I may feel about cruelty – even if we develop a taste for it – it remains wrong, wrong in all possible worlds. And no matter how disinclined you or I may be to show compassion, the goodness of compassion retains its authority over us and demands our admiration and our compliance, whether we like it or not.

Now all these cases I have mentioned, our vivid awareness of natural beauty, our responses to the mysterious power of music and our sense of awe before the authoritative demands of morality – all these may described by the believer as revelations of the sacred, as intimations of the divine reality that is the source of all truth, beauty and goodness. But it is also striking that they do not necessarily present as supernatural or miraculous irruptions in to the natural world; they are in a way perfectly 'natural'. They are not, to be sure, everyday or routine occurrences, since they characteristically raise us up to something higher than our mundane habits and inclinations; but the relevant experiences depend on faculties and sensibilities that are an integral part of our human heritage. Except in tragic cases where these sensibilities have been irretrievably damaged by trauma or abuse or serious illness, such heightenings, or intensifications, transforming the way in which we experience the world, can come to all of us, from time to time, and if we honestly interrogate ourselves we are hard pressed to deny it.

I want to suggest that these experiences fall, simply and uncomplicatedly, into the category of awareness of God by means of the natural light. They are, if you like, natural intimations of the transcendent, glimpses of the sacred dimension that forms the ever present horizon of our natural human existence. I am, to be sure, here

---

[35]	Knud E. Løgstrup, *The Ethical Demand* [*Den Etiske Fordring*, 1956], ed. H. Fink and A. MacIntyre (Notre Dame, Ill.: University of Notre Dame Press, 1997).

[36]	Pascal, *Pensées*, no. 131.

somewhat widening the traditional extension of the phrase 'natural light', since that is normally taken to be the natural light of *reason*: the terms *lumen naturale* and *lux rationis* are virtually interchangeable in many Christian writers.[37] But *that* I think is simply an instance of an intellectualist bias that is prevalent among many philosophers and theologians. If something can't be turned into an argument or a logical intuition, then it is supposed to be not worth its salt – or else it is allowed because it is construed as something supernatural that, as Descartes put it, 'whisks us up at a stroke to infallible faith'.[38] But the kinds of experience I have been speaking of are on the one hand not supernatural short cuts; yet on the other hand they are not exercises of our rational or inferential faculties, but something much more spontaneous and direct and intuitive. They are *natural glimpses of the divine.*

But even if they are not themselves arguments or intuitions of the intellect, can these glimpses at least be the *basis* for intellectual inference to God? Well, in a sense perhaps they can, in the following sense: since it is a rational requirement, a requirement of intellectual integrity, to take proper account of all aspects of our experience, any worldview that wantonly ignores, or fails properly to accommodate, these aspects of our experience is to that extent intellectually weakened in comparison with its theistic competitors. Yet in another sense I am inclined to say that construing such experiences as grist for an inferential mill would be a distortion. For if we take on board the lessons of Pascalian epistemology, we should see that there is not here a body of evidence from which there is a logical or probabilistic conclusion to be drawn by anyone who responsibly attends to the data. In the first place, no one can be compelled to have, or to acknowledge, such experiences: they require a certain kind of focused attention, a certain motivational stance which might best be described as a listening or attunement.[39] And in the

---

[37]    The notion of *lux rationis* or 'the light of reason', found in Descarte's *Regulae* [c. 1628] (AT X 368: CSM I 14), becomes, in the *Meditations, lumen naturale,* 'the natural light' (for example AT VII 40: CSM II 28).

[38]    René Descartes, *Preface* to the 1647 French translation of the *Principles of Philosophy*, AT IXB 4: CSM II 181.

[39]    Compare Heidegger's term *Stimmung* (cf. *Being and Time* [*Sein und Zeit*, 1927], trans. J. Macquarrie and E. Robinson (New York: Harper and Row, 1962), H 137), as interpreted by George Steiner: 'Metaphysical techniques of argument and systematization prevent us from "thinking the question of being", from putting our thoughts into the vital register of interrogation (I use "register" to recall the notion of *Stimmung*, of tuning and accord between question and being) ... [This] underlies Heidegger's "counter-logic", the peculiar design to replace the aggressive inquisitorial discourse of Aristotelian, Baconian and positivist investigation with an unresolved, even circuitous, nevertheless dynamic dialectic. In Aristotelian analysis, nature is made to bear witness; Bacon tells of putting natural phenomena on the rack so as to make them yield objective truths. In French *la question* signifies judicial torture. In Heidegger's "questioning of being", an activity so central that it defines, or should define, the human status of man, there is neither enforcement nor a programmatic thrust from inquisition to reply ... To question truly is to enter into harmonic concordance with that which is being questioned. Far from being initiator and

second place, they are not 'data' presented for our speculative assessment and inference. Rather, we ourselves are part of the evidence, as we open ourselves to something that is resistible, something that does not compel our assent, but which if we are responsive has the power to transform us – not in such a way as to enhance our store of knowledge, or to allow us to make better inferences, but so as to irradiate our lives with meaning and value that we cannot create for ourselves.

In this sense, to come full circle back to the Pauline dictum with which we began, God's power and divine nature are indeed manifest in what he has created – in the beauty and wonder of creation, in the glory of the works of music and art that celebrate that creation, and in the majesty of the moral law that inspires the human race, made in his image, with awe and longing. Nothing in logic or ordinary observation compels us to see things in such a transfigured light, so when such manifestations fail to occur, or for various reasons pass people by, or are interpreted in a sceptical or deflationary way, there is no point in issuing condemnations about their having 'no excuse'.

And the context, in any case, is quite unlike that of ordinary human reasoning, scientific investigation or speculative inquiry. In the very special character of our distinctive human responses to the transcendent there is always an implied call, a call to change, and to bring our weak and wasteful lives into closer harmony with the enduring source of being and value. The standard Christian view is that we cannot do that unaided, and that our salvation requires faith, and a voluntary act of openness to divine grace. But the special theology of faith and grace builds on the ordinary natural responses that are already at work in our experience of the natural and human world. So there is a link between the natural and the supernatural light, a bridge between the workings of nature and of grace, which together have the power to guide us home to our ultimate source and end. Or, if you will forgive me for allowing the last word to Wordsworth, this time from a different but equally famous poem, the Intimations Ode:

> Hence in a season of calm weather
> Though inland far we be,
> Our Souls have sight of that immortal sea
> Which brought us hither.[40]

The 'sight' that Wordsworth refers to is not 'objective evidence', but neither is it 'insider knowledge', restricted to the club of believers or the saved. It arises out of a pattern of response that is part of our ordinary natural human heritage: we only

---

sole master of the encounter, as Socrates, Descartes and the modern scientist-technologist so invariably are, the Heideggerian asker lays himself open that which is being questioned and becomes the vulnerable locus, the permeable space it its disclosure' (George Steiner, *Heidegger* (London: Fontana Press, 1992, 2nd edn), p. 55).

[40]    William Wordsworth, 'Ode: Intimations of Immortality, from recollections of early childhood', from *Collected Poems* [1815].

need to find the time to attune ourselves to it, and allow ourselves to glimpse its true meaning.

Chapter 3

# A Robust Reformed Epistemology

Anthony Bolos

## Introduction

Recent literature in religious epistemology has overlooked a significant debate in mainstream epistemology. In short, theories in religious epistemology have failed to consider the value problem. This paper, then, hopes to rectify this omission by arguing that one of the most influential accounts of religious epistemology – Reformed epistemology – fails to adequately account for the final value of knowledge. Reformed epistemology fails to account for the final value of knowledge in that it is susceptible to the same problems that all reliabilist accounts of knowledge face; namely, the swamping problem. This problem threatens to undermine any attempt to account for the value of knowledge over and above the value of true belief for, as it stands, the swamping problem claims that there is no real difference in value between true belief and knowledge. In the end, an agent is epistemically no better off with knowledge than with mere true belief.

However, there is a reasonable way out for the Reformed epistemologist. Once the swamping problem is properly understood, I argue that the Reformed epistemologist is in a good position to account for the value of knowledge. This comes by way of endorsing the achievement thesis whereby knowledge is seen as a cognitive achievement. In this essay, I highlight two different ways one can understand the achievement thesis. First, a cognitive achievement can be understood as success from ability that is always *primarily* creditable to the agent. Or, second, a cognitive achievement can be understood as success from ability that is at least *partially* creditable to the agent. How one understands the achievement thesis will depend on the role the *sensus divinitatis* plays in the belief-forming process.

Further, the Reformed epistemologist is in a good position to meet the requirements for the *strong* achievement thesis.[1] The strong achievement thesis argues that an achievement should be understood in terms of overcoming some obstacle whereby the agent's belief is the result of some ability that can be credited to the agent. The account I propose not only meets the requirements of the strong achievement thesis, but also retains a distinctive feature of Reformed epistemology in that the belief in question can be said to overcome the obstacle of cognitive

---

[1]    The strong vs weak achievement thesis won't be considered in detail. For a basic overview see Duncan Pritchard, 'Achievements, Luck and Value', *Think* 25 (2010).

malfunction that, as Plantinga states, is brought about by sin. It is an achievement because it overcomes an excessively hostile environment that is not conducive to belief in God given the cognitive consequence of sin. In the end, whichever version of the achievement thesis is correct, it is possible to provide an account of Reformed epistemology where the final value of knowledge is adequately demonstrated. I will present several different positions with regard to the achievement thesis. What I will claim is that the Reformed epistemologist is in a good position to account for the final value of knowledge regardless of the position one takes with respect to the various positions within the achievement thesis.


## Reformed Epistemology and the Nature of Knowledge

Reformed epistemology is a thesis about the nature of (religious) knowledge. And within Reformed epistemology, Alvin Plantinga's account has become one of the most discussed within the philosophical literature.[2] Plantinga's account revolves around a parity argument whereby the agent's belief in God might be basic just in case the belief in question was brought about in the same way as other beliefs we take to be basic. Perceptual beliefs, for example, are thought to be basic in that the acceptance of the perceptual experience is immediate and non-inferential. In other words, the perceptual belief is immediate and isn't accepted on the basis of any other beliefs. Thus, Plantinga asks, if perceptual beliefs (as well as memory and a priori beliefs) are basic, why can't belief in God be basic?

According to Plantinga, belief in God might be basic if the belief comes about in the same way that other basic beliefs arise. Thus, there needs to be some faculty similar to your perceptual faculty that gives rise to this immediate and non-inferential belief. The faculty that is similar to the perceptual faculty, it is claimed, is the *sensus divinitatis*. This faculty, then, gives rise to belief in God when occasioned by some event or experience. Plantinga notes that the working of this faculty is triggered by any number of circumstances (for example, beauty, grandeur, guilt and so on),[3] and that in the same way that you seem to 'find yourself' with the certain perceptual beliefs, theists, given the right circumstances, also seem to 'find themselves' with belief in God. Thus, belief in God should enjoy the same epistemic status that perceptual beliefs enjoy.

If the above account is correct, then Plantinga's description of theism as properly basic provides the theist with an account of how their belief in God can be warranted without that particular belief being inferred from evidence or argument. But Reformed epistemology isn't *only* an account of warranted belief; it is also

---

    [2]   For different accounts of Reformed epistemology see Alvin Plantinga and Nicholas Wolterstorff (eds), *Faith and Rationality* (Notre Dame, Indiana: University of Notre Dame Press, 1983).

    [3]   Alvin Plantinga, *Warranted Christian Belief* (Oxford: Oxford University Press, 2000), p. 174.

a claim about knowledge. If the theist holds a warranted belief, then this might constitute knowledge *if true*. In short, the theist can be said to have knowledge if the belief is produced by a properly functioning faculty that is working in an appropriate environment according to its design plan.[4] And this faculty, the *sensus divinitatis*, gives rise to belief in God in an immediate and non-inferential fashion when occasioned by some event or experience.

None of this of course is without controversy. One might reject Plantinga's parity argument or object to some feature of his understanding of warrant.[5] Regardless of whether Plantinga's account of the nature of knowledge is correct, what I am most concerned about in this chapter is how a Reformed epistemologist might answer the value problem in light of their account of the nature of (religious) knowledge. Given this, what is relevant are the similarities Plantinga's account of warrant has with simple reliabilism. A common component amongst reliabilist theories of knowledge is their agreement that a reliable belief-forming faculty is a *sufficient* condition for knowledge. Other reliabilists, such as Alvin Goldman and John Greco, discuss knowledge in terms of a reliable belief-forming process[6] or agent.[7]

This observation is important given that if Plantinga's account of the nature of knowledge is a reliabilist one, it will then be subject (*prima facie* at least) to many of the same objections that trouble all versions of reliabilism. And some of the most important problems relating to the value problem have been directed at reliabilist theories.[8] Thus, classifying Reformed epistemology as reliabilist will bring us one step closer to identifying the issues that face Reformed epistemology concerning the value problem.

## Knowledge and the Nature of Value

A comprehensive epistemology ought to include answers to the questions of the nature of knowledge and of its value. With Reformed epistemology, so far anyway, we have an answer to the nature question, but not the value question. However, why assume that we need an answer to the value question just because the nature question has been answered? The reason for this, I think, is that the two are

---

[4]   Plantinga, *Warranted*, p. 178.

[5]   For overviews and critiques see Jonathan Kvanvig (ed.), *Warrant in Contemporary Epistemology* (London: Rowman & Littlefield, 1996).

[6]   See Alvin Goldman, 'Reliabilism: What is Justified Belief?' in Louis Pojman (ed.), *The Theory of Knowledge* (Belmont: Wadsworth, 2003), p. 265.

[7]   See John Greco, 'Agent Reliabilism', *Nous* 33 (1999), pp. 273–96.

[8]   See Linda Zagzebski, 'The Search for the Source of the Epistemic Good', *Metaphilosophy*, 34 (2003), pp. 12–28. See also Jonathan Kvanvig, *The Value of Understanding and the Pursuit of Understanding* (Cambridge: Cambridge University Press, 2003), pp. 46–52.

linked.[9] If a successful answer to the nature question tells us how we are to obtain knowledge, a successful answer to the value question ought to tell us, among other things, why obtaining that *knowledge* is something we ought to value. Without the latter, the former becomes irrelevant. After all, if arriving at true belief is just as epistemically praiseworthy as arriving at knowledge then the nature question, while possibly interesting, becomes less relevant.

So if the value and nature questions are linked, how should Reformed epistemology answer the value question? First, we need to be clear on what exactly the value question involves. There are three main problems that arise while discussing the value question:[10]

- The *primary value problem* is the challenge to explain why knowledge is more valuable than mere true belief.
- The *secondary value problem* is the challenge to explain why knowledge is more valuable than that which falls short of knowledge.
- The *tertiary value problem* is the challenge to explain why knowledge has a different kind of value than that which falls short of knowledge.[11]

While each problem presents unique difficulties for the value question, it is the third problem that concerns us here. What makes the tertiary problem so relevant is that in answering the tertiary problem, one finds an answer to the other two problems. The reason for this is that in discussing what *kind* of value knowledge has, we will be able to see why it is to be desired over mere true belief and that which falls just short of knowledge.

What precisely, then, is the kind of value that gives knowledge its distinctive epistemic place? We have, at minimum, four options to choose from: instrumental value, extrinsic value, intrinsic value and final value. The three I want to briefly discuss, however, are instrumental, intrinsic and final value.[12] In the end, I conclude that the kind of value that we are going to look for in the case of knowledge is final value.

Instrumental value might be defined as something that is valued often because of some other desired good that comes as a result. Money is a good example of

---

[9]    See John Greco, *Achieving Knowledge* (Cambridge: Cambridge University Press, 2010), p. 91. See also Jonathan Kvanvig, *Value*, pp. ix–xvii.

[10]    The following discussion on value will follow closely Pritchard's work on this topic; see Duncan Pritchard, Alan Millar, and Adrian Haddock (eds), *The Nature and Value of Knowledge* (Oxford: Oxford University Press, 2010), chapters 1–3.

[11]    Ibid., 3–8.

[12]    I'm setting aside a discussion on extrinsic value because the issues surrounding the value of knowledge have never really involved any debate on extrinsic value. The primary issues surrounding the value of knowledge have usually pitched intrinsic value and instrumental value against each other. In other words, the options are usually intrinsic or instrumental value. As I will discuss later, this isn't quite right.

something that has instrumental value. We value money not because it, as an object, is an end in and of itself to be valued; rather, we value money because it often helps us acquire or achieve our desires – it is a *means* to an end.[13] However, there is nothing particularly distinctive about instrumental value. Justification, for example, is said to have instrumental value. And even if one can successfully demonstrate that knowledge has more instrumental value than true belief, this kind of comparison puts the discussion back on the continuum that we are hoping to avoid. Thus, instrumental value gets us no closer to answering the question of distinctive value.

Intrinsic value, however, is a more plausible candidate. In many earlier discussions about the value of knowledge, the kind of value discussed is intrinsic value. For something to have intrinsic value, it is said to have value for its own sake. As Christine Korsgaard puts it, to say that something is intrinsically valuable is to say that it has 'its goodness in itself'.[14] In other words, its value is derived from properties that are internal to the object in question. This rules out, then, the possibility that something has value because of its relational or external properties. Further, the value of the object in question does not, if intrinsically valuable, derive its value from some instrumental good that comes as a result.[15]

Intrinsic value, then, is a possibility when it comes to determining what kind of value knowledge has. However, I wish to argue that this is not the kind of value that knowledge has. This is a good thing given that a discussion on the intrinsic value of knowledge would lead to a discussion on intrinsic value scepticism. By denying that knowledge has intrinsic value, we avoid a difficult debate concerning even the possibility of whether anything (let alone knowledge) has intrinsic value.[16] This leaves us, then, with one final option: final value.[17]

---

[13]   Of course it is always possible that someone might value money as an end. I take it that these would be special cases and that generally money is the kind of thing that is valued because it might, for example, fulfill our desires.

[14]   Christine M. Korsgaard, 'Two Distinctions in Goodness', *The Philosophical Review* 92/2 (1983), p. 170.

[15]   With Korsgaard, I agree that it is best to keep the categories of value as intrinsic vs extrinsic and final vs instrumental. However, if something is intrinsically valuable, it is, by most accounts, finally valuable (that is, non-instrumental). As we will see in the next paragraph, however, something can be finally valuable without being intrinsically valuable. See Wlodek Rabinowicz and Toni Rønnow-Rasmussen, 'A Distinction in Value: Intrinsic and For Its Own Sake', *Proceedings of the Aristotelian Society* 100 (2000), pp. 33–51.

[16]   For a discussion on this see Shelly Kagan, 'Rethinking Intrinsic Value', *Journal of Ethics* 2 (1998), pp. 277–97.

[17]   Note here that I am not conceding to the intrinsic value sceptic. The only point I am making is that it is an added benefit of my account that we are not trying to account for the intrinsic value of knowledge, as this would take us into a debate about the coherence of intrinsic value. As will become apparent in the next section, final value really is the only option in accounting for the distinctive value of knowledge. This is because knowledge is valuable given its relational properties (for example, its relationship to cognitive achievements).

The kind of value that knowledge has, I think, is final value. If something is finally valuable, it is non-instrumentally valuable and valuable as an end, and not merely a means to an end. Further, it is important to note that not everything that has final value has intrinsic value. The key difference is that final value allows for its value to come from some external property. In other words, something is said to be finally valuable because of its relational properties and not merely because of its internal properties. For example, what makes the first car ever built by Henry Ford valuable is different from what makes a 2012 Maserati valuable. Ford's earliest model (the Model T) had a top speed 40mph, needed to be started by a hand crank and when the fuel tank was running low could only climb steep hills in reverse. A new Maserati, however, boasts a top speed of over 180mph, starts at the push of a button and has expensive leather and wood trim throughout. We value the Maserati because of what it offers us – comfort, speed and modern styling. The Model T, however, isn't valued for its comfort, speed or modern styling. It has value because of something external to it; or, put another way, it is valuable because of its relational properties. (For example, it is valuable because of the time and place it came from, or because of its relationship to an important piece of US history.) Thus, Ford's Model T might have final value without having intrinsic value – that is, if it hadn't been one of the first cars built in Detroit its value would be questionable.

The kind of value that knowledge has, then, is final value. This is because knowledge is thought to be valuable for its own sake and is thought to have non-instrumental value. If this is true, and knowledge is indeed non-instrumental and valuable for its own sake, then where does this *final* value come from? And how can the Reformed epistemologist account for the final value of knowledge?

**The Swamping Problem**

Before discussing the source from which knowledge derives its final value, Reformed epistemology, like any reliabilist theory of knowledge, is immediately faced with an important problem; namely, the swamping problem. The swamping problem is supposed to show that true belief, whether reliably or unreliably formed, is, ultimately, what we value. The reason for this is that a reliable faculty adds nothing to the *value* of a true belief. What we as epistemic agents are aiming at, in the end, is a true belief. Thus, when an unreliable faculty happens to produce the desired end (for example, true belief), the value of the end in question remains the same. It shouldn't make any difference in terms of value whether we have a true belief as a result of a reliable faculty or a true belief as a result of an unreliable faculty. They both have given us what we want – namely, a true belief. Thus, we only value reliable faculties because of what they produce. In other words, we value reliable faculties *only* as a means to true belief.

To see this more clearly, consider an example by Linda Zagzebski.[18] In this example, we have two equally great cups coffee. One cup was made from a reliable coffee-making machine and the other was made from an unreliable coffee-making machine. The reliable machine routinely produces great cups of coffee while the unreliable machine routinely produces bad cups of coffee. In this case, however, both machines have produced great cups of coffee. The problem, then, is that it seems we ought to value both equally given that they both contain the desired end – the desired end being a great cup of coffee. And given that the desired end is a great cup of coffee, it shouldn't matter that one of the cups comes from an unreliable coffee-making machine. What this example shows, then, is that where the coffee comes from is irrelevant to its value. In other words, what is of value is the great cup of coffee and not the process that brings about the great cup of coffee. The similarities to the discussion on the value of true belief and knowledge are obvious. The value of two equally true beliefs is the same regardless of the process that produced these true beliefs.

Before attempting to offer a solution to the swamping problem, it will be important to point out exactly what the swamping problem implies and what assumptions are implicit in the argument. As noted above, it was initially thought that the swamping problem was only a problem for reliabilism. Zagzebski's version of the swamping problem illustrates this belief nicely. However, it is clear that the swamping problem is not simply a problem for reliabilism.[19] After all, you could just plug in any epistemic property or condition for knowledge and the force of the swamping argument still stands. The reason for this is that the property in question plays the same role with regard to true belief as any other property that is paired with true belief. Consider, for example, the belief that epistemic properties are only instrumentally valuable in that they bring us closer to true belief. Thus, whatever the property in questions is, it seems that this property will play the same role with regard to truth in that the property will serve as merely a means to an end (that end being a true belief). Take justification, as opposed to reliability, for example. We think justification is valuable because it is usually a good indicator of the proximity of truth. Of course justification for some proposition $p$ doesn't entail the truth of $p$, it does, in many cases, put the agent on better epistemic footing than those who believe $p$ without the appropriate justification. Justification, then, is instrumentally valuable. This being the case, it seems that any epistemic property (whether it be reliability, warrant, justification and so on) will only be instrumentally valuable insofar as it helps you achieve some other epistemic good.[20] In this case, the epistemic good in question is true belief.

---

[18]   Zagzebski, 'The Search for the Source of the Epistemic Good', pp. 12–28.

[19]   See Duncan Pritchard, 'The Value Problem for Knowledge' in Pritchard et al. (eds), *The Nature and Value Knowledge*, pp. 8–11.

[20]   See Duncan Pritchard, 'Veritism and Epistemic Value' in Hilary Kornblith and Brian McLaughlin (eds), *Alvin Goldman and His Critics* (Blackwell, forthcoming).

Thus, it seems that the swamping problem isn't merely a problem for reliabilism, but also for any account where epistemic properties are understood to only have instrumental value in relation to true belief. The swamping argument does of course make this implicit claim. We have, then, what appears to the first assumption of the swamping problem:

(1)   Once the fundamental epistemic good in question is attained, no epistemic property that is merely instrumental can be added to confer additional value.

This seems right and the swamping problem is convincing in this regard. Whether we are concerned about a true belief or a great cup of coffee, once the end is attained, the instrumental property that helps us attain this end doesn't make this end any more valuable.[21] Consider, again, which equally great cup of coffee you would prefer: the one from the reliable coffee maker or the one from the unreliable coffee maker? For most, it wouldn't make any difference. Thus, I think we can easily concede (1).

However, the swamping problem makes another very important point:

(2)   The fundamental epistemic good is true belief.

In (1), it was simply stated that once the fundamental epistemic good in question is attained, no epistemic property that is merely instrumental can be added to confer additional value. However, (1) doesn't state what the fundamental epistemic good is (though, it is implied in the above paragraph).[22] The swamping problem, then, assumes the truth of (2). Veritism, or epistemic value T-monism as it is sometimes referred to, is the belief that there is one fundamental epistemic good – namely, true belief.[23] In other words, what we are aiming at and hoping to acquire as agents

---

[21]   I take it that one might reasonably think there is value in the process, but this is, I think, independent of the value that concerns the end in question. For example, if there are two equally great houses that have the same value (in this case, market value), how you come into possession of these houses matters little to the true value of the houses. Imagine that one of the houses was gained through a random game of chance (you won the house through an email lottery) and the other house was one that you built over many years as the result of your skill and effort. The former was gained through a process that holds little value, while the latter was gained through what many would consider a valuable process. The home you own because of your skill and effort is something you can be proud of, perhaps even brag about. All this, though, is in spite of the fact that both houses have the same market value.

[22]   I think it is best to keep (1) and (2) apart. After all, I might concede (1) and not (2). I might think, for example, that the (1) is true but that the fundamental good in question is something other than true belief (for example, knowledge).

[23]   Pritchard uses the phrase epistemic value T-monism in his *Nature and Value of Knowledge*. However, in his recent essay on the swamping problem ('Veritism and Epistemic Value') he uses veritism to represent the idea that truth is the fundamental epistemic good. See also, Michael DePaul 'Value Monism in Epistemology' in Matthias Steup (ed.),

is the accumulation of true beliefs. As such, we hope to avoid false beliefs. As Marian David puts it, 'the sole basic epistemic value, or good, is true belief; and the sole basic epistemic disvalue, or bad, is false belief'.[24]

I think there is good reason to assume that true belief is the fundamental epistemic good at which we are aiming.[25] However, I will leave these considerations aside for moment. What is most important is determining whether the swamping problem does in fact assume veritism and what this might imply for the force of the swamping problem. To begin, it is important to note that the swamping problem isn't really an argument for veritism. It is simply an argument about the value of knowledge vs true belief, *given* the truth of the veritist position. The way the swamping problem is set up, we are told to compare some desired end (for example, good coffee) with the desired epistemic end (for example, true belief). As (1) and (2) suggest, then, what is really going on in the example is a discussion about conferring additional value to the fundamental epistemic good that is true belief. Thus, there can be little discussion, I think, on whether the swamping problem does in fact assume the veritist position.

From this, we are now in a position to discuss the conclusion that follows from (1) and (2):

(3)   Thus, given (1) and (2), knowledge is of no more value than true belief.

What (3) is saying is simply that if (1) and (2) are true, then (3) seems to follow. After all, how can anything be more epistemically valuable than the fundamental epistemic good? I take it that (3) is what most conclude should be taken to be the force of the swamping problem.[26] Thus, we have, taken together, the following argument:

(1)   Once the fundamental epistemic good in question is attained, no epistemic property that is merely instrumental can be added to confer additional value.

---

*Knowledge, Truth, and Duty: Essays on Epistemic Justification, Responsibility, and Virtue* (Oxford: Oxford University Press, 2001), pp. 170–183.

[24]   Marian David, 'Truth as the Primary Epistemic Goal: A Working Hypothesis' in Matthias Steup and Ernest Sosa (eds), *Contemporary Debates in Epistemology* (Oxford: Blackwell, 2005), p. 308.

[25]   See, however, Jonathan Kvanvig, 'Truth is not the Primary Epistemic Good' in Matthias Steup and Ernest Sosa (eds), *Contemporary Debates in Epistemology*, pp. 286–95.

[26]   Zagzebski, in 'The Search for the Source of the Epistemic Good', claims, for example, that given the swamping problem 'we cannot explain what makes knowledge more valuable than true belief' (p. 14). Though, it is important to note that Zagzebski sees the problem as being the result of using a 'machine-product model of belief' and believes her virtue-based belief model avoids the swamping problem. However, so long as you take truth to be the primary epistemic good it is hard to see, as discussed above, how this is not a problem for any account of knowledge.

(2)    The fundamental epistemic good is true belief.

(3)    Thus, given (1) and (2), knowledge is of no more value than true belief.

Given the above reasoning, it seems that if we are going to account for the distinctive value of knowledge (over and above that of mere true belief) we need to deny (3). One thing to keep in mind, however, is that just because (3) seems to be a conclusion about the value of knowledge over and above that of true belief (and not specifically a question about the final value of knowledge), it is still imperative that an answer be provided concerning the value of knowledge over and above that of mere true belief. This is because our inability to provide an answer as to why knowledge is more valuable than mere true belief will mean that we also cannot provide an answer to the question of distinctive value. Yet, it is also important to note that even if we can provide an answer concerning the value of knowledge over and above that of mere true belief, it doesn't mean in turn that we have accounted for the distinctive value of knowledge.

Given this, what are the options, then, if we are to hold on to the intuition that knowledge is of distinctive value? The first option we have is deny (1). I'm going to ignore this possibility here since I take the real source of (1) to be the belief that (2) is true.[27] Rejecting (2), then, seems to be the obvious choice if we are going to ultimately deny (3).

Yet, how exactly should one go about rejecting (2)? First, we need to get clear on what exactly (3) entails. In claiming that true belief is the fundamental epistemic good I am claiming that the good in question, true belief, is ultimately non-instrumentally valuable. For example, (1) makes that claim that justification is only instrumentally valuable in that we value it as a means to true belief. True belief, however, is to be valued as an end. Its value is not derived from its relation to any other good.

Further, in claiming that the fundamental epistemic good is true belief, I am claiming that true belief is the primary epistemic goal at which we are aiming. If something is the primary or fundamental epistemic goal, it seems to follow naturally that this goal would also be the fundamental epistemic good. This assumption runs the other way as well. If I take true belief to be the fundamental epistemic good, it seems to follow that I ought to take true belief to be my primary epistemic goal. This being the case, it follows, then, that true belief is not only the fundamental epistemic good, but also the primary epistemic goal.[28] After all,

---

[27]    For an argument that targets something similar to what (1) claims, see Alvin Goldman and Erik J. Olsson, 'Reliabilism and the Value of Knowledge' in Adrian Haddock, Alan Millar and Duncan Pritchard (eds), *Epistemic Value* (Oxford: Oxford University Press, 2009), pp. 19–41. For a summary and critique of this argument, see Pritchard, 'Veritism and Epistemic Value', pp. 8–14.

[28]    In the literature, it seems that many simply assume the two are synonymous. Saying that true belief is the primary epistemic goal is to simply endorse the idea that true belief is the fundamental epistemic good. I have kept them apart, however, in order to keep

it would seem odd to claim that the primary epistemic goal is true belief while the fundamental epistemic good at which we are aiming is something different. I take it, then, that the important question to ask about (2) is why one should *assume* that true belief is the primary epistemic goal.[29] Why not knowledge, for example? Knowledge, after all, has been the primary issue both ancient and contemporary philosophers have been concerned with.

A thorough defence of why true belief is the primary epistemic goal (as opposed to knowledge) will take us beyond the scope of this section. In the end, what we are really looking for is a response that will guide us in ultimately rejecting (3). Thus, the real question is whether (2) does in fact imply (3). I contend that it doesn't, and therefore the swamping problem is of little concern to the question of the distinctive value of knowledge.

Where then, does this leave us with regard to the swamping problem? If we accept that true belief is the fundamental epistemic good, I think there is a very easy solution to the swamping problem.[30] Here is a recap of what is going on in the swamping problem:

(1)　Once the fundamental epistemic good in question is attained, no epistemic property that is merely instrumental can be added to confer additional value.

(2)　The fundamental epistemic good is true belief.

(3)　Thus, given (1) and (2), knowledge is of no more value than true belief.

The solution I am presenting argues that the conjunction of (1) and (2) does not entail (3). As was mentioned above, the swamping problem is really a thesis about epistemic value. And (2) is simply a specific claim about epistemic value, namely veritism.

Thus, what one should conclude from the swamping problem isn't:

(3) given (1) and (2), knowledge is of no more value than true belief,
but rather:

(3*) given (1) and (2), knowledge is no more *epistemically* valuable than true belief.[31]

---

the distinction clear. However, I take it that what we ought to be aiming at as agents is just whatever the fundamental epistemic good in question is.

[29]　I prefer to use 'primary epistemic goal', but one could just as easily ask why true belief is the 'fundamental epistemic good'. Whatever phrase one uses, one is going to be defending, ultimately, the same thing.

[30]　This solution that I give below is first offered by Pritchard in 'Veritism and Epistemic Value'.

[31]　See Pritchard 'Veritism and Epistemic Value', MS, p. 15.

And of course (3*) is something a veritist can happily concede. Thus, we now have a revised swamping problem:

(1)   Once the fundamental epistemic good in question is attained, no epistemic property that is merely instrumental can be added to confer additional value.
(2)   The fundamental epistemic good is true belief.
(3*)   Given (1) and (2), knowledge is no more epistemically valuable than true belief.

It now appears that we have a harmless conclusion for the thesis that we are trying to defend – namely that knowledge is of more *general* value than true belief. This conclusion should come as no surprise since all through the discussion of the swamping problem we have been primarily concerned with epistemic value as opposed to general value.

With the real force of the swamping problem settled, we are now in a position to once again discuss the question of the general value of knowledge. And as discussed above, the real question that we need to answer is what it is that makes knowledge distinctively valuable over and above anything that falls short of knowledge.

## Achieving Knowledge

How, then, can knowledge be said to have final value? Following Greco, let's say that an achievement is a kind of success from ability.[32] What this means, then, is that an agent can be said to achieve something if the achievement comes by way of some ability that can be credited to the agent. Consider the following example:

> *Mt Everest*: Edmund and Didier both have a desire to reach the top of Mount Everest. Let's assume that the goal of each person was to reach the summit. Edmund, however, successfully climbs Mount Everest by starting at the base. Didier, on the other hand, realizes his goal by taking a helicopter ride to the summit.

While it is valuable to reach the top of Mount Everest (for example, you are at the highest point on the planet), surely the person who has reached the peak of Mount Everest by starting at the base has achieved something more significant than the person who takes a helicopter to the top. This is because, I think, we value the effort and ability of the person who started at the base. In other words, we value achievements more than mere success. And while Didier has successfully reached

---

[32]   See John Greco, *Achieving Knowledge* (Cambridge: Cambridge University Press, 2010).

his goal, the success is not due to his abilities. The credit, in the case of Didier, is due to the helicopter and not the abilities of Didier. Edmund, on the other hand, has successfully climbed Mount Everest because of his abilities. It is creditable to Edmund that he successfully used his abilities to reach the summit.

Now, there is some ambiguity in this example that needs to be clarified. You might think that Didier has met the conditions that are set forth in defining an achievement. After all, he does deserve some credit for reaching the peak. He chose a helicopter instead of a car, he might have chosen a clear day instead a stormy windy day, or he might have chosen an expert pilot as opposed to a novice. These things are all certainly of credit to Didier. However, what we want from an understanding of achievement is a result that is down to Didier's agency – one where the success in question is clearly down to his ability. In other words, what we want from a definition of achievement is one where the success in question produces a result that is *primarily creditable* to the agent.[33] In the above example, then, only Edmund's manner of reaching the peak can be said to be *primarily creditable* to him. In the case of Didier, his success is primarily due to the proper functioning of something external to him – namely, the helicopter.

Achievements, then, are a kind of success from ability whereby the success is primarily creditable to the agent. With this definition in mind, then, we might have an answer to the swamping problem and a working account of the final value of knowledge. In the swamping problem, the intuition seems to be that successfully attaining truth just is the highest epistemic good. Knowledge, in a sense, gives us nothing that truth hasn't already given us. However, if we think of knowledge as a cognitive achievement, then the difference between the two becomes apparent. True belief can be attained by means of luck or in the absence of a cognitive achievement. There needn't be any cognitive achievement on the part of the agent in order to successfully attain the true belief. True belief is similar to Didier in the Mount Everest case. The goal of reaching the peak was realized, but not in any way that is primarily creditable to Didier. True belief, then, can be attained, in many cases, in a manner that is not primarily creditable to the agent. And given that knowledge is an achievement, and achievements are indeed valuable, knowledge can be said to have final value.[34]

If knowledge is a cognitive achievement (and thus finally valuable), in order for the Reformed epistemologist to account for the value of knowledge it needs to be demonstrated that knowledge, as explained by Reformed accounts, is in fact a

---

[33]   See Duncan Pritchard, 'Anti-Luck Virtue Epistemology', *The Journal of Philosophy* (forthcoming). For more on the primary credit/of credit distinction see Pritchard, *Nature*, pp. 40–41.

[34]   As noted above, the kind of value in play here is final value as opposed to intrinsic value. This is because the value that knowledge has is derived from some property external to it (for example, achievements).

cognitive achievement.[35] *Prima facie*, this seems problematic. This is because on Reformed accounts, it's not entirely clear if the agent can be credited for the true belief. Consider the following example:

> *Sceptic*: Sceptic Jon isn't convinced by any of the arguments that are traditionally associated with theism. Sceptic Jon, however, becomes believer Jon while observing some majestic sunset. He comes to believe in God on the model provided by Plantinga. It is some experience – a majestic sunset for example – that triggers the *sensus divinitatis*, which in turn gives rise to the belief that God exists. Jon, lacking direct control over his beliefs, simply finds himself believing in God.[36] But let's assume that Jon is not alone. He is enjoying the sunset with sceptic Jane. Sceptic Jane, like Jon, isn't convinced by any of the arguments that are traditionally associated with theism. Sceptic Jane is in the same exact environment as Jon. Yet sceptic Jane finds herself with no such belief. For Jane, the majestic sunset doesn't trigger the belief that God exists.

What is interesting about this example, I think, is that two people with similar beliefs about God enjoy the same sunset. Yet one comes away a theist, while the other remains a sceptic. It seems, *prima facie* anyway, that Jon's believing is really down to luck. After all, Jon has no control or knowledge of the faculty that gives rise to his belief in God. It just so happens that Jon's cognitive faculty, the *sensus divinitatis*, stopped malfunctioning while sceptic Jane's cognitive faculty, the *sensus divinitatis*, continued to malfunction. If Jon's belief in God is true, then Jane's continued scepticism is a result of bad epistemic luck.[37] And if Jane's continued scepticism is a result of bad epistemic luck, then perhaps Jon's belief is a result of good epistemic luck. In which case, Jon's belief in God is not a cognitive achievement.[38]

While the above example raises some important questions, I think there is a way around this sort of objection. There is an important story to be told, I think, with regard to the *sensus divinitatis* and the nature of cognitive achievements in that the *sensus divinitatis* is like any other faculty. It is similar to other faculties in that it malfunctions when not exercised in the appropriate environment. Perceptual

---

[35]   In this chapter I will assume that the achievement thesis (or something similar) is correct. The argument that follows, then, is conditional on the truth of the achievement thesis.

[36]   Plantinga is a non-voluntarist and argues that we do not control what we believe. See Alvin Plantinga, 'Positive Epistemic Status and Proper Function' in *Philosophical Perspectives* 2 (1988), p. 37.

[37]   For a similar argument see Linda Zagzebski 'Religious Knowledge and the Virtues of the Mind', in Linda Zagzebski (ed.), *Rational Faith: Catholic Responses to Reformed Epistemology* (Notre Dame, Indiana: Notre Dame University Press, 1993), pp. 199–223.

[38]   Note here that I am assuming, of course, that this belief is true.

faculties, for example, malfunction with age and fail to be reliable when not used in the environment for which they were designed. Attempting to use your perceptual faculties in the ocean, for example, would not produce the same result as using your perceptual faculties on a clear sunny day. The same goes for the *sensus divinitatis*. It is prone to malfunction. But what exactly, if anything, causes the malfunctioning of the *sensus divinitatis*? The answer to this, according to Plantinga, is the cognitive consequences of sin. Sceptic Jane's failure to believe, then, is the result of cognitive dysfunction brought about by sin. Believer Jon's new-found belief is the result of a properly functioning *sensus divinitatis*.

So far, then, we have an account of the dysfunction of the *sensus divinitatis*. However, we still need some non-lucky account of why Jon's faculty started functioning properly. Also, we need some reason for believing that Jon's belief is a cognitive achievement (after all, a properly functioning faculty might be down to luck as well). Dealing with the latter first, Jon's belief in God can be seen as an achievement if the belief comes by way of some ability that can be credited to the agent. Further, and slightly stronger, achievements might be understood in terms of the overcoming of some obstacle to belief.[39] Meeting this stronger condition on achievements, the obstacle that is overcome is the hostile environment in which Jon finds himself, an environment that is not conducive to belief in God because of the cognitive consequences of sin. Meeting this stronger condition on achievements, the obstacle that is overcome is the hostile environment in which Jon finds himself. An environment that's not conducive to belief in God because of the fallen nature of humans. Much needs to be said about this, but let's say that the hostile environment is the result of sin. And let's say that sin affects the way in which the *sensus divinitatis* would have normally operated. So before sin, knowledge of God would have been undisputed. Because of sin, however, the *sensus divinitatis* malfunctions and therefore belief in God is disputed.

The above description of the *sensus divinitatis* draws heavily from the Calvinist notion that even though humans are born with this faculty called the *sensus divinitatis*, it is inoperative. Thus, humans are born with the *capacity* to believe in God, but the capacity for belief is hindered by the human condition. The human condition, sin, is more than just a statement about humans and their dysfunctional faculties. The human condition affects both the inhabitants and the *environment* that humans inhabit. By this I mean that there are certain obstacles present in the environment that make belief in God challenging. These obstacles to belief might include the problem of evil, divine hiddenness or lack of religious experience: so perennial problems in philosophy of religion like the problem of evil and divine hiddenness are, in effect, a result of the human condition. Given the problems that the human condition generates, then, the environment we inhabit isn't conducive to belief in God. Thus, when one does believe in God it can be said to be an achievement. In fact, it's a strong achievement in that you've overcome the hostile environment that arises from the cognitive consequence of sin.

---

[39] See strong achievements versus weak achievements in Pritchard, *Nature*, pp. 31–47.

So far, then, only one of the conditions of achievement has been met. What remains to be seen, however, is whether this belief is something that can indeed be credited to the agent. Consider perception for example. It could be argued that any belief that is formed via perceptual faculties is creditable to the agent given that this faculty is an internal property of the agent. Notice that on externalist accounts the agent needn't know anything about this faculty or have any access to the operations of this faculty. And given that Reformed epistemology does provide an externalist account, the same reasoning applies to the *sensus divinitatis*. Returning to the above example, Jon needn't know anything about the *sensus divinitatis* or have access to the workings of this faculty. Thus in the same way that perceptual beliefs are creditable to the agent, beliefs that arise as a result of the *sensus divinitatis* are creditable to the agent given that both faculties are internal properties of the agent.

However, it was stated above that achievements need to be *primarily creditable* to the agent. In other words, the belief in question needs to be a result of the cognitive ability of the agent. And this cognitive ability needs to be *primarily creditable* to the agent. Thus if we are to claim that knowledge on the Reformed account amounts to a cognitive achievement, it needs to be established that the belief in question is *primarily creditable* to the agent. One reason for thinking that it's not *primarily creditable* to the agent is that it's not clear on Reformed accounts whether the belief is due to God or the agent. There is extensive discussion in Reformed literature about God being primarily responsible for the belief of the theist. The noetic effects of sin are so severe that God needs to intervene if the agent is to have knowledge of him. Thus, it is God, *through* the *sensus divinitatis*, who is primarily responsible for the belief of the agent. This might explain, from the example above, why Jon believes and Jane doesn't. It's ultimately down to God's choosing.[40] If this is the case, then the problem of credit becomes apparent. If God is primarily responsible for the agent's believing, then knowledge of God isn't an achievement and demonstrating the value of knowledge on Reformed accounts will be difficult.

However, this notion of 'primarily creditable' is rather vague and might be challenged. Consider the following example:

*Emie*: Let's imagine that there is a small child named Emie. Emie can walk on her own most of the time, but like most children she has trouble when the ground is uneven or littered with obstacles (for example, rocks). In other words, under normal conditions Emie's ability to walk is apparent. However, the environment isn't always a friendly one and she

---

[40]    Whether this is just or fair is a discussion that unfortunately goes beyond the scope of this paper. Briefly, however, you might think that God's intervention in the case of Jon (as opposed to that of Jane) is not necessarily arbitrary. Even though we don't have access to the reasons behind the choice, it does not follow that God does not have *good* reason to intervene in the case of Jon and not Jane.

now finds herself on a trail that is uneven and strewn with large rocks. However, she still needs to go from point A to point B. She stands to her feet and wobbles along. As her father, I notice that she isn't going to make it on her own so I stand behind her. I catch her when she falls and hold her arms as she navigates the obstacle. In due course, Emie arrives at her destination.

Now, Emie's successful arrival at point B isn't *primarily* due to her abilities. In fact, it seems that her success could be primarily creditable to me. Without me, she wouldn't have reached her destination. Despite this, however, I think the intuition here is that for Emie this is still an achievement; regardless of the fact that her success is not primarily creditable to her agency. This, I think, is because of the hostile environment in which Emie has found herself. There are some environments that are so *excessively* hostile in relation to one's ability, that all that is required is some exercise of the relevant ability in order for that success to be considered an achievement. The same goes for knowledge of God in this case. Perhaps the human condition is so severely distorted by the cognitive consequences of sin that the environment is *excessively* hostile in relation to one's cognitive ability. Thus, the cognitive success in question need not be *primarily* creditable to the agent, but only *partially* creditable to the agent.

There are many ways, then, that the cognitive success in question might be partially creditable to the agent. Perhaps putting yourself in the right environment might suffice. After all, certain environments are more conducive to belief in God than others. This might involve, for example, participating in the sacraments. Or perhaps being open-minded is a virtue and despite the excessively hostile environment you find yourself in, the virtuous agent won't rule out the possibility of theism. You're not hostile to the idea of theism despite the excessively hostile environment you find yourself in. These might be ways, then, in which partial credit can be attributed to the agent.

However, if one wants to retain the idea of primary credit then the above arguments aren't going to be persuasive. After all, if the notion of primary credit is abandoned then Didier's success in the Mt Everest case might count as an achievement. Perhaps, then, to retain the notion of primary credit a weaker understanding of the *sensus divinitatis* is needed. Whatever the weaker notion entails, though, it should still retain its distinctive Reformed character. Thus, the *sensus divinitatis* should still be seen as a cognitive faculty that malfunctions due to the cognitive consequences of sin. If sin did not exist, belief in God via the *sensus divinitatis* would be uncontroversial. Further, in order to retain the distinctive Reformed character, the weaker version must allow God to play *some* role in the belief formation process. Where the weaker notion might differ, however, is in the understanding of the role God plays at the time of the belief.

The stronger understanding of the *sensus divinitatis* claims that God must intervene given the severity of sin's effects on the human condition and hence on the *sensus divinitatis*. The cognitive consequences of sin are so great that the *sensus divinitatis* is unable, without divine intervention, to produce true beliefs about God. God, in a sense, causes and maintains the proper functioning of the *sensus divinitatis*. On the weaker account, though, God might be seen as merely the enabler of the proper functioning of the *sensus divinitatis*. Like impaired perceptual faculties, the *sensus divinitatis*, with the right care and attention, can begin to produce reliable results about the world. If doctors can prescribe the right medications to fix impaired perceptual faculties, perhaps God can provide the way in which to repair the malfunctioning *sensus divinitatis*. In other words, the *sensus divinitatis* is a malfunctioning faculty that needs to be nurtured and the way to nurture this faculty comes from God. This would make God merely the *enabler* of the properly functioning faculty as opposed to the *reason* for the properly functioning faculty. A child is not born knowing that 1+1=2, despite the possibility of this truth being arguably innate; the child must be nurtured by his parent or teacher in order to understand this truth.

So in what ways can one nurture the *sensus divinitatis*? The answer is similar to the one provided above concerning partial credit. As stated above, by putting yourself in the right environment and being open-minded one might nurture the *sensus divinitatis*. In the end, the nurturing of the *sensus divinitatis* enables the faculty to overcome the excessively hostile environment in which it finds itself.

In summary, the weaker understanding of the *sensus divinitatis* makes God the enabler of the belief. And by doing this, the cognitive success in question (for example, belief in God) can be attributed *primarily* to the cognitive ability of the agent (like perception, for example). If this is the case, then the conditions for achievement are met and the Reformed epistemologist is in a good position to account for the final value of knowledge.

## Conclusion

I have argued that the Reformed epistemologist needs to offer some account of the value of knowledge. The reason for this is that any account of the nature of knowledge ought to also provide an account of the value of knowledge. One way in which the Reformed epistemologist might account for the value of knowledge is by endorsing the achievement thesis. In doing this, the Reformed epistemologist can either adopt a strong understanding of the *sensus divinitatis* or a weak understanding of the *sensus divinitatis*. In adopting the former, the Reformed epistemologist must drop the notion of primary credit and accept the idea that partial credit is all that is necessary for the achievement thesis. The other possibility that is available is to adopt the weak understanding of the *sensus divinitatis*, which maintains the idea that primary credit is a necessary condition for achievement. Either possibility, however, demonstrates a way in which the Reformed epistemologist might account for the value of knowledge.

Chapter 4

# Oracles, Obstacles and Revelations

Charles Taliaferro

**Introduction**

In this chapter I am principally concerned with removing or challenging some obstacles that get in the way of recognizing divine revelation. I am writing from the perspective of the Cambridge Platonists, a group that includes Ralph Cudworth, Henry More and other philosophers who flourished in and around Cambridge University (but were not unknown at Oxford) in the middle of the seventeenth century. They were especially important for their articulation of a form of Christian theism in the early modern era, contemporaneous with the birth of modern science, and many of the terms that are current in contemporary philosophy of religion were coined by the Cambridge Platonists ('theism', 'consciousness' and even the term 'philosophy of religion' appear to have been introduced into English by them).[1]

The terrain of this chapter is to begin by contrasting two conceptions of reality and experience, one that reflects secular naturalism, and one that became (for at least one of the subjects involved) the beginning of Christian faith. After briefly reviewing what has become known as the argument from religious experience (in its theistic formulation), the burden of this paper is to remove some obstacles standing in the way of accepting the experiential evidence for a Cambridge Platonist vision of reality and experience.

The difference between secular naturalist versus Cambridge Platonist philosophies may be compared to two evening parties. A secular naturalist-style party may be imbued with humour, friendship, romance and more. These goods, however, are enjoyed while all that is outside the dinner party is hostile and bleak. The scene is akin to Virginia Woolf's portrait of a dinner party in *To the Lighthouse*. After a rough start, the dinner party comes to life:

> Now all the candles were lit up, and the faces on both sides of the table were brought nearer by the candlelight, and composed, as they had not been in the twilight, into a party round a table, for the night was now shut off by panes of glass, which, far from giving any accurate view of the outside world, rippled it

---

[1]    I offer an account of Cambridge Platonism in *Evidence and Faith: Philosophy and Religion Since the Seventeenth Century* (Cambridge: Cambridge University Press, 2005), chapter one. See also *Cambridge Platonist Spirituality* co-edited by myself and Alison Tepley (New York: Paulist Press, 2005).

so strangely that here, inside the room, seemed to be order and dry land; there, outside, a reflection in which things wavered and vanished, watery.

Some change at once went through them all, as if this had really happened, and they were all conscious of making a party together in a hollow, on an island; had their common cause against that fluidity out there.[2]

The trouble with such a dinner party in the secular naturalist framework is that the party and dinner partners all pass or seem to pass (especially if memories fade) into oblivion. At the end of the dinner party, there is a haunting passage in which one of the main characters, Mrs Ramsey, realizes that, in a sense, as she looks at the party as she departs, it is already gone. 'With her foot on the threshold she waited a moment longer in a scene which was vanishing even as she looked, and then, as she moved and took Minta's arm and left the room, it changed, it shaped itself differently; it had become, she knew, giving one last look at it over her shoulder, already the past'.[3]

Compare Woolf's dinner party with the following account by the British poet W.H. Auden, of an experience after a summer dinner that proved to be a vital element in his rethinking Christianity:

One fine summer night in June 1933 I was sitting on a lawn after dinner with three colleagues, two women and one man. We liked each other well enough, but we were certainly not intimate friends, nor had any one of us a sexual interest in another. Incidentally, we had not drunk any alcohol. We were talking casually about everyday matters when quite suddenly and unexpectedly, something happened. I felt myself invaded by a power which, though I consented to it, was irresistible and certainly not mine. For the first time in my life I knew exactly – because, thanks to the power, I was doing it – what it means to love one's neighbour as oneself. I was certain, though the conversation continued to be perfectly ordinary, that my three colleagues were having the same experience. (In the case of one of them, I was able to later confirm this.) My personal feelings towards them were unchanged – they were still colleagues, not intimate friends – but I felt their existence as themselves to be of infinite value and rejoiced in it.

Auden goes on to reflect further on the meaning and extent of that experience:

I recalled with shame the many occasions on which I had been spiteful, snobbish, selfish, but the immediate joy was greater than the shame, for I knew that, so long as I was possessed by this spirit, it would be literally impossible for me deliberately to injure another human being. I also knew that the power would, of course, be withdrawn sooner or later and that, when it did, my greeds and

---

[2] Virginia Woolf, *To The Lighthouse* (New York: Harcourt Inc., 1955), p. 97.

[3] Ibid., p. 111.

self-regard would return. The experience lasted at its full intensity for about two hours when we said good-night to each other and went to bed. When I awoke the next morning, it was still present, though weaker, and it did not vanish completely for two days or so. The memory of the experience has not prevented me from making use of others, grossly and often, but it has made it much more difficult for me to deceive myself about what I am up to when I do. And among the various factors which several years later brought me back to the Christian faith in which I had been brought up, the memory of this experience and asking myself what it could mean was one of the most crucial, though at the time it occurred, I thought I had done with Christianity for good.[4]

For Auden, the encounter with this loving power was something dynamic, hinting at something transcendent and unwavering. Auden felt as though a very real power had acted upon him and brought him a kind of revelation or disclosure: the infinite value of his companions. It is interesting that while reflection on this experiential disclosure of love was part of the process that brought Auden to Christian faith, the experience took place at a time when he was quite sceptical about Christianity and religious faith in general. Auden's after-dinner experience is very much in line with the spirituality of the Cambridge Platonists.[5] The Cambridge Platonist Ralph Cudworth believed that more is needed to come to an awareness of God than scholarship or the intellect. There is an essential experiential element:

> Ink and paper can never make us Christians, can never make a new nature, a living principle in us, can never form Christ, or any true notions of spiritual things in our hearts … Cold theorems and maxims, dry and jejune disputes, lean syllogistical reasonings could never yet of themselves beget the least glimpse of true heavenly light, the least sap of saving knowledge in any heart.[6]

Instead, Cudworth writes, 'The secret mysteries of a divine life' must be 'kindled from within' the soul.[7]

Let us now turn to consider the argument from religious experience and then turn to some recent obstacles to taking experiences like Auden's seriously in an evidential fashion that might bear on theism.

---

[4]  W.H. Auden, 'The Protestant Mystic' in *Forewords and Afterwords* (New York: Random House, 1973), p. 69.

[5]  For further work on the Cambridge Platonists, see W.R. Inge, *The Platonic Tradition in English Religious Thought* (New York: Longmans Green and Co., 1926); G.A.J. Rogers et al. (eds), *The Cambridge Platonists in Philosophical Context* (Dordrecht: Kluwer, 1997); Benjamin Carter, *'The Little Commonwealth of Man': The Trinatarian Origins of True Ethical and Political Philosophy of Ralph Cudworth* (Leuven: Peeters, 2011).

[6]  Ralph Cudworth, 'A Sermon Before the House of Commons' in Taliaferro and Tepley (eds), *Cambridge Platonist Spirituality*, p. 60.

[7]  Ibid.

## Principle of Critical Trust

There are a range of philosophers today who believe that, in the absence of strong reasons for doubting experiences like Auden's, we should trust these experiences as evidencing a divine reality. The principle at work here has been called the *principle of credulity* or the *principle of charity* – sometimes articulated as the dictum that we should trust appearances unless we have positive reasons for doubting them.[8] Another way to positively approach religious experiences would be to presume they are innocent (reliable) until proven guilty (unreliable). Following Kai-Man Kwan, I suggest using the term *critical trust*, such that if a person seems to experience a reality, and the person has some reason to think that the object of experience exists or at least its existence is possible, then the person has reason to trust such an experience as reliable.[9] The trust is *critical* insofar as it is not a principle of gullibility on which *anything goes*. Also, the experience here is understood to be *observational*; an ostensible and apparent experience of X involves X appearing to be present or for X to be revealed or disclosed as real. On this view, the appearance of X is not the experience of a judgement that some state of affairs is true. There is a difference between a person reporting that it appears to her that God exists (as the result of an argument, for example) versus reporting that God appears to her. Perhaps one helpful way to mark the evidential difference would be to compare two persons who are reading the Bible, a secular naturalist and a 'believer' who experiences Scripture as an authentic revelation or disclosure of the divine. In the first case, the reader may experience the God of the Bible, the way one experiences a character in a novel (readers may love Gandalf as he appears in *The Lord of the Rings* trilogy) but in the case of the believer, she may have what she believes to be an authentic encounter with (or disclosure of) God or the things of God (awareness of the mercy of God, for example) *through* the Bible.[10]

---

[8]     See, for example, William Alston, *Perceiving God* (Ithaca: Cornell University Press, 1991); Caroline Franks Davis, *The Evidential Force of Religious Experience* (Oxford: Clarendon Press, 1989); Jerome Gellman, *Experience of God and the Rationality of Theistic Belief* (Ithaca: Cornell University Press, 1997); Gary Gutting, *Religious Belief and Religious Skepticism* (Notre Dame: University of Notre Dame Press, 1983); Richard Swinburne, *The Existence of God* (rev. edn, Oxford: Oxford University Press, 1991); William Wainwright, *Mysticism: A Study of Its Nature, Cognitive Value and Moral Implications* (Madison: University of Wisconsin, 1981); Keith Yandell, *The Epistemology of Religious Experience* (Cambridge: Cambridge University Press, 1993); H.D. Lewis, *Our Experience of God* (New York: Macmillan, 1959); and Nelson Pike, *Mystic Union* (Ithaca: Cornell University Press, 1992).

[9]     See Kai-Man Kwan's excellent book *The Rainbow of Experiences, Critical Trust, and God: A Defense of Holistic Empiricism* (London: Continuum, 2011).

[10]     I am thereby characterizing the religious experience as something more akin to perceptual appearing than merely phenomenal appearing as one finds in what is known as phenomenal conservativism. Chris Tucker defends this principle: 'If it seems to a subject that P, then the subject thereby possesses evidence which supports P' (in his 'Phenomenal

Before digging into critical objections to trusting ostensible religious disclosures of the divine, I suggest a point that has been defended by William James on up to Paul Helm in our own day: we should only reluctantly adopt a method of inquiry that presumes from the outset that a divine disclosure or encounter is unnatural, a violation or contortion of nature or a violation of the very nature of religion. Assuming that experiences like those of Auden have some good, if indeed such experiences are veridical, we have reason not to employ a philosophical method that renders them fatuous from the outset. A similar, though controversial point is worth noting in the philosophy of mind: assuming (as I think we should) that first-person experiential states can be good (and are certainly morally significant), we should not adopt a philosophical method which would not allow us (in principle) to recognize such states.[11] The next section aims to remove some of these obstacles that stand in the way of acknowledging experiences like Auden's as veridical. I then conclude with reflections on an interesting argument from Anthony Kenny that challenges the William James–Paul Helm admonition to be disposed to be open to divine revelation. In what may be called an argument from humility, Kenny argues that, on the grounds of humility, we should be disposed to agnosticism rather than theism.

## Revelation and the Obstacle Course

From time to time, obstacles to accepting revelation claims have been set up. Let us consider two briefly – the philosophical worry about oracles, and what was known as 'enthusiasm' – and then spend a little more time on David Hume, and two contemporary thinkers, who define 'revelation', 'experience', 'God' and 'history' in ways that make the experiential encounter with God unnatural, absurd, anti-religious or a conceptual monstrosity.

### *Philosophers and Oracles*

One reason why philosophy may have flourished in ancient Greece is because philosophical questions were not addressed by oracles or by officially recognized divine revelation. If oracles had endorsed philosophical views (for example, Apollo tells us that justice is not as important as beauty), philosophers might be in even greater danger than they were of accusations of impiety if they questioned

---

Conservativism and Evidentialism in Religious Experience' in K.J. Clark and R.J. VanArragon (eds), *Evidence and Religious Belief* (Oxford: Oxford University Press, 2011), p. 52). I am sympathetic with this principle, but the kind of appearing I am identifying involves the ostensible appearing or encounter with a divine reality (as seen in the report by Auden) as opposed to someone like Auden simply thinking something like 'there is divine love'.

[11]    A defence of this claim here would be next to impossible, but see Stewart Goetz and Charles Taliaferro, *A Brief History of the Soul* (Oxford: Blackwell, 2011).

such divinely revealed precepts. We have no reason to think that the Oracle of Delphi was ever asked a philosophical question. Philosophers like arguments. This became apparent to me when one of my professors complained about a rival at Harvard University that he was good on pronouncements, but short on arguments: 'He thinks he's the bloody Oracle of Delphi!!'

In reply, ancient philosophers took at least one pronouncement of the Oracle of Delphi seriously. A friend of Socrates was told by the Oracle that Socrates was the wisest person in Athens. This pronouncement seems to be what motivated Socrates to philosophically challenge others about the nature of wisdom. It should also be noted that Jewish, Christian and Muslim philosophers worked fruitfully through the medieval era until today, balancing revelation claims with independent philosophical reflection that did not draw on revelation. Ignoring reports of divine revelation would be like practicing a philosophical inquiry into consciousness, without asking the other persons about their thoughts, feelings, and so on.

*The Danger of Enthusiasm*

In the seventeenth century the term 'enthusiasm' was used to refer to states of mind in which persons may be especially prey to unwarranted beliefs. The worry, expressed with perhaps the greatest urgency by David Hume and Immanuel Kant, was that courting revelation claims would lead to waves of irrational beliefs.

In reply I suggest there is no safe place for what used to be called enthusiasm. I know followers of Hume and Kant today who seem entirely subject to waves of irrationality.

*Hume's Thesis is that Revelation is Unnatural*

Hume famously argued that miracles are violations of the laws of nature. There was something unnatural or invasive about reported events in which God is revealed. Hume's case against the rationality of belief in miracles has been much discussed.[12] But what is less widely appreciated is that the same strategy Hume employed against signs of divine intelligence were used by him in favour of doubting reports of intelligence among black Africans.

Here is Hume's famous characterization of miracles and his judgement that they cannot reasonably be thought to occur:

> A miracle is a violation of the laws of nature; and as a firm and unalterable experience has established these laws, the proofs against a miracle, from the very nature of the fact, is as entire as any argument from experience can possibly be imagined ... And as a uniform experience amounts to a proof, there is here a direct and full proof, from the nature of the fact, against the existence of any

---

[12]    See, for example, John Earman, *Hume's Abject Failure: The Case Against Miracles* (Oxford: Oxford University Press, 2000).

miracle; nor can such a proof be destroyed, or the miracle rendered credible, but by an opposite proof, which is superior.[13]

Hume holds that all of our experiences that miracles do not occur (we do not routinely observe persons being resurrected) count against reports of a resurrection:

> A wise man ... proportions his belief to the evidence. In such conclusions as are founded on an infallible experience, he expects the event with the last degree of assurance, and regards his past experience as full *proof* of the future existence of that event. In other cases, he proceeds with more caution: He weighs the opposite experiments: He considers which side is supported by the greater number of experiments: to that side he inclines, with doubt and hesitation; and when at last he fixes his judgment, the evidence exceeds not what we properly call *probability*. All probability, then, supposes an opposition of experiments and observations.[14]

But note that Hume's case against divine intelligence runs parallel to his case against the reliability of testimony that Africans or blacks are intelligent.

Hume so defined what it is to be a Negro (and so did Kant) so as to make *black intelligence* as unreasonable as believing in *divine intelligence*. I need to be really clear here: I am not arguing that Hume's case against miracles should be rejected because he was a racist. I am, rather, pointing out that his strategy of ruling out divine intelligence is interestingly similar to his case against intelligence among some humans, and this raises an important point about values in our inquiry. Here is a notorious passage from Hume's work:

> I am apt to suspect the Negroes and in general all of the other species of men (for there are four or five different kinds) to be naturally inferior to the whites. There never was a civilized nation of any other complexion than white, nor even any individual eminent either in action or speculation. No ingenious manufactures amongst them, no arts, no sciences. On the other hand, the most rude and barbarous of whites, such as the ancient Germans, the present Tartars, have all still something eminent about them, in their valour, form of government, or some other particular. Such a uniform and constant difference could not happen, in so many countries and ages, if nature had not made an original distinction betwixt these breeds of men. Not to mention our colonies, there are Negro slaves dispersed all over Europe, of which none ever discovered any symptoms of ingenuity, though' low people without education will start up amongst us, and distinguish themselves in every profession. In Jamaica indeed they talk of one Negro as a man of parts and learning; but 'tis likely he

---

[13]  David Hume, 'Of Miracles' in *An Enquiry Concerning Human Understanding* (second edition, ed. L.A. Selby-Bigge (Oxford: Clarendon Press, 1902), pp. 127–8.

[14]  Ibid., pp. 110–111.

is admired for the very sheer accomplishments like a parrot, who speaks a few words plainly.[15]

For Hume, there has been a uniform and constant association of whites and superior intelligence, non-whites and inferior intelligence. He acknowledges reports of exceptions but dismisses this talk in light of his view of the regular, uniform, exceptionless character of nature. He is so convinced of this that he offers an explanation of ostensible anomalies. It is more probable that blacks merely simulate intelligence, the way a bird may merely simulate language, without being intelligent; presumably both may be accounted for within the bounds of what Hume conceives the laws of nature to be.

When it came to miracle narratives, Hume was convinced that a reckless imagination and wish fulfillment were at work. Primitive people have a natural love of wonder, surprise and agreeable emotions. Hume appears to think that reports of black intelligence are prompted by the motives behind reported miracles: wish fulfillment, love of wonder, surprise and agreeable emotions. Belief in miracles erodes common sense, whereas belief in black intelligence erodes the British Empire.

As it happens, the man from Jamaica was Francis Williams (1702–70), who had a degree from Cambridge University, headed a school and was known for his Latin poetry. When Hume was in Britain there were roughly 10,000 blacks living in London. A black American poet, Phillis Wheatley, went to London where she publicly wrote and recited poetry. Hume's judgement was fixed against reports of nonwhites and miracles because they were deemed improbable in light of the number of experiences of what he countenanced as nature's exceptionless course.[16]

It seems to me that matters need to be reversed. I presume we (all readers of this chapter and book) agree that persons of all races should be treated with dignity and charity, that we should be quick to recognize and respond to intelligence, ingenuity and skill. And if the evidence at some point seems less than ideal as it

---

[15]   David Hume, 'Of National Characters' in T.H. Green and T.H. Grose (eds), *The Philosophical Works of David Hume*, Vol. 3, (London: Longmans, 1886), p. 252. Unfortunately, Hume's position was not just of academic interest. Hume's authority is appealed to and defended in such pro-slavery texts as the anonymously authored *Personal Slavery Established by the Suffrages of Custom and Right Reason* (1773), Richard Nisbet's *Slavery Not Forbidden by Scripture* (1773) and in Edward Long's three-volume, extensive racist text *The History of Jamaica*. Some attacks on slavery took issue with Hume: see James Beattie's *Essay on the Nature and Immutability of Truth* (1770) and James Ramsey's *An Essay on the Treatment and Conversion of African Slaves in the British Sugar Colonies* (1784).

[16]   So prevalent in the black tradition has this sort of imitation supposedly been, that literary historians often refer to the poetry published before Paul Laurence Dunbar's dialect verse as part of a single 'Mockingbird School'. I first developed a case for seeing Hume's case against miracles with his case for white supremacy with Anders Hendrickson in a co-authored paper 'Hume's Racism and His Case against Miracles' in *Philosophia Christi* 4/2 (2002), pp. 427–42.

perhaps did for some in the eighteenth and early nineteenth centuries, Pascal's wager seems ready at hand to motivate a person to be open to such evidence. Pascal in the seventeenth century and William James in modern times, as noted earlier, stressed the importance of values in inquiry: if we have some reason to think there is value to some belief (such as the belief in God or the belief in the dignity of all people) we should not adopt a form of inquiry that will rule out from the outset attaining such valuable beliefs. Similarly, unless we have positive reasons for thinking theism is incoherent, we should not characterize the ostensible experience of the divine as unnatural.

The case of the Cambridge Platonists was the exact opposite of Hume. They believed we should treat as natural and good (albeit with critical trust) ostensible divine experience and should also be open to the intelligence and goodness of fellow humans, notwithstanding one's superficial differences. The Cambridge Platonist Peter Sterry's invocation to openness is typical of those in the movement:

> Do you so believe that in every encounter you may meet under the disguise of an enemy, a friend, a brother, who, when his helmet shall be taken off, may disclose a beautiful and well known face, which shall charm all your opposition into love and delight at the sight of it.[17]

In *The Problem of Slavery in Western Culture*, David Brian Davis credits Cambridge Platonism as laying the groundwork for rejecting the racism and white supremacy of their day. Davis summarized the Cambridge Platonist outlook as follows:

> For beneath a superficial diversity of cultures one might find a universal capacity for happiness and contentment, so long as man's natural faculties had not been perverted by error and artificial desire. We must look to primitive man, said Benjamin Whichcote, if we would seek man's moral sense in its pristine state. Natural law, said Nathanial Culverwel, is truly recognized and practiced only by men who have escaped the corruptions of civilization. If traditionalists objected that savages were ignorant of the Gospel, the answer was that heathen might carry within them the true spirit of Christ, and hence be better Christians than hypocrites who knew and professed all the articles of faith.[18]

On not defining 'experience', 'history' and 'revelation' so as to make revelation or the disclosure of God in experience impossible, unnatural or implausible,

---

[17]    Peter Sterry, 'A Discourse of the Freedom of the Will' in Taliaferro and Tepley (eds), *Cambridge Platonist Spirituality*, p. 181.

[18]    David Brian Davis, *The Problem of Slavery in Western Culture* (Ithaca: Cornell University Press, 1966), p. 351. Whichcote and Culverwel were Cambridge Platonists.

Samuel Fleishacker and Wesley Wildman both employ categories that seem prejudiced against recognizing experiences of God or divine revelation:

> To call God speaking on Sinai (or as Jesus in the Galilee, or, through the angel Gibreel, to Muhammad) an 'historical fact' is to say that historical methods of investigation would suffice to establish it. But they would not. The very idea of God is the idea of a being beyond all nature, who can control nature itself … No amount of historical evidence could ever prove that that being appeared at a point within the natural course of things. Indeed, the mere idea that they could prove such a thing is a betrayal of the idea of God, a suggestion that God is just one being in the universe among others. For God's appearance in history to be pinned down by scientific investigation would be for God to be subject to the forces of the universe, rather than to be the source of or governor of those forces. A god who can be studied by science is an idol, rather than God, even if there is just one such god, and to believe that the unique God in or on whom the universe is supposed to rest can be known scientifically is to reduce monotheism to idolatry.[19]

Fleishacker goes on to caricature divine revelation:

> Even if, say an apparently disembodied voice, accompanied by thunder and mysterious trumpet blasts, once uttered remarkably accurate prophecies and deep nuggets of moral wisdom, that would indicate just that there are powers in the universe beyond those with which we are acquainted. Erich von Däniken's hypothesis, in *Chariots of the Gods*, that all supposed religious revelations are really records of visits to earth by intelligent creatures from outer space is very silly, but as an empirical explanation of Sinai, it is better than the hypothesis that the speaker was God. (A better explanation is, of course, the Humean one: that the very event attested to by the Torah is excellent reason to disbelieve the testimony.) At best, evidence that the event at Sinai took place as described might be evidence for a superhero god. It is very unlikely, but we just might be able to show that a creature rather like Spiderman or Dumbledore killed all the Egyptian firstborn, split the Red Sea for the Israelites, and produced a grand sound and light show at Mount Sinai. That would fall far short of showing that an all-powerful, all-wise and all-good source of the universe had done these things, or had spoken to human beings. The notion of a power over-turning the usual course of events, whose presence can yet be determined by scientific means, is just a notion of an unusual, surprising power within the universe, a sort of magic or a force hitherto relegated to science fiction. The notion of God speaking, or otherwise intervening in human history, defies our very conception of how nature works, and of what a historical event is. So the hypothesis that

---

[19]   Samuel Fleishacker, *Divine Teaching and the Way of the World* (Oxford: Oxford University Press, 2011), p. 26.

> God has spoken to us can neither be confirmed nor disconfirmed by the findings
> of historians, or other scientists.[20]

In *Religious and Spiritual Experiences* Wesley Wildman similarly describes experiential revelation as conceptually impaired. According to Wildman, the experiential encounter with God in theistic tradition is the encounter with 'disembodied intentionality'. God, like angels and ghosts are 'discarnate intentional beings'. In rejecting theism, naturalists hold that there are 'no disembodied forms of intentionality, no disembodied powers'.[21] I offer five replies succinctly.

First, the idea that if God is the God of nature, then God cannot be manifested in or experienced in the natural world seems entirely ungrounded. If God can control nature, wouldn't it rather seem to be a limitation of divine agency if God cannot act in the created order?

Second, describing revelation or religious experience in terms of 'disembodiment' seems at the very least misleading. 'Disembodiment' is the contrary of 'embodiment' and it suggests something impaired, damaged or un-anchored. One may think of the experience of God as the encounter with something incorporeal but not disembodied. (Recall that for integrative dualists a person is incorporeal and yet embodied.)

Third, the idea that if God is experienced, then God would become or could become an idol is at least peculiar. A thing need not be experienced to be an idol (someone might even worship the absence of religion) and many things can be experienced without risk of idolatry (myself, for example!). Moreover, on some accounts, God experiences (or is at least cognitively aware of) God's self. Would that mean God might become an idol for God?

Fourth, I know of no reason to think that an experience of X entails that X is merely one thing of possibly many things of the same species.

Finally, the term 'history' can be used to refer to that which is studied or confirmed through historical inquiry, but it can simply mean 'the past'. Someone can believe that (for example) Jesus rising from the dead happened as an historical fact without (a) claiming to prove this, or (b) without claiming that it can be established through historical inquiry. We believe many things intelligibly about the past and present without claiming to prove or know or settle the matter through science or philosophy (free will, moral realism …).

There are many more objections that need to be explored for a full case to be made for a theistic argument from religious experience: these include objections from the challenge of religious diversity and verification. I have addressed such matters elsewhere, but propose to focus on only one more obstacle that goes to the

---

[20]    Ibid.

[21]    Wesley Wildman, *Religious and Spiritual Experience* (Cambridge: Cambridge University Press, 2011), p. 27.

heart of the James-Helm thesis of remaining open methodologically.[22] Anthony Kenny has advanced what may be called an argument from humility to the effect that, as a matter of principle, agnosticism should be preferred to theism. Let us turn to this argument in a final section.


## The Humility Objection

In 'Faith, Pride and Humility', Kenny argues that humility requires that agnosticism be preferred over theism:

> There is, beyond doubt, a virtue – let us call it rationality – which preserves the just mean between too much (credulity) and believing too little (scepticism). From the viewpoint of an agnostic both the theist and the atheist err by credulity: they are both believing something – the one a positive proposition, the other a negative proposition – in the absence of the appropriate justification. On the other hand, from the point of view of theism, the agnostic errs on the side of scepticism: that is, he has no view on a topic on which it is very important to have a view. Internally, there is no way of settling whether it is the agnostic who errs on the side of scepticism, or the theist who is erring on the side of credulity.
>
> But if we look at the matter from the viewpoint of humility it seems that the agnostic is in the safer position. The general presumption that others are in the right will not help us here; for others are to be found in both camps, and there is no obvious way to decide to which of them one should bow. But there is one important difference. The theist is claiming to possess a good which the agnostic does not claim to possess: he is claiming to be in possession of knowledge; the agnostic lays claim only to ignorance. The believer will say he does not claim knowledge, only true belief; but at least he claims to have laid hold, in whatever way, of information that the agnostic does not possess. It may be said that any claim to possess gifts which others do not have is in the same situation, and yet we have admitted that such a claim may be made with truth and without prejudice to humility. But in the case of a gift such as intelligence or athletic skill, those surpassed will agree that they are surpassed; whereas in this case, the theist can only rely on the support of other theists, and the agnostic does not think that the information which the theist claims is genuine information at all. Since Socrates philosophers have realized that a claim not to know is easier to support than a claim to know.[23]

Is Kenny's case for agnosticism successful? If he is right, we should perhaps begin with a presumption of agnosticism. I believe Kenny's argument faces certain problems.

---

22  See Charles Taliaferro and Jil Evans, *The Image in Mind* (London: Continuum, 2011).

23  Anthony Kenny, *The Unknown God* (London: Continuum, 2004), pp. 108–9.

An agnostic may or may not think of her suspension of belief as a gift; perhaps she may feel she earned it. But either way, I suggest the agnostic implicitly claims to have a good that is not possessed by others. (Though perhaps a thorough agnostic might be a radical sceptic and claim to not be sure whether or not she has a good or even whether or not theists and atheists have what they believe are gifts.)

Consider two points in reply. First, agnostics (and sceptics in general, historically) may be viewed as claiming to have a good: intellectual integrity or cognitive prudence. Alternatively, they claim not to have the impairment of false beliefs. Sceptics may be thought of as having 'information' (namely they know more about the limits of cognition) not possessed by others.

Second, Kenny's analogy with athletic and intellectual skill seems problematic. Historically and in our own day, theists can and have deeply admired naturalist arguments as well as agnostic arguments. A naturalist need not abandon naturalism in claiming that some theistic argument is deeply impressive. I suggest that humility seems to require that all parties seek a fair and generous hearing, rather than requiring the a priori adoption of one stance (scepticism) among others.

Rather than conceive of the theism-naturalism debate as one between competing athletes, I commend the image of an imaginative and non-polemical dialogue among friends. I began this chapter with two images: the dinner party with Virginia Woolf and an after-dinner religious experience with W.H. Auden. I end with an image of an ideal philosophical comradeship taken from Augustine's *Confessions*. In the place of imagining philosophers and theologians as athletes, why not adopt this alternative?

> When I was with my friends, my mind was occupied with our talking and laughing, exchanging kindnesses, reading good books together, now joking, now being serious, disagreeing without animosity as one might disagree with one's own self (and finding that our rare disagreements seasoned our usual concord), teaching and learning from one another, sorely missing those who were gone and welcoming with joy those who came. These and such like signs coming from hearts that loved one another, through mouth and tongue and a thousand gracious gestures, were the kindling of a fire that melted our minds together and made the many of us one.[24]

---

[24]    Augustine, *Confessions* (trans. J.W. Ryans; New York: Doubleday, 1960), 4.8.13.

Chapter 5

# Belief in a Good and Loving God: A Case Study in the Varieties of a Religious Belief

Gabriel Citron

## 1 Introduction

In the early 1950s Antony Flew contributed a short but thought-provoking paper to a symposium entitled 'Theology and Falsification'.[1] Flew concluded his paper with the following question:

> Just what would have to happen not merely (morally and wrongly) to tempt but also (logically and rightly) to entitle us to say 'God does not love us' or even 'God does not exist'? I … put to the succeeding symposiasts the simple central questions, 'What would have to occur or to have occurred to constitute for you a disproof of the love of, or of the existence of, God?'[2]

Flew gives the impression that he takes this question to confront the religious believer with a fatal dilemma. For he seems to think that, on the one hand, the believer will not want to say that his belief in a good and loving God is falsifiable, because then he would most likely need to admit that it had actually already been falsified; and he seems to think that, on the other hand, neither will the believer want to say that his belief in a good and loving God is *not* falsifiable, because this would mean that the belief has no informational content, and this would put it beyond the pale of orthodoxy. Many philosophers of religion have taken up Flew's challenge. Most picked one or other of the horns of Flew's dilemma and denied that the chosen horn had the consequences that Flew seemed to think it had; and some tried to occupy a position somewhere between the two horns, denying that Flew had laid out all the options.

John Hick, for example, embraced the second horn of the dilemma, insisting that religious belief – and specifically belief in 'the existence of … a loving God'[3] – is unfalsifiable:

---

[1]    Antony Flew, 'Theology and Falsification' in Antony Flew and Alasdair Macintyre (eds), *New Essays in Philosophical Theology* (London: SCM Press, 1955), pp. 96–9.

[2]    Ibid., p. 99.

[3]    John Hick, *Faith and Knowledge* (Ithaca: Cornell University Press, 1970), p. 168.

> Would *any* conceivable happening compel the faithful to renounce their religious
> belief? … [I]s there any *logical terminus*, any definite quantum of unfavourable
> evidence in face of which it would be demonstrably irrational to maintain theistic
> belief? It does not appear that there is or could be any such agreed limit. It seems,
> on the contrary, that theism is to this extent compatible with whatever may occur
> … It follows from this conclusion that theism is not an experimental issue.[4]

Hick denied, however, that the unfalsifiability of religious beliefs means that
they lack informational content. At the other extreme, Randal Rauser insists that
religious beliefs – including the belief that God loves us – are falsifiable, in ways
similar to scientific beliefs:

> [P]articular Christian beliefs are eminently falsifiable. That is, they could in
> principle be shown to be false … [O]ne could provide evidence that God does
> not love anybody. Perhaps, for instance, we could argue that there is such a high
> distribution of evil in the world that it seems likely that God does not love any
> of his creatures … [T]he belief that 'God loves me' is in principle as vulnerable
> to epistemic defeat as beliefs about the natural world.[5]

Rauser insists, however, that though belief in a good and loving God is falsifiable, it
has not, in fact, been falsified. The final example I will note is that of Basil Mitchell,
who seems to think that belief in a good and loving God somehow straddles both
horns of the dilemma:

> The theologian surely would not deny that the fact of pain counts against the
> assertion that God loves men. This very incompatibility generates the most
> intractable of theological problems – the problem of evil. So the theologian *does*
> recognize the fact of pain as counting against Christian doctrine. But it is true
> that he will not allow it – or anything – to count decisively against it; for he is
> committed by his faith to trust in God.[6]

Mitchell thereby hopes to gain the best of both worlds for the belief that God loves
us – for he can take it both to attain informational content by being falsifiable to
some degree, and to avoid actual falsification by his appeal to trust.

I take these three responses to be broadly representative of the range of
positions available amongst mainstream analytic philosophers of religion, and
I do not intend to discuss them in any detail, apart from to draw attention to

---

    [4]   Ibid., pp. 148, 158.

    [5]   Randal Rauser, 'How to show that "God loves me" is false', *The Tentative Apologist*,
19 September 2009, http://blogs.christianpost.com/tentativeapologist/2009/09/how-to-
show-that-god-loves-me-is-false-19/ (accessed: 6th December 2011).

    [6]   Basil Mitchell, 'Theology and Falsification' in Flew and Macintyre (eds), *New
Essays*, p. 103.

a quality shared by all three. Namely, that however much they may disagree in their respective answers to Flew's question, they are all, nonetheless, in complete agreement about there being only one correct answer. Though each of the philosophers quoted disagrees over *what* the logic of belief in a good and loving God is, they all agree that it has only one logic – that the logic of belief in a good and loving God is uniform. Consider how Hick asks 'Would any conceivable happening compel the faithful to renounce their religious belief?', and in doing so simply assumes that the same answer will apply to all of 'the faithful'. Rauser talks of 'the belief that "God loves me"' in a way that makes it clear that he thinks that this belief comes in only one variety, and that logical properties can be ascribed to 'the belief' *simpliciter*. And Mitchell talks of what '[t]he theologian surely would not deny' and what 'the theologian *does* recognize' – apparently taking it for granted that all theologians are in agreement over the nature of God's love of humanity and the nature of people's belief in that love. In their responses to Flew's challenge each of these philosophers is taking it for granted that all instances of belief in a good and loving God are of one and the same kind.

The aim of this paper is to challenge this consensus by showing that belief in a good and loving God can come in multiple different logical varieties – ranging from being an evidentially grounded and empirically falsifiable ontological hypothesis, all the way to being a belief which is both non-groundable and non-falsifiable, and more akin to an attitude than to an hypothesis. The existence of multiple logical varieties of this belief is important to recognise, because failure to do so can lead to inadvertent misevaluations and inadvertent distortions. Misevaluation can come about because different logical varieties of the belief that there is a good and loving God may deserve different evaluations; but if someone is unaware that more than one variety of the belief exists, then he is likely to make illegitimately universal judgements – whether positive or negative. He might say, for example, that 'the belief that there is a good and loving God is rational' or 'is irrational' – unaware that there are varieties of the belief that he has not examined, but which are nonetheless included in his judgement. Distortion can come about because when such a person does come across a variety of the belief which is different from the variety that he takes to be the sole one, he is likely try to assimilate the new belief – against the grain of its nature – to the only logic of the belief that he knows, thereby skewing it. This, in turn, will mean that he is likely to make misevaluations of specific instances of the belief as well as on the universal level. If philosophy of religion is to engage in understanding and evaluating religious beliefs it is essential that it recognise that those beliefs often come in multiple logical varieties. I will show how this variety exists in the case of belief in a good and loving God, not only so as to correct generalisations – of the kind we saw just above – about this belief, but also with the hope that this will give the reader a feel for how common the phenomenon of logical variety may be in the family of religious beliefs more generally.

I will do this by putting forward a number of simple examples of belief in a good and loving God which can act as what Wittgenstein called '[c]entres of variation'[7] for the broad range of the varieties of this belief. Some of the examples will be taken from reports of actual people's beliefs, some will be imaginary, and others will be hybrids of the two. These examples are not intended to be premises in, or evidence towards, any sort of argument for the existence of logical variety in the belief in question – such as an argument from the authority of the examples, or an argument from the number of examples collected. In fact, I am not trying to make an argument at all, in any usual sense. Rather, my intention is simply to lay out examples of different possible kinds of belief in a good and loving God – and in so doing to implicitly ask the reader: 'Does this sound natural, or seem familiar, to you? Does this example ring true, as a form that this belief does actually take?' None of the examples is intended to *force* the reader to admit anything – on pain of irrationality – as proofs and arguments are usually meant to do. Rather, the examples are intended to bring about a recognition in the reader – to provoke or prompt a recollection – that belief in a good and loving God really does come in a variety of logical kinds. I take this to be one aspect of the method that Wittgenstein is referring to when he says that '[l]earning philosophy is *really* recollecting. We remember that we really used words in this way',[8] and therefore that '[t]he work of the philosopher consists in assembling reminders for a particular purpose'.[9]

## 2    First Centre of Variation: Beliefs in a Good and Loving God Which Are Empirically Falsifiable Both with Regard to Truth and with Regard to Proof

We can begin by considering some simple examples of beliefs in a good and loving God which are empirically falsifiable. Consider the following report from a 1983 study of religious parents' responses to the early death of one of their children:

> EXAMPLE 1:
>
> [O]ne woman explained: 'I turned away from (my beliefs) because I kept thinking, "How could there be a God?" ...' ... Often this type of ... [reaction] was described by those who had expected divine intervention to heal their children and were bitterly disappointed when the children died instead. As one father explained: 'I used to be a member of the church until after the death ...

---

[7]    See Ludwig Wittgenstein, *Wittgenstein's Nachlass: The Bergen Electronic Edition* (Charlottesville: InteLex, 2003), item 157b, p. 13r; and Ludwig Wittgenstein, 'Wittgenstein's Philosophical Conversations with Rush Rhees, 1939–50: from the notes of Rush Rhees' (ed. Gabriel Citron), *Mind* (forthcoming), conversation §20.

[8]    Ludwig Wittgenstein, *The Big Typescript: TS 213*, trans. and ed. C. Grant Luckhardt and Maximilian AE Aue (Oxford: Blackwell, 2005), §89, p. 309.

[9]    Ludwig Wittgenstein, *Philosophical Investigations*, trans. GEM Anscombe (Oxford: Blackwell, 1999), §127.

People had faith that Amy would live and it did not happen. So I changed my beliefs. Why believe in something that contradicts yourself?'[10]

The father in this passage had a belief in a good God which had very clear parameters. According to his belief, the existence of a good and loving God was incompatible with the early death of his daughter. So, when she did die – contrary to his expectation, and the expectation of some members of his church – he found this to 'contradict' his belief. In other words, his belief in a good and loving God was one which was falsifiable by a certain very specific empirical state of affairs, and indeed it was falsified when that state of affairs came about, so he dropped his belief in God. Consider, also, the following comments by a Jew who survived the Nazi concentration camps:

EXAMPLE 2:

I lost my faith and stopped believing in God when I saw the Nazis take pious, innocent, bearded religious Jews out to the courtyard and butcher and slaughter them for sport, having competitions and playing games with these Jews as they murdered them for their amusement – like huntsmen sporting with animals – and leaving others, less pious than they, unharmed. How can you believe anything after you've seen something like that?[11]

For this man there was a specific state of affairs which he found to be incompatible with his belief in a good and loving God – namely, the injustice of the torture of the pious during the Nazi Holocaust, while the impious were left unharmed. This brought him to give up his belief as it had been falsified by what he saw happening around him.

These examples of beliefs in a good and loving God are evidently falsifiable because their holders reported them to have been actually falsified by certain occurrences.[12] But a belief in a good and loving God can be falsifi*able* even though the believer does not take it to have been falsifi*ed*. Consider, for example

---

[10]  Judith Cook and Dale W. Wimberley, 'If I Should Die before I Wake: Religious Commitment and Adjustment to the Death of a Child', *Journal for the Scientific Study of Religion* 22/3 (1983), p. 227.

[11]  Reeve Robert Brenner, *The Faith and Doubt of Holocaust Survivors* (New York: The Free Press, 1980), p. 114.

[12]  It is important to note that the mere fact that someone ceases to believe in a good and loving God as a result of the obtaining of a certain empirical state of affairs does not by itself show that the belief in question must have been an empirically falsifiable one – for the empirical state of affairs may have been merely the *cause* of the person's ceasing to hold the belief. Rather, a belief will count as an empirically falsifiable one if the obtaining of an empirical state of affairs is the *reason why* the person gave up their belief, or the reason why they ought to. Thus it is significant that the father in Example 1 explicitly identified the unexpected death of his daughter as the reason why he stopped believing.

(EXAMPLE 3), the case of someone whose young daughter is in critical condition in hospital, after being run over by a drunk driver. The father thinks to himself: 'If she dies, there cannot be a God – for God would never let such a child die so young, so pointlessly'. Or he may think to himself something like: 'If God lets her die, then He couldn't possible exist'. Or perhaps: 'If she dies here, I couldn't possibly go on believing in God – but then I'll be left utterly bereft: without my daughter, and without my Father too' – and at that thought the distraught father may begin to pray even more fervently than before. In these cases, the believer envisages – and clearly articulates – a concrete state of affairs which he considers to be incompatible with the existence of a good and loving God. We may wonder that the death of his daughter should be, for him, a falsifying condition for his belief, given that countless men's daughters have died early and unjustly throughout history, and given that he surely knows this fact very well. We may wonder at this fact, but such it is: until this kind of tragedy faced him head-on, somehow it did not have the same power for him, and now that it is facing him, no other tragedy has any room in his mind.

It should be noted that a person may hold a falsifiable but unfalsified belief in a good and loving God – as in Example 3 – but without articulating, or even thinking of, the conditions that they would count as being falsifying. Perhaps they could be prompted to articulate those conditions by means of probing questions. Or perhaps they could be provoked to make conscious those conditions when confronted with the immanent possibility of one of the conditions' instantiation – such as with the father in Example 3. But it is possible that they never bring these conditions to consciousness at all, let alone articulate them. One's belief's being falsifiable is a dispositional matter, and someone can have a disposition despite its never being manifested.[13]

The examples of beliefs presented in this section can be described as empirically falsifiable both with regard to truth and also with regard to proof. They are empirically falsifiable with regard to truth, in that for each of them there are describable empirical states of affairs the obtaining of which are taken to be incompatible with the truth of the beliefs in question; and they are empirically falsifiable with regard to proof, in that if those describable empirical states of affairs were to obtain, they would be easily identifiable and observable, and therefore able to be submitted as proof against the truth of the beliefs in question.

I take Examples 1, 2, and 3 to mark out one centre of logical variation for beliefs in a good and loving God. As with all the examples that I will present in the course of this chapter, the question that readers must ask themselves is whether these examples ring true as ways that religious believers sometimes actually talk about and treat their beliefs in a good and loving God. If some of them do ring true then this should already make it clear that there is something seriously deficient in the descriptions of the logic of belief in a good and loving God given by both Hick and Mitchell in section 1 – that 'theism is … compatible with whatever

---

[13]	This also applies to the other varieties of the belief that we will see in the succeeding sections.

may occur'[14] and that 'the theologian ... will not allow ... anything ... to count decisively against' the 'assertion that God loves men'.[15] These universal statements have completely ignored the kinds of belief in a good and loving God which we have seen exemplified in this section.

Let us now turn to some further examples of belief in a good and loving God – but examples whose logic seems slightly different to those of the beliefs just presented.

## 3   Second Centre of Variation: Beliefs in a Good and Loving God Which Are Empirically Falsifiable with Regard to Truth, But Not with Regard to Proof

Consider the following remarks from a sermon given – in 1912 – by the then popular American preacher, James Russell Miller (1840–1912):

EXAMPLE 4:

Sometimes there is *inscrutable mystery* in the difficult experiences through which godly people are led. A few years ago a happy young couple came from the marriage altar, full of hope and joy ... A year later a baby came and was welcomed with great gladness. From the beginning, however, the little one was a sufferer. She was taken to one of the best physicians in the land. After careful examination, his decision was that her condition is absolutely hopeless ... What comfort can we give to such mothers as this? Yes, it is hard to look upon the child's condition, so pathetic, so pitiful, and to remember the doctor's words: 'Absolutely hopeless!' Is there any comfort for this condition? Can this mother say that God is leading her in the path of life? Is this experience of suffering, part of that path? Does God *know* about the long struggle of this mother? Does he know what the doctor said? Yes – he knows all. Has he then no *power* to do anything? Yes – he has all power. Why, then, does he not cure this child? We may not try to answer. We do not know God's reasons. Yet we know it is all right. What good can possibly come from this child's condition, and from the continuation of this painful condition year after year? We do not know. Perhaps it is for the sake of the mother and father, who are being led through these years of anguish, disappointment and sorrow. Many people suffer *for the sake of others*, and we know at least that these parents are receiving a training in unselfishness, in gentleness, in patience, in trust ... Let us never be afraid, however great our sufferings, however dark life is. Let us go on in faith and love, never doubting, not even asking *why*, bearing our pain and learning to sing while we suffer. God is watching, and he will bring good and beauty out of all our suffering.[16]

---

[14]   Hick, *Faith and Knowledge*, pp. 148, 158.

[15]   Mitchell, 'Theology and Falsification', p. 103.

[16]   JR Miller, 'You Will Not Mind the Roughness', *Grace Gems*, http://jameslau88. com/you_will_not_mind_the_roughness.htm (accessed: 13th July 2011).

Miller's sermon deals with what is almost the paradigmatic prima facie falsifier of belief in a good and loving God – the suffering of an innocent child. Miller 'defuses' this prima facie falsifier, however, by insisting that God will 'bring good and beauty out of all our suffering'. In other words, God is morally justified in allowing or causing the suffering in question because He is only do so in order to bring about from it an outweighing good. Miller even suggests one possibility of a good that God may have intended by the child's suffering: 'Perhaps it is for the sake of the mother and father, who … are receiving a training in unselfishness, in gentleness, in patience, in trust'. However, Miller is very clear that this is just one possibility, and that, in fact, we are in no position to know what good God intends to bring from any given suffering. If the parents buckle under the stress of caring for their sick child, and their marriage falls apart with recriminations and bitterness, Miller would simply insist that we are not in a position to know what goods will sprout, perhaps in some distant way, at some distant time, from the tragedy of the child and that of his parents' marriage – but we should have faith that some worthwhile good certainly will result. The kind of goods that Miller believes God will bring to flourish from sufferings are all perfectly intelligible and describable causal consequences of the evils in question – it is just that, given the complexity of the goods that God can bring from given evils, and given our limited capacities, we will never be in a position to be able to identify whether or not they have come about. Thus Miller has put forward a defuser of the prima facie falsifier of the child's suffering – but his defuser is such that it is not itself easily falsified.

The defuser appealed to in this kind of belief need not only be that the prima facie falsifier will allow for an outweighing good of some sort, but could equally well be that it might allow for the avoidance of a significantly greater evil. Consider the following summary of the responses of some religious parents who had been bereaved of children:

> EXAMPLE 5:
> Parents who spoke of religion and their beliefs … also spoke of God having some reason for their child's death … A few parents suggested their child may have had some sort of abnormality and they had to trust that God knew best: 'I accepted that God knew there was something wrong and that's why she had died. And He knew that, whatever was wrong, we couldn't handle it, between ourselves, that it was His will'.[17]

The kinds of evil that the parent may think their child's death avoided could all have been easily imaginable and describable. However, we would never be in a position to confirm whether or not one or other of these maladies really lay in the child's future – for the wrong could have been some subtle physical disease, and it could equally have been an undetectable latent moral disorder, or spiritual sickness.

---

[17]    Kathleen Gilbert, 'Religion as a Resource for Bereaved Parents', *Journal of Religion and Health* 31/1 (1992), pp. 22–3.

The kind of defusers that we have seen used in the above two examples can be applied very broadly to all evils – taking evils universally to happen either so as to causally bring about outweighing goods or to effect the avoidance of greater evils. If we asked a believer (EXAMPLE 6) who appeals to such defusers whether or not there is a state of affairs which he would take to falsify – to be inconsistent with – the existence of a good and loving God, he might reply: 'Of course there is! – Namely, a state of affairs in which there was suffering which did not allow for any outweighing good or for the avoidance of any greater evil. That is, if there were suffering which was pointless. And it is not hard to imagine a case of such suffering – such as a person dying young, when, on the one hand, he would actually have gone on to have had a wonderful life, bringing joy to all around him, and where his death, on the other hand, does not lead to any material, moral, or spiritual growth by any others. Such random and meaningless suffering would be completely incompatible with the existence of a good and loving God – but we humans can never be in a position to identify any suffering as being meaningless in that way, because we can never see the whole picture. And this is precisely what it means to have *faith* in God: to trust in Him, that He is there, guiding everything around us for the best, even when that cannot be seen'.

How, then, do the logics of the beliefs exemplified in this section compare with those of the beliefs exemplified in the previous section? The beliefs in the previous section were empirically falsifiable both with regard to truth and proof, whereas the beliefs of this section are empirically falsifiable with regard to truth but not with regard to proof. For though there are describable empirical states of affairs the obtaining of which are taken to be incompatible with the truth of this section's beliefs, those states of affairs could never be *shown* to obtain. There are therefore some similarities between the beliefs of this section and the previous one, but also some significant differences.

## 4    Third Centre of Variation: Beliefs in a Good and Loving God Which Are Not Empirically Falsifiable, but Which Are Philosophically Falsifiable

There is yet another form that belief in a good and loving God can take – but which is not empirically falsifiable at all. Believers whose beliefs are of this third variety acknowledge that there are many prima facie falsifiers of their belief in a good and loving God, but they defuse these falsifiers by claiming that all evils bear a necessary relation to certain goods which outweigh them, which provide an explanation (or a possible explanation) for why a good and loving God would allow the evils to happen. Richard Swinburne's belief in a good and loving God seems to be of this kind:

EXAMPLE 7:
[T]he good of individual humans (and in so far as they are capable thereof, the good of animals) consists (as well as in their having thrills of pleasure) in their

having free will to choose between good and evil, the ability to develop their own characters and those of their fellows, to show courage and loyalty, to love, to be of use, to contemplate beauty and discover truth – and if there is a God it consists above all in voluntary service and adoration of him in the company of one's fellows, for ever and ever. All that … cannot be achieved without quite a bit of suffering on the way … [O]f each … [moral and natural evil] it is the case that by allowing it to occur God makes possible a good which he could not otherwise make possible without allowing it (or an equally bad state) to occur. Every moral evil in the world is such that God allowing it to occur makes possible (given the assumption that humans have free will) the great good of a particular choice between good and bad. Every bad desire facilitates such a choice. Every false belief makes possible the great good of investigation, especially cooperative investigation, and the great good of some of us helping others towards the truth. Every pain makes possible a courageous response (in all except animals caused to respond badly, and humans who do not yet realize what is the good response), and normally the goods of compassion and sympathetic action. And those animal pains to which animals are caused to respond badly, and those human pains to which humans respond with self-pity in ignorance of what a good thing a courageous response would be, still provide many opportunities and much knowledge for others. We can respond to the self-pitying humans by helping them to do better; their failure is our opportunity. And all animal pain gives knowledge and opportunity for compassion to animals and humans if they know of it … Each bad state or possible bad state removed takes away *one* actual good. Each small addition to the number of actual or possible bad states makes a small addition to the number of actual or possible good states.[18]

According to Swinburne the evils in the world are the necessarily possible side-effects of the existence of free will, and the value of the existence of free will outweighs the evil which stems from it; and furthermore, sometimes evils are themselves necessary conditions for the opportunity for moral and spiritual character development, and the value of this opportunity outweighs the evils which are necessary for it. We must note that Swinburne's defuser is not the fact that people *actually do* a certain minimal amount of good as a result of their free will, or that they *actually develop* their moral and spiritual characters to a certain minimal degree as a result of the evils that challenge them. If this was his defuser then it would itself be open to empirical falsification – namely, by a preponderance of immoral uses of our freedom, and a preponderance of selfish and cowardly responses to our own and others' suffering. But Swinburne's defuser does not commit him to any empirical states at all, for his defuser relies on the value of the mere existence of free will and of the mere existence of the opportunity for moral and spiritual character development – and not on whether that freedom

---

18    Richard Swinburne, *Providence and the Problem of Evil* (Oxford: Clarendon Press, 1998), pp. xii, 217–8.

or opportunity are used well or badly. Thus, whatever happens in the world, Swinburne will not take his belief in a good and loving God to have been falsified – for he thinks that all evils can be accounted for by their necessary relation to the values of free will and opportunity for moral and spiritual growth.

However, the fact that Swinburne's belief is not empirically falsifiable does not mean that it is utterly unfalsifiable – for it relies on the truth of all manner of contested philosophical positions, and these positions could perhaps be shown to be false by philosophical proof and argument. One of the philosophical premises on which Swinburne's defusers depend is his set of axiological judgements regarding various relative value-weightings; another is his moral judgement regarding whether it is permissible for an agent to inflict suffering on one being for the benefit of another. Swinburne, in fact, explicitly acknowledges that his defusers 'will only convince fully those readers who come to accept many of the moral views [which I have] advocated ... about which actions and states of affairs are good'.[19] Swinburne can hold that his philosophical judgements are not false, but are nonetheless philosophically falsifi*able*. Holding a philosophical position in a falsifiable manner may involve being able to state clearly which other philosophical positions would be incompatible with one's own; and perhaps even more than that, being able to explain what kind of arguments could be made in order to convince one of one of those incompatible philosophical truths. Thus, Swinburne could acknowledge that a strong deontological ethics – which held that killing others was always forbidden, no matter what good end one hopes to achieve thereby – would be incompatible with his defuser. He may even be able to point to precisely how a Kantian argument would need to be bolstered in order to convince him of the truth of that deontological principle. He believes that the argument cannot be bolstered in the necessary ways, but he is open to being shown otherwise. Thus, though his belief in a good and loving God is not open to empirical falsification of any sort – either with regard to truth or with regard to proof – it is nonetheless open to falsification of some sort, namely, philosophical falsification.

## 5 Fourth Centre of Variation: Beliefs in a Good and Loving God Which Are Non-Falsifiable

The final cluster of examples that I will bring is of beliefs in a good and loving God which seem to be of a radically different kind to any of the preceding. Consider the following passage from a sermon given by Rabbi Shimon Schwab (1908–95) who managed to escape Nazi Germany for America in the 1930s:

> EXAMPLE 8:
> There are so many who ask the question 'Why?' There's no doubt that all the troubles which befall the Jewish people, are by no means accidental. They are

---

[19] Ibid., p. xii.

punishments for our historic sins, such as assimilation, beginning in ancient times and continuing through our most recent past. However, this does not explain the massive holocaust which was allowed by the Holy One (blessed be He) to take place. We do not dare give any explanations, nor do we even search for answers. We do not ask the questions that so many ask: How come so many righteous ones, holy ones, and pure ones were choked to death in gas chambers? What was the sin of one million Jewish children who were murdered in cold blood? Why were all those millions of innocent Jews by virtue of their ignorance – slaughtered like sheep? As to the masses of Torah Jews, they all did repentance, and they all were already purified by their sufferings. How come the prayers of those righteous ones and holy ones and all those thousands of penitents were not answered? And on the other hand, many non-believers – violators of the Torah – were saved. The answer is: silence! We do not dare ask.[20]

It is clear that Rabbi Schwab is deeply troubled by the suffering, destruction and injustice of the Holocaust. However, he does not allow those things to actually bring any falsifying force to bear on his belief in a good and loving God. He says that 'We do not ask the questions that so many ask', rather, when the question is raised we say: '[S]ilence!'. Thus, he recommends that – despite the seeming falsifying force of the Holocaust – we nonetheless retain our belief in a good and loving God. No attempt is made to defuse the falsifying force of the Holocaust for belief in a good and loving God, rather its falsifying force is simply shut down or refused. Rabbi Schwab considers it to be irreligious or impious to even try to consider how it could be that a good and loving God could allow the Holocaust, and instead of trying to *understand* the compatibility of a good and loving God and the Holocaust we are forcefully exhorted to simply *accept* their compatibility.

This approach is exemplified even more forcefully in a sermon of Rabbi Kalonymous Kalman Shapira (1889–1943), which he preached to his fellow prisoners from the depths of the Warsaw Ghetto, in December 1941:

EXAMPLE 9:
[O]ne's faith must … involve an act of self-surrender … Now when [the notion of] self-surrender is applied to the context of faith, the meaning is this: even at a time when God's presence is hidden, one believes in Him; one believes that everything comes from Him, everything is good, everything is just, and all the sufferings are full of God's love for Israel. To our sorrow, we see now that even among those people who had been firm believers, certain individuals have had their faith weakened. They pose questions, saying in effect, 'Why have You forsaken us? If the suffering is being inflicted upon us in order to bring us closer

---

[20]    Quoted in Chaim Rapoport, *The Messiah Problem: Berger, The Angel, and the Scandal of Reckless Indiscrimination* (Ilford: Ilford Synagogue, 2002), p. 171 fn. (I have silently translated Hebrew words into English, and taken out some italicisations.)

to Torah and divine service, [why do] we see the opposite happening?! The Torah and everything sacred are being destroyed.' Now if the Jewish person speaks this way as an expression of prayer and supplication, as he pours out his heart before God, that is good. But if, God forbid, he is posing questions; or even if he is not [actively] questioning, but, in the depths of his heart, his faith, God forbid, is weakened, then God help us! Faith is the foundation of everything; when one's faith is, God forbid, weakened, then, God forbid, he is torn away and separated from Him ... In reality, however, what place is there for arguments, God forbid, and questions? ... [O]ne must surrender his soul, his self, his attachments. Then his faith will not be weakened; he will believe with perfect faith that everything is [transpiring] with justice and with the love of God for Israel.[21]

According to Rabbi Shapira there are sufferings which are so great – and so purely destructive – that no reason or explanation could possibly be given for them which would accommodate them within the system of our beliefs about God and His workings. No answers can be given, no defusers can be provided – but we must bind ourselves to God nonetheless, with a faith that is above reason and rationality. Even to go so far as to 'pose questions' in one's heart about God's justice is to manifest a blasphemous impairment of faith, and to 'tear oneself away' from God. In short, arguments or questions on the matter are ruled out as religiously and spiritually suicidal. Indeed, in serving God we must submit not only our wills to Him, but our whole selves – including our reason – and thus we overcome any falsifying power of the suffering around us by an act of faithful surrender to God despite that suffering. If we do that then we see that everything – even the worst torture and suffering – 'is [transpiring] with justice and with the love of God for Israel'. Thus, Rabbi Shapira advocates a belief in a good and loving God which is utterly non-falsifiable, which sets itself in the face of even the most radical apparently falsifying evidence. It seems that for Rabbi Schwab and Rabbi Shapira, the whole issue of falsifiability is taken to be entirely inappropriate to their belief in a good and loving God.

I would like to bring one further example in this section, because it will show that it is possible for utterly non-falsifiable beliefs to nonetheless look a lot like beliefs that are falsifiable. Consider the following remarks by Rabbi Emil Fackenheim, who was briefly interned at the Sachsenhausen concentration camp from which he escaped and fled to Britain, but whose brother was killed in the Holocaust:

EXAMPLE 10:
There is no experience, either without or within, that can possibly destroy religious faith. Good fortune without reveals the hand of God; bad fortune, if it

---

[21]  Sermon of 15 December 1941, quoted in Nehemia Polen, *The Holy Fire: The Teachings of Rabbi Kalonymous Kalman Shapira, the Rebbe of the Warsaw Ghetto* (Lanham: Rowman and Littlefield, 2004), pp. 82–4.

is not a matter of just punishment, teaches that God's ways are unintelligible, not
that there are no ways of God.[22]

The believers exemplified in section 3 thought they could describe and outline
the kinds of reasons that God might have for allowing or causing evil – they did
not think that God's reasons were unintelligible or unfathomable, rather they
just thought that we humans are not in a position to know which of the reasons
suggested was actually God's reason on a particular occasion. Rabbi Fackenheim
speaks similarly of God having reasons for allowing or causing evils – but he adds
the caveat that these reasons are not merely beyond our ability to *know*, but, rather,
completely beyond human capacity even to *comprehend.*

As with all the falsifiable varieties of the belief, Rabbi Fackenheim may even
say that there are states of affairs which would be incompatible with the truth of
his belief in a good and loving God: namely, if all the suffering and evil of this
world took place but without there being any reason for it. This is almost identical
to what the believer in Example 6 said. But in this case, the same words are being
used with a different grammar: for the believer in Example 6 could describe the
kind of thing that he meant by such phrases as 'suffering with no reason behind it'
– namely, suffering which was not causally related in the right way to outweighing
goods or greater evils. But Rabbi Fackenheim could not say anything at all about
what is covered by 'suffering with no reason behind it' – for when he talks of God's
reasons he adds the caveat that these reasons are completely unintelligible to the
human mind. But if the kinds of thing that might count as reasons for suffering
are utterly beyond our understanding and imagination, so too must be the kinds of
situation that would count as being *lacking* in reasons. Rabbi Fackenheim could
not describe – in anything other than the most formal terms – a state of affairs (be it
empirical, philosophical, or of any sort) that would be incompatible with the truth
of his belief, let alone any state of affairs which could be identified and observed
to obtain. Thus, when we scratch the surface of the kind of belief presented in
Example 10, we find that though it is expressed in ways that makes it sound quite
similar to certain falsifiable forms of the belief in a good and loving God, to all
intents and purposes it is actually entirely non-falsifiable.

If the cluster of examples set out in this section ring true as ways that religious
believers sometimes actually talk about and treat their beliefs in a good and
loving God, then this will have made clear that there is a logical variety of this
belief which is entirely non-falsifiable – non-falsifiable both empirically and
philosophically, and both with regard to truth and proof. This shows that there
is something seriously deficient in Rauser's remarks – quoted in section 1 – that
'the belief that "God loves me" is in principle as vulnerable to epistemic defeat as
beliefs about the natural world'.[23] This universal statement has completely ignored

---

22    Emil Fackenheim, 'On the Eclipse of God' in Emil L Fackenheim, *Quest for Past
and Future: Essays in Jewish Theology* (Boston: Beacon Press, 1968), p. 231.

23    Rauser, 'How to Show'.

the kinds of belief in a good and loving God which we have seen exemplified in this section.

Furthermore, just as it is possible for people to have an empirically falsifiable belief in a good and loving God without having consciously articulated to themselves what exactly they would take to falsify the belief, so too it is possible to have an entirely non-falsifiable belief in a good and loving God without having brought the fact of its non-falsifiability to consciousness – for as I said in section 2, whether or not a believer holds his belief falsifiably is largely a matter of his dispositions.

That said, it should be noted that in all the examples set out above, the element of non-falsifiability was very much present and conscious to the believers who expressed their beliefs. More than that, these believers often explicitly took the difference between falsifiable and non-falsifiable varieties of belief in a good and loving God to be one laden with religious significance – for according to the believers quoted in this section, holding a belief in God's goodness and love which is falsifiable is actually blasphemous, or, at the very least, something sinfully hubristic or a terrible weakening of one's faith. Thus, the distinction between empirically falsifiable and entirely non-falsifiable varieties of belief in a good and loving God is not merely a neutral one which is helpful for philosophical housekeeping, but rather one of enormous *religious* significance. In fact, religious communities have to hand an array of pejorative descriptions for disapproved-of forms of given religious beliefs – such as 'primitive', 'childish' or even 'superstitious', 'unorthodox', 'heretical' or 'idolatrous'. It turns out that making distinctions between different varieties of a given belief is actually a very common practice within religions.


## 6   The Nature and Significance of the Differences Between the above Centres of Variation

The beliefs in the four clusters of examples arrayed above in sections 2–5 differ with regard to their degree and kind of falsifiability, up to and including beliefs that are entirely non-falsifiable. As Wittgenstein says, '[i]f someone says he believes something then we can't always tell what he believes merely from the words he uses … It is so often a matter of finding what things are connected with what he says'.[24] To say that one belief differs from another with regards to its degree and kind of falsifiability is simply to point out one way in which different 'things are connected with' each of the two beliefs. Insofar as the degree and kind of falsifiability of a given belief is a part of its logic, the beliefs of the four clusters of examples arrayed above differ in their logics. How significant these logical

---

[24]   Ludwig Wittgenstein, 'Wittgenstein's Saturday Discussions: 1946–1947' in Ludwig Wittgenstein, *Ludwig Wittgenstein: Public and Private Occasions*, trans. and ed. James C Klagge and Alfred Nordmann (Lanham: Rowman and Littlefield, 2003), p. 404.

differences are taken to be will be a function of how significant the differences with regard to degree and kind of falsifiability are taken to be.

As it happens, the difference between a belief that is observably empirically falsifiable and one that is entirely non-falsifiable is one that is usually very significant to us. For example, a belief that is observably empirically falsifiable can be used to predict the obtaining or non-obtaining of certain observable empirical states of affairs, whereas an entirely non-falsifiable belief cannot ground any such predictions. Moreover, an observably empirically falsifiable belief can be contradicted by the obtaining or non-obtaining of observable states of affairs, and therefore found to be false, whereas an entirely non-falsifiable belief cannot be found to be false in any such way. Furthermore, observably empirically falsifiable beliefs directly connect to, and interact with, a whole host of other beliefs that we have – namely, our other empirical beliefs about the world, what makes it up and what happens in it – in ways which entirely non-falsifiable beliefs do not. Since these matters of proof and evidence, predictive power, truth and falsity, consistency of belief and the like play significant roles in our lives, the logical difference between observably empirically falsifiable beliefs and entirely non-falsifiable ones is a significant one. Thus, talk of falsifiability or non-falsifiability is really shorthand for an interlocking web of qualities which are usually fundamental to the logic of our beliefs. Falsifiability is not a logical quality that belongs narrowly or especially to beliefs of the natural sciences; rather, it speaks much more broadly to the issues of the extent to which a belief is sensitive to reality, and the kind of reality it is sensitive to (empirical, scientific, metaphysical and so on, or none at all).[25] Thus, if both some of the beliefs exemplified in section 2 (observably empirically falsifiable ones) and some of those exemplified in section 5 (entirely non-falsifiable ones) were recognised by the reader as being kinds of belief actually held by some religious believers, then it will have been recognised that belief in a good and loving God comes in more than one logical variety.

By saying that the beliefs exemplified in section 2 and in section 5 are of different logical varieties I am saying nothing more than that their logics are different in significant ways. Because significance is interest-relative, the matter of categorising beliefs in a good and loving God in logically fine-grained ways will always be open to disagreement. I have placed two distinct logical categories between those of observably empirically falsifiable beliefs and entirely non-falsifiable ones – namely, those of sections 3 and 4. But if one wanted to deny that the differences between those two intermediate clusters were significant enough to warrant their being counted as distinct logical varieties, this would be fine – as long as the logical differences between them were noted and not glided over.

---

[25]  Thus I could just as well have shown the logical variety amongst beliefs in a good and loving God by focussing on other logical qualities such as, for example, the given beliefs' degree of groundedness or non-groundedness in evidence, and the kinds of evidence involved. Falsifiability or otherwise is a convenient and dramatic way of looking at the logical differences between beliefs, but it is by no means the only one.

As Wittgenstein says in a slightly different context: 'Say what you choose, so long as it does not prevent you from seeing the facts'.[26]

Now, it might be objected to the above that one cannot necessarily learn about the content of a belief from its ramifications, and therefore that one cannot say that one belief has a different logic from another just because it implies or is implied by different kinds of thing. Simple reflection, however, will show that this objection must be misguided. For whether or not a belief implies that one's child will survive his illness, or whether or not it implies that certain kinds of good must eventually come about, will be a matter of the content of the belief in question. The content of a belief and its inferential ramifications are internally related – they are mutually constitutive of one another.

A second, more promising objection, grants that the content of a belief is internally related to its degree and kind of falsifiability. What it calls into doubt is that the degree and kind of falsifiability that a believer takes his own belief to have – and treats it as having – is necessarily an accurate reflection of the degree and kind of falsifiability that the belief *actually* has. The basis for this objection is the recognition that a believer can be mistaken or confused about the logic of the belief that he holds. For example, a believer in a good and loving God could take his belief to be observably empirically falsifiable simply because the various possible philosophical defusers of those prima facie empirical falsifiers have never occurred to him. Thus, he takes his belief to be – and treats it as being – observably empirically falsifiable, when in actual fact it is only philosophically falsifiable. This is indeed a good observation, and I would not want to deny that people can sometimes be mistaken or confused about the logic of their own beliefs – and therefore treat them in a way that is not fitting for that belief and in a way which therefore does not inform us accurately about the belief.

However, though such mistakes or confusions are possible, this fact cannot be used to deny that there are multiple logical varieties of belief in a good and loving God. For though a person can sometimes be mistaken or confused about the logic of his own belief, there are plenty of cases in which it would be very unreasonable to claim this. Consider someone who is suspected of being mistaken or confused about the logic of his belief. Imagine that the person who suspects the believer of being mistaken or confused proceeds to explain to the believer the alternative logic that the former takes to be the correct one for the believer's belief, and the believer shows that he clearly understands this alternative logic. For example, a person who takes his belief in a good and loving God to be observably empirically falsifiable may be suspected of simply not having realised that his belief is actually only philosophically falsifiable, because he has not realised that all prima facie empirical falsifiers can be defused by means of a good philosophical theodicy. The believer who has this explained to him, and who understands it clearly, may react in one of two ways. He may be grateful and admit that he hadn't thought of that, and that it therefore turns out that in actual fact his belief is not, and never

---

[26]  Wittgenstein, *Philosophical Investigations*, §79.

was, observably empirically falsifiable at all. However, another believer may fully understand the form of the belief that is only philosophically falsifiable, and deny that this is his belief. This believer may insist that his belief is one that is observably empirically falsifiable – for if God really is a good Father then there are certain obvious and observable things that He simply will not allow. The believer may add that if anyone denies this, then clearly they must mean by 'good and loving' something quite different to what he, the believer, means. If this is the believer's reaction, then it would seem difficult to claim that this may be a case in which he is mistaken or confused about the logic of his belief. After all, if a person fully understands a given variety of a belief, then his honest denial that this is the variety of the belief that he holds will itself be partly constitutive of the fact that the belief he holds is not of that logical variety.[27] There is a degree of radical misunderstanding of a belief which it does not make sense to attribute to a person. For at a certain point it makes no sense to attribute to someone a belief of a variety which they completely and utterly misunderstand, and it makes sense, instead, to admit that they actually understand their belief perfectly well, only that they hold a different variety of the belief to the one that we initially thought they held.

We can therefore imagine each of the believers of the above examples being confronted clearly with the logics of the alternative varieties of the belief, and being asked if, perhaps, they might not be mistaken about the nature of their belief. We can imagine cases in which the believers might agree that they were mistaken, but we can equally imagine cases in which they would not admit to any such mistake or confusion. And since this reaction is perfectly intelligible, the objection that the way a believer treats his belief may be out of sync with its true logic does not threaten to collapse the multiple different varieties that I have laid out above into only one.

The above reasoning applies to distinctions between logical varieties of any degree of fine- or coarse-grainedness. But when it comes to logical varieties which are radically different – such as the difference between observably empirically falsifiable beliefs and entirely non-falsifiable ones – the idea that a person could hold a belief of one of these kinds but mistakenly treat it as though it were of the other becomes extremely hard to understand. With Wittgenstein, we might want to say that '[f]or a blunder, that's too big'.[28] This means that at the very least the fact that some believers treat their belief in a good and loving God as observably empirically falsifiable, and others treat theirs as entirely non-falsifiable, should show that there is more than one logical variety of the belief.

---

[27]    Ruth Garrett Millikan, in a different context, observes that 'there is … a tendency for the object of one's thought to become whatever one takes it to be' ('On Unclear and Indistinct Ideas', *Philosophical Perspectives* 8 (1994), p. 75). Similarly, there is a tendency for the logic of one's belief to become – at least partially – whatever one takes it to be.

[28]    Ludwig Wittgenstein, 'Lectures on Religious Belief' in Ludwig Wittgenstein, *Lectures and Conversations on Aesthetics, Psychology, and Religious Belief*, ed. Cyril Barrett (Oxford: Blackwell, 1966), p. 62.

## 7    Conclusion and Further Directions

The aim of this paper has been to show that belief in a good and loving God is not logically uniform, but, rather, that it can and does come in multiple logical varieties. Analytic philosophy of religion seems often to work on the assumption that all religious beliefs are logically uniform (that is, that all instances of belief in God are of the same logical kind as each other, and all instances of belief in the afterlife are of the same logical kind as each other, and the like). The most effective way to undermine this presumption of uniformity is to present examples of a range of different logical varieties of a given belief and simply to ask: 'But do not religious believers also hold beliefs like this?' I hope that in working through the range of examples arrayed above the reader will not just get a sense of the logical varieties of belief in a good and loving God, but also a sense of how easy it would be to lay out a similar range of logically varied examples for other core religious beliefs – such as belief in miracles, in God's creation of the world, in the efficacy of petitionary prayer, in the afterlife and many more.

It is important to recognise the existence of logical variety in religious beliefs – as I mentioned in my introduction – because failure to do so often leads both to misevaluations and to distortions of the beliefs in question. Therefore, since philosophers of religion spend so much of their time trying to provide either elucidations or evaluations of religious beliefs, the recognition of the logical variety of many religious beliefs ought to be fundamental to much of what philosophers of religion do.

However, more than simply helping us to avoid misevaluating and distorting religious beliefs, recognising the existence of logical variety is also important for a further reason – for logical variety is the foundation upon which further important logical qualities rest, so that failure to recognise logical variety will almost certainly lead to failure to recognise these second-level qualities as well. Thus, the logical variety exhibited by the belief in a good and loving God often gives rise, in turn, to people holding that belief in a way that is indeterminate, mixed or fluid between those different varieties. That is, someone's belief in a good and loving God may hover indeterminately between more than one logical variety of the belief; or it may mix together some of the logical characteristics of different varieties of the belief; or it may change from having one logical character to another and perhaps back again. The fact that people's religious beliefs are often logically indeterminate, mixed or fluid will be masked by the fact that the belief is always expressed by the same sentence regardless; and yet, these logical qualities are very common amongst religious beliefs, and account for much of the real-life complexity and messiness that is characteristic of religious beliefs as actually held.

Sometimes, of course, indeterminacy, mixedness and fluidity will be manifestations of doxastic vices, such as confusion or evasion on the part of the believer. At other times, however, they can constitute doxastic virtues of positive religious significance. For example, certain kinds of indeterminacy and mixedness can be the result of the multi-layered nature of some religious beliefs; and certain kinds of fluidity can be manifestations of processes of religious growth or of a natural ebb and flow in religious life. There is no room here to enter into a full discussion of the nature and significance of the qualities of logical indeterminacy, mixedness and fluidity, in religious belief. But I hope that in highlighting the logical variety that exists in one central religious belief I have not only brought attention to that variety itself, but also helped to lay some groundwork for a more detailed study of the important logical qualities that derive from it.[29, 30]

---

[29]   I have made a brief start in discussing the qualities of logical indeterminacy, mixedness and fluidity in my paper 'Simple Objects of Comparison for Complex Grammars: An Alternative Strand in Wittgenstein's Later Remarks on Religion', *Philosophical Investigations* 35/1 (2012), especially sections 3 and 5; and, with some overlap, I also touch on them in my paper 'Religious Language as Paradigmatic of Language in General: Wittgenstein's 1933 Lectures' in Nuno Venturinha (ed.), *The Textual Genesis of Wittgenstein's Philosophical Investigations* (London: Routledge, 2013), especially section 5.

[30]   I would like to thank Stephen Mulhall, Rachel Bayefsky, Michael McGhee, Adrian Moore, Dani Rabinowitz and David Citron for helpful comments on earlier drafts of this paper; and to thank the Arts and Humanities Research Council for funding the doctoral research on which this paper is based.

# PART II
## Divine and Human Minds

# Chapter 6

# Belief Formation and Biased Minds

Olli-Pekka Vainio and Aku Visala

According to an old joke, philosophy deals with questions that can never be answered and religion with answers that can never be questioned. Based on this evaluation, philosophy of religion appears to be something even more suspect than its individual components. As jokes often do, this one also has a hint of truth in it. Even if we acknowledge that the aforementioned situation is ideal neither for philosophy nor religion, our knowledge acquisition is limited in ways that makes us less than perfect reasoners. Our minds have certain limitations that constrain both what they can do and how. Often we are limited by time and resources: we just cannot go checking all the necessary facts. In addition, non-conscious cognitive processes restrict us and guide our thinking in various ways. These factors, at least to some extent, help us to understand why it is so hard to reach consensus in philosophical debates. The hard question that arises is: what can philosophy (and philosophy of religion, especially) do if our minds are not well suited for philosophizing?

## Disagreement in Philosophy

It is a truth generally acknowledged that philosophers of high standing must have considerable disagreements with other philosophers. A brief look at a recent survey among professional philosophers reveals the fact of widespread disagreement in a drastic way. The following answers were drawn from a group of approximately 1,000 professional philosophers:[1]

| Topic | Accept or lean towards |
| --- | --- |
| Abstract objects: | Platonism (40%), nominalism (37%) |
| Free will: | compatibilism (59%), libertarianism (14%), no free will (12%), other (9%) |
| Epistemic justification: | externalism (42%), internalism (26%) |
| Laws of nature: | non-Humean (51%), Humean (24%), other (18%) |
| Meta-ethics: | moral realism (56%), anti-realism (28%), other (18%) |
| Mind: | physicalism (56%), non-physicalism (27%), other (16%) |
| Time: | A-theory (15%), B-theory (26%), other (58%) |
| Zombies: | conceivable but not metaphysically possible (35%), metaphysically possible (23%), inconceivable (16%), other (25%) |

---

[1]  The survey, including a lot more questions and answers, can be found at www.philpapers.org/surveys.

Many interesting points could be made in response to these results. We make only one, namely that in the case of most philosophical problems, we seem to have two or three mutually exclusive positions that battle for dominance. With respect to most problems, there is no consensus.

Some philosophers, most notably Colin McGinn and Peter van Inwagen, have suggested that this state of affairs obtains because philosophical questions and problems are difficult for beings who have minds like ours. In his *Problems in Philosophy*, McGinn argues that our cognitive capacities are such that they make it difficult to access the truth in certain domains of knowledge. These domains include such fundamental topics as the nature of free will, consciousness and the relationships of language and reality and of mind and body. Such domains are then labelled as 'philosophical' as opposed to commonsensical, scientific or something else. There is, however, nothing 'mysterious', McGinn claims, about these questions: they are neither confusions nor self-evidently true or false. They are answerable in principle, but given our limited cognitive capacities they are more or less unanswerable *for us*.

Since, for McGinn, our access to philosophical truths is severely limited, he is not surprised that philosophers find it hard to agree. What is more, he also emphasises the central role played by our extra-philosophical knowledge or our rational *intuitions* in our philosophizing. He writes:

> Philosophical theses can sometimes be assented to, but often they can expect only to be taken seriously. We may hope to find sufficient reason actually to believe a philosophical proposition, but often enough the best we can do is to get ourselves into a position to regard the proposition with respect ... A good deal of philosophical debate consists in persuading others to take seriously a hypothesis one has come to find attractive for reasons that defy summary statement or straightforward demonstration ... The relation between evidence (argument) and truth is very often not close enough to permit full-blown assent.[2]

These 'reasons that defy summary statement and straightforward demonstration' guide our philosophical inclinations so as to make us appreciate and defend some particular philosophical theory because its assumptions have certain intuitive plausibility for us.[3] In what follows, it is just these reasons that we aim to identify and discuss.

---

[2]	Colin McGinn, *Problems in Philosophy* (Oxford: Blackwell, 1993), p. 1. See also Peter van Inwagen, *The Problem of Evil* (Oxford: Oxford University Press, 2006), pp. 37–55.

[3]	There are many views as to what these 'philosophical intuitions' actually are. One possibility assumes the existence of some a priori rational faculty that produces beliefs about, say, mathematics and conceptual or linguistic connections. Another theory is that intuitions are nothing more than deeply held beliefs – beliefs that come mostly from non-philosophical or non-scientific sources such as common-sense and everyday perception.

## Various Ways of Knowing

What are the forces that shape our extra-philosophical intuitions so as to produce disagreement? We can begin to answer this question if we stop thinking about our minds as calculators that simply process information according to logically valid inferences. Research in cognitive psychology and cognitive science suggest that the human mind processes information in various ways. Not only are these ways more complex than philosophers normally think, they are also, for the most part, outside our direct voluntary control. This fact, we will argue, goes some way towards explaining why our philosophical reasoning so often leads to disagreement.

Here we want to focus on one aspect of human cognition – its multi-layered nature. Many cognitive scientists talk about two general types of information processing, *reflective* and *intuitive*. This is particularly evident in what are often called *dual-process models* of cognition. Psychologists like Daniel Kahneman argue that many cognitive problems arise due to the fact that we are caught between these two information processing strategies.[4]

The evidence for the dual-process model of cognition comes from many different sources, the most important of which are developmental studies and the study of practical rationality and cognitive biases. The dual-process model claims that there are two fundamentally different information processing strategies in human cognition. The first strategy we call the *high-court strategy* or *the reflective strategy* and the second the *bureaucracy strategy* or the *intuitive strategy*.[5]

According to the high-court strategy, we can understand information acquisition as a sort of judicial process. The basic idea is that the epistemic subject receives or collects evidence and formulates a proposition or a set of propositions on the basis of this information. Then this set of propositions is brought before the 'belief-judge' and the 'belief-attorney' presents all available evidence for and against it. Finally, the judge presents his verdict: either the set in question is accepted in which case it turns into a set of beliefs held by the epistemic subject, or it is discarded.

In the high-court strategy, acquiring new beliefs is based on analysis of evidence and coherence and the exercise of reflective reasoning and inference. In this mode, we basically choose our beliefs as if our consciousness was like a guard standing at the gate of our mind. Only propositions that are accompanied with sufficient evidence and coherence are let through the gate. Finally, the model implies that there is one single process and a single set of norms of rationality through which all propositions have to pass.

In contrast, when reasoning in bureaucratic mode, there is no single, unified process of belief acquisition or a single set of norms of rationality for all new information. Rather, the epistemic subject automatically acquires and processes

---

In the former sense, as one might expect, one's view of what philosophical intuitions are has a significant impact on how one understands the nature of philosophical inquiry.

4    See Daniel Kahneman, *Thinking. Fast and Slow* (London: Allen Lane, 2011).

5    In Kahneman's terms, these are called System 1 and System 2.

information in different ways all the time and the information acquired triggers certain beliefs without any conscious effort. There is no judge or jury in the mind, only a large number of independent systems that process information and send their processed information to other systems as facts. In the high-court strategy, every piece of evidence and inference is transparent to the epistemic subject and every belief is treated equally. In bureaucratic processing, there are all sorts of things going on of which the 'head of the investigation' knows nothing about. The bureaucratic processing is, thus, driven by factors that are mostly out of our conscious reach.

When we are thinking about philosophical work, it is tempting to think that philosophizing takes place in high-court mode. Unfortunately, this is not the case. The dual process model of cognition gives a partial explanation of the problem of why people find different solutions to philosophical dilemmas convincing: they have been influenced by different experiences that in turn make some solutions easier to accept than others.

High court and bureaucracy modes are not sealed off from each other so that we use only either one of these two.[6] Even in the cases where we are able to reason conscientiously, we cannot forget what we have learned in our more bureaucratic moments. If we think of our lives as narratives – that is to say, as very long and time-consuming knowledge acquisition processes – it becomes easy to see how complex our cognitive structure is and how different people can acquire different convictions about relatively similar matters.

In fact, often we do not even need a long time span to develop a 'cognitive bias' towards one particular solution.[7] In an interesting study, Linda Babcock and George Loewenstein gave the same court case to two groups for investigation and judgement.[8] Group A was divided between plaintiffs and defendants, group B was not. Both groups had the same, somewhat ambiguous, evidence. In group A, those who were given the role of plaintiff saw the evidence as supporting their case. Simultaneously, those in the role of defendant drew an opposing

---

[6]   Unsurprisingly, there is some disagreement among psychologists as to how this relation between different systems and their exact nature should be framed. For an overview, see Gerd Gigerenzer, *Rationality for Mortals* (Oxford: Oxford University Press, 2008), pp. 3–20. It is not necessary in this context to wander any deeper into this field of questions. Suffice it to note that contemporary psychologists are moving away from mind-as-a-computer models towards more embodied models where the inherent limitedness of human reasoning is acknowledged.

[7]   Cognitive biases are natural inclinations that make us favour certain perspectives, arguments and views over others. In popular discourse, 'bias' usually has a negative connotation, but in cognitive psychology it merely refers to models of reasoning that are often helpful for humans from the viewpoint of survival. Thus biases are neither good nor bad as such, and they can both help us to find the truth or keep us from finding it.

[8]   Linda Babcock and George Loewenstein, 'Explaining bargaining impasse: the role of self-serving biases' in *Journal of Economic Perspectives* 11 (1997), pp. 109–26.

conclusion and claimed that the evidence favoured their case. In group B the interpretations of the evidence were less clear and less biased towards either side. The lessons appear to be that if we currently inhabit a clearly defined identity (even an imagined one), we will automatically interpret the available evidence as supporting our case, and that it is harder for us to take into account opposing arguments and see their rationales.

Relatively natural and universal intuitive beliefs create different kinds of biases in our information processing. For example, we have biases that make us automatically prefer views that are simple and cohere with the beliefs that we already have. The bigger the difference between our beliefs and some new piece of information the more reluctant we are to adopt the new piece of information. Further, we tend to neglect disagreement because it creates cognitive dissonance which in turn makes us uneasy. We also overemphasise our own intelligence: studies suggest that 70 per cent of humans think that they are smarter than average. Then there is the fact that we persistently overemphasise the rationality of the particular choices we make. Even when we try to reason reflectively and conscientiously, we favour solutions that appear simpler to us, which confirm our previously held convictions, and which challenge those convictions to the least possible degree. These are called *conservation, confirmation* and *simplification* biases. These biases normally help us to reason our way relatively reliably and quickly through everyday challenges, but it is easy to see how they can work against us when we attempt to reason more abstractly and generally.[9] Summing up, there is wide agreement in the cognitive study of rationality over the fact that human cognitive faculties are naturally biased towards certain outcomes. Our information processing systems do more than simply record and save information, they select relevant information, discard non-relevant information and sometimes even distort the outcomes of information processing. These distortions are relatively stable across large groups of individual humans; some even seem to be common to all human beings.

Against such a dark background the crucial question is this: what can philosophy in general, or philosophy of religion in particular, do? What role is there left for reasoning when our faculties are biased and to a great extent unsuitable for the task they are set to undertake?

## The Vagueness of Philosophical Inquiry

Perpetual and widespread disagreement in philosophy pertains not only to preferable answers to philosophical questions, but also to what philosophy is

---

[9]   See, for example, Gilbert Harman, 'Practical Aspects of Theoretical Reasoning' in A.E. Mele and P. Rawling (eds), *The Oxford Handbook of Rationality* (Oxford: Oxford University Press, 2004), pp. 45–56; Scott Plous, *The Psychology of Judgment and Decision Making* (New York: McGraw-Hill, 1993).

and how it should be done. Indeed, in this sense philosophy as a discipline is rather peculiar compared to, say, a science like psychology or biology. In these disciplines, virtually all practitioners agree on what the subject matter is and there is widespread agreement over methods of enquiry. Further, the subject matter of psychology or biology is not a psychological or biological question per se. All this is false in philosophy. Not only do philosophers disagree wildly about the subject matter of philosophy, they also disagree about the methods of enquiry.

Philosophical reflection on the nature of philosophy is quite popular nowadays and is sometimes referred to as *meta-philosophy*. In order to bring some kind of clarity to the issue, we look at how different views answer the following questions:

(1)   Are there philosophical truths, and if there are, what are they like?
(2)   Is there a distinct method in philosophy, and if there is, what is it like?
(3)   Is there progress in philosophy and does it matter whether philosophy makes progress?

The question of the nature of philosophy and its methods is, of course, an ancient one. The classical *rationalist* view is that rational reflection gives us access to deep truths about reality that are otherwise inaccessible to us. It is philosophy, as opposed to, say, science or common sense that ultimately tells us how the world is. For the rationalist, philosophical truths are a priori truths that we can access via rational reflection and intuition. They are truths that pertain to ultimate reality behind what we can see or hear. Rational reflection is also a priori in the sense that it does not depend on observation or any other type of empirical knowledge. Instead, rational reflection is seen as a special kind of capacity that can access non-empirical truths.

Opposed to the rationalist, there has been the *empiricist* who thinks that philosophical truths are empirical and hence a posteriori truths. Philosophical truths are not accessed via some specific a priori capacity but rather by inference from observation. Further, there is no specific philosophical subject matter: there are no philosophical truths that pertain to some non-observable realm or ultimate reality. We may have philosophical truths about the world but they are accessed via observation. From this, it follows that the philosophical method cannot be completely a priori.

In the contemporary scene, the main meta-philosophical schools are *naturalism* and *non-naturalism*.[10] The basic distinction between these views is, roughly, that the naturalist sees philosophy as an extension of science whereas the *non-naturalist* emphasises the differences between science and philosophy. Although the non-naturalist is in the tradition of rationalism and the naturalist in the tradition of empiricism, both usually deny the rationalist idea that philosophy gives us access to some non-empirical ultimate reality that is otherwise inaccessible to us. Instead,

---

[10]   The following discussion is mostly based on Hans-Johann Glock, *What is Analytic Philosophy?* (Cambridge: Cambridge University Press, 2008), especially chapters 2 and 5.

in contemporary meta-philosophy, philosophy is normally seen as a *second-order discipline* that consists of reflecting, clarifying and organising truths we already have obtained through science, everyday observation and reasoning.

Still, the naturalist and the non-naturalist disagree over several issues. First, for the naturalist, there are no philosophical truths apart from scientific truths. Thus, the proper subject matter of philosophy is the interpretation and reflection of scientific truths. As Rudolf Carnap originally put it, philosophy provides the logical grammar of science. Similarly, later naturalists such as W.V.O. Quine insisted that traditional philosophical disciplines, such as epistemology, need to be *naturalized*, that is, turned into branches of science. In the case of epistemology, it would be psychology that would provide us with a naturalized epistemology. Similar development has also been going on in the philosophy of mind in the last 30 years as cognitive science and cognitive psychology have replaced (or at least profoundly shaped) much traditional philosophising about the mind and the body.

In opposition to this, the non-naturalist normally insists that although philosophy is a second-order discipline, the subject matter is not just scientific truths, but all other truths as well. For the naturalist, the set of all truths is scientifically accessible, whereas for the non-naturalist it is not (or at least he is not committed to the claim that all truths are scientific truths). The non-naturalist insists that there are non-scientific truths as well: these might be linguistic, conceptual, logical or common sense truths of some type or another. Thus, the non-naturalist does not think that science necessarily needs a particular philosophy to support it; the job of the philosopher is broader than that of a scientist. For Wittgenstein and his followers, the philosopher clarifies and reflects on the use of language.[11] For many contemporary non-naturalists, such as Michael Dummett drawing on Gottlob Frege, philosophy deals with conceptual and logical truths.[12] Finally, a contemporary Kantian can see the subject matter of philosophy residing in the conditions of our experience of the world. Most non-naturalists, thus, seem to think that at least some truths obtainable via philosophy (although not pertaining to some peculiar ultimate world) are a priori truths or some kind of synthetic a priori truths that are not accessible through science. These truths are usually seen as truths about most general laws of thought (Dummett) or the meanings of sentences (Wittgenstein).

Second, the naturalist thinks that philosophy does not have a specific method of inquiry, but rather that philosophical methods are reducible to scientific methods. The non-naturalist disagrees. Resembling the traditional rationalist, the non-

---

[11]   A Wittgensteinian view of philosophy is outlined in, for example, Peter Hacker, 'Analytic philosophy: beyond the linguistic turn and back again' in M. Beaney (ed.), *The Analytic Turn: Analysis in Early Analytic Philosophy and Phenomenology* (London: Routledge, 2007).

[12]   See Michael Dummett, *The Nature and Future of Philosophy* (New York: Columbia University Press, 2010).

naturalist thinks that there is a special capacity that is applied in philosophising. This could be some sort of rational intuition as traditionally thought or the possession of linguistic or conceptual competence as the Wittgensteinians and some other linguistic philosophers would have it.

In sum, given the naturalistic view of philosophy, philosophy either ultimately reduces to science or gets eliminated by it. Contrary to this, on the non-naturalist view even a complete future science would not solve all philosophical problems and questions.

There are also middle-ground views that reject bits of both naturalism and non-naturalism. One of the most well-known is the Oxford philosopher Timothy Williamson's view that seeks to avoid the mistakes of what Williamson calls 'crude empiricism (naturalism) and crude rationalism (non-naturalism)'.[13] According to him, philosophy is, to the dismay of the naturalist, truly an armchair discipline. This is clearly closer to the non-naturalist view of philosophy than to the naturalist. However, contrary to the non-naturalists, Williamson emphasises that the philosophical subject matter is seldom purely a priori, conceptual or linguistic as the non-naturalist claims. Further, he argues that clear-cut distinctions between the a priori and the a posteriori, and between the conceptual and the empirical are very difficult to make. Thus, philosophical questions consist of questions and problems whose nature is unclear or *vague* to us and which resist our normal repertoire for answering questions. If this is what philosophical questions are, there is no single set of philosophical truths. Instead, some philosophical question might turn out to be empirical, whereas others might resist empirical treatment.

It follows from Williamson's view of philosophical questions that although conceptual or linguistic analysis is important in philosophy, the subject matter of philosophy is not really (or at least clearly) conceptual or linguistic. This point is well made when Williamson writes that 'although philosophers have more reason than physicists to consider matters of language or thought, philosophy is in no deep sense a linguistic or conceptual inquiry, any more than physics is. But it does not follow that experiment is an appropriate primary method for philosophy'.[14] In other words, the subject matter of philosophy is not simply conceptual or linguistic but much closer to our everyday and scientific issues. Here the naturalist is on the right track. At the same time, however, philosophical progress is best achieved by rigorous use of semantic and logical methods, although the subject matter itself is not necessarily semantic or linguistic. In this way, Williamson thinks, we bring clarity to previously unclear and vague questions.

Further, Williamson thinks that there is no single philosophical method, no rational intuition or linguistic competence through which philosophical knowledge is acquired. Nor are philosophical methods just scientific methods.

---

[13]   Williamson's idea of philosophy is best explained in his *The Philosophy of Philosophy* (Oxford: Blackwell, 2007).

[14]   Williamson, *The Philosophy of Philosophy*, p. 21.

Instead, philosophers can use all our ways of acquiring knowledge: common sense, perception, logic and science. What the philosopher does is to use all these rigorously and systematically. In this sense, philosophy is much closer to our everyday and scientific ways of acquiring knowledge but without reducing into either science or everyday reasoning.

Finally, some brief points about philosophical progress. Williamson endorses the non-naturalist idea of true philosophical, not just scientific, progress. Although Williamson is very critical of the current state of analytic philosophy, especially with respect to its methodology, he still thinks that some progress has been made and can be made in the future:

> In many areas of philosophy, we know much more in 2007 than was known in 1957; much more was known in 1957 than in 1907 … Although fundamental disagreement is conspicuous in most areas of philosophy, the best theories in a given area are most cases far better developed in 2007 than the best theories in that area were in 1957, and so on.[15]

Later, he continues the same thought: 'It seems likely that some parts of contemporary analytic philosophy just pass the methodological threshold for some cumulative progress to occur, however slowly, while others fall short of the threshold'.[16] Thus, through rigorous work on philosophical methods and rules of inquiry there is progress to be made in the future.[17]

## Implications for Philosophy of Religion

In the light of what has been said, it is no wonder that philosophers disagree. They are driven by their conflicting intuitions, restricted by time and resources and by their biased minds. They have different ideas about what they do, and about how and why they do it. Even the Williamsonian solution, which seems to fit quite nicely with the psychological picture we painted earlier, leaves many things open. Williamson's approach provides a system that makes it possible to engage a wide

---

[15] Williamson, *The Philosophy of Philosophy*, pp. 279–80.

[16] Williamson, *The Philosophy of Philosophy*, p. 288.

[17] Dummett shares Williamson's cautious view of philosophical progress: 'philosophy is a sector in the quest of truth, or, more accurately, a search for a clearer understanding of the truths we already know'. If there is no progress in philosophy, then we do not get any closer to truth by philosophy and we should abandon the whole enterprise. Increasing truth-likeness of philosophical theories is, therefore, necessary for the meaningfulness of philosophical inquiry. If there is no progress, philosophy is not worth wasting any time on. Nevertheless, Dummett readily admits that progress in philosophy is slow, and 'the path toward the goal of philosophy … is a meandering one that twists and turns upon itself' (*The Nature and Future of Philosophy*, pp. 148–9).

range of questions with multiple tools while maintaining philosophical rigour. In a way this helps us outflank some of our biases since we are not at the outset restricted by methodological or other meta-level assumptions.

If we take Williamson's view of philosophy seriously and apply it to philosophy of religion, at least the following points might characterize the discipline:

(1)  Progress might be made by focusing on careful analysis of religious questions using the tools of logic and semantics before attempting to answer them.

(2)  However, philosophy of religion is not just linguistic or conceptual analysis of how religious people use language. A successful theory in philosophy of religion could tell us, for example, the cases when we have or we do not have religious knowledge, or that given empirical facts x, y, z, some religious propositions are either false or true, or maybe more or less probable.

(3)  It is not possible to define at the outset the borders and methods of the discipline. In other words, very simple models (like a Wittgensteinian language-based approach or Quinean naturalism) are not optimal tools for the task, even if they may have their own legitimate place in solving some particular problems.

In addition to these more abstract considerations, several practical consequences will result. In the following, we mention three related issues.

*No Hope of Consensus*

First, as long as we have the kind of brains we do, we must acknowledge that with respect to problems that involve strong, mutually conflicting intuitions and reflective reasoning, consensus is highly unlikely. This includes most philosophical problems such as the problem of free will, the mind-body problem and the existence of God. In these cases and many others, the interplay of personal histories, conflicting natural intuitions, ever-active biases and ambiguous nature of philosophical enquiry make complete agreement highly unlikely. Philosophy of religion is not an exception. Since the issues that philosophy of religion deals with are loaded with personal significance and require great amounts of reflective thought, we should not expect disagreements to vanish any time soon.

Here, a critical question arises. If philosophy cannot produce agreement, does it mean that philosophy is meaningless and does not make progress? Our answer is negative. Philosophy is not meaningless and complete agreement is seldom necessary for progress towards truth. Disagreements abound in domains that we generally take to be reliable sources of knowledge – or at least think that there is truth to be had in that domain. Scientists disagree with each other constantly, but yet we do not abandon the scientific search for truth. Further, we do not abandon political discourse just because there is perpetual disagreement about what the best course of action is. The same goes with ethical and moral issues. We keep doing philosophy, science and politics despite the fact that consensus on specific problems is not in sight.

*The Need for Communal Enquiry*

Second, in order to combat the individual and pan-human biases that seek to distort our philosophical and scientific attempts to get to truth, communal effort is needed. The best way to resist our biases so far has been the development of communally shared rules of reasoning and methods of assessing evidence.[18] Through such inter-subjective efforts, scientists, for example, are able to form theories and come to conclusions about which theories are best supported by evidence. This communal effort is crucial for all forms of reflective thinking, especially philosophy. Without inter-subjectivity, communal criticism and shared rules of reasoning, we would all fall prey to our own favourite ideas.

Given the need for communal inquiry for progress, the ever-continuing fragmentation of contemporary philosophy is deeply problematic. The fragmentation also reminds us that there is a downside to communal effort. The larger a community of high-level reflective thinkers becomes, the more likely it is to split up into schools and cliques. In this sense, communal effort is a double-edged sword: on the one hand, it is a necessary prerequisite for intellectual work, but on the other hand, it creates disagreement and makes fragmentation more likely. Nevertheless we want to emphasise that despite its problems communal effort seems to be the only even somewhat successful way to get closer to truth in science, philosophy and other domains of reflective thinking.

*The Role of Philosophy of Religion*

Our third point has to do with philosophy of religion and the religious relevance of its results. If the cognitive scientists are correct, religious belief comes naturally to human beings. Human beings have several cognitive biases and information processing tendencies that make them susceptible to religious, as opposed to non-religious, ideas.[19] Given the deeply entrenched nature of religion

---

[18]    Richard P. Larrick, 'Debiasing' in Derek Koehler and Nigel Harvey (eds), *Blackwell Handbook of Judgment and Decision Making* (Oxford: Blackwell 2004), pp. 316–37.

[19]    See, for example, Justin Barrett, *Cognitive Science, Religion and Theology: From Human Minds to Divine Minds* (West Conshohocken, PA: Templeton Press, 2011). There are, of course atheists and non-believers, but usually a great deal of reflective thinking is needed in order to get into this position. In addition, some psychologists claim that atheism and non-belief require substantial cultural scaffolding whereas religious belief does not. If the theories of cognitive science are correct, we can infer that non-belief will spread slowly and only in special cultural conditions; see Justin L. Barrett, *Why Would Anyone Believe in God ADD ?* (Lanham, MD: Altamira, 2004), pp. 108–18.

and religious belief, philosophy of religion has an important function in keeping the disagreements between believers and non-believers – as well as between different kinds of believers – civilized and polite. Analytic philosophy and analytic philosophy of religion can offer tools for a cultural conversation. Even if philosophical discourse cannot promise consensus, by getting people to reflect on their views and the views of others, philosophy of religion can secure a state where conflicting views are given fair hearing, subjected to critical discussion and possible improvement.

The deeply entrenched nature of religious ideas should also make us think about how prevalent and widely dispersed philosophy of religion's discussions and their outcomes can become. Given the way the human mind works, highly abstract arguments and theories of philosophical natural theology are quite unlikely to be adopted by most believers. This conclusion creates a problem for certain theories in religious epistemology. Several evidentialists have suggested that we need consciously accessible evidence and procedures if we are to come to justifiably believe anything about religious issues. However, if most actual religious beliefs are formed intuitively and very few people are able to engage in critical reflection on their intuitive-level processing, strongly evidentialist-orientated natural theology will only affect a fraction of believers.[20] Would the evidentialist then say that most believers are irrational in their religious belief?

If religious belief is largely a product of intuitive-level processing instead of sophisticated theories and arguments of natural theology, what then is the point of doing philosophical theology? As some philosophers of religion working in the Reformed tradition have suggested, instead of producing religious belief, philosophical theology could function as a reflective way to deal with *defeaters* for intuitive-level religious belief.[21] As many psychologists have pointed out, intuitive beliefs can be challenged and replaced by reflectively acquired beliefs in the process of conscious critical reflection. Given the plurality of religious and non-religious creeds in Western societies, almost all religious believers at some point of their lives encounter information that casts doubt on their beliefs. This should trigger a reflective process of evaluation and reformulation in the believer and this is where natural theology could come in.

Finally, the function of philosophical and natural theology could be to shape – in Charles Taylor's terms – the *social imaginary* of a culture or a society. A social imaginary is a mental space which specifies what worldview options are available for an individual to affirm or reject. Before modernity the social imaginary contained only a few options. Now, because of the postmodern state of our Western cultures and societies, the social imaginary has almost incomprehensibly

---

[20]    For discussion, see, for example, James Ross, 'Willing Belief and Rational Faith' in Kelly James Clark and Raymond J. VanArragon (eds), *Evidence and Religious Belief* (Oxford: Oxford University Press 2011), pp. 13–21.

[21]    See, for example, Alvin Plantinga, *Warranted Christian Belief* (Oxford: Oxford University Press, 2000), pp. 357–73.

many options.[22] To complicate things even further, many of these options are both mutually contradictory and yet also apparently rational.[23]

The important thing is that persistent argumentation and debate can, despite its abstract and reflective nature, *keep ideas within the social imaginary*. Of course, some ideas deserve to be forgotten and thrown out of our imaginary, but if this happens undeservedly due to contingent social factors, misguided intuitions or false arguments, some problems will likely occur. It is the task of philosophy of religion to keep account of what is rejected or affirmed, and on what grounds: this way we may also come to acknowledge *why* we are disagreeing and *what* it is that we are disagreeing about. Maybe this could be one humble but relatively reasonable goal, for philosophical inquiry – for creatures with minds like ours.

---

[22]    Charles Taylor, *A Secular Age* (Cambridge, MA: Harvard University Press, 2007).

[23]    For a detailed discussion of the meaning of rationality, see Robert Audi, *Rationality and Religious Commitment* (Oxford: Oxford University Press, 2011). We use 'rational' here in Audi's sense to refer to views that are not clearly false. It is therefore a very minimal concept. According to Gary Gutting, the situation depicted in this essay should not lead us towards scepticism. A situation where we seem to have good arguments on both sides of a debate and neither side is making clear philosophical errors should lead us to conclude that both options are rational and therefore possible. Consequently, we are not committing a philosophical crime if we commit ourselves to some particular solution even when we disagree with our epistemic peers. See Gary Gutting, *What Philosophers Know: Case Studies in Recent Analytic Philosophy* (Cambridge: Cambridge University Press, 2009), pp. 232–3.

Chapter 7

# When Does God Know?
# Open Theism, Simultaneous Causation, and Divine Knowledge of the Present

Benjamin H. Arbour

For the sake of constructing a *reductio ad absurdum*, I assume that open theists are right to conclude in the face of the dilemma of freedom and foreknowledge (hereafter DFF) that God lacks exhaustive foreknowledge. From this assumption, I show why open theism logically entails the impossibility of divine knowledge of the present. I do so by arguing that open theism's response to the DFF together with the metaphysics of free will and the metaphysics of time required in order for open theism to be properly motivated as a response to the DFF entails not only that God lacks knowledge of the future, but also that God lacks knowledge of any present truths involving free will. Because omniscience entails knowledge of all truths, I take as obvious that this is an undesirable conclusion for any theist. Hence, if my argument holds, open theism should be rejected.

**Defining the Dilemma**

Philosophers have long puzzled as to how the following three truths form a coherent set:

(1)   God's knowledge is infallible, and thus cannot be wrong.
(2)   God knows at $t1$ that an agent $S$ will do an action $A$ at $t3$.
(3)   $S$ is free to refrain from doing $A$ at $t3$.

In an effort to clarify why open theists reject divine foreknowledge of future contingents, allow me to introduce some definitions of theirs, as well as what is widely held to be the most successful argument for the incompatibility of significant freedom and divine foreknowledge.

To oversimplify things, libertarians maintain that a person is free with respect to some action just in case that person possesses the ability to act in mutually exclusive ways with respect to that action.[1] Thus, if $S$ is free with respect to $A$, then it is within $S$'s power to either do $A$, or to refrain from doing $A$. Bringing time into play so as to clarify the nature of the DFF, if it is within $S$'s power to refrain from doing $A$ at $t3$, then it is within $S$'s power at $t3$ to bring it about that God was wrong in believing at $t1$ that $S$ would do $A$ at $t3$. But, from premise (1), God is an infallible knower, so $S$ cannot truly have the power to bring it about that God was wrong. Some have suggested that $S$'s freedom does not require that $S$ have at $t3$ the ability to bring it about that God was wrong, but rather that $S$ has at $t3$ the ability to bring it about that God believed something different at $t1$ than God actually believed.[2] But counterfactual power over the past strikes many – including all open theists – as counterintuitive, so I shall set this issue aside in the present chapter.

The common intuition of temporal asymmetry – that the past is relevantly different from the future, such that we can causally influence what happens in the future while we cannot presently causally influence the past – entails, according to open theists, that we lack any sort of counterfactual power over the past.[3] That is, we cannot presently cause things that comprise history to have been different than they in fact were.[4] Because open theists believe humans possess free will as understood by libertarians (hereafter LFW), and because they are not persuaded that any other solution to the DFF succeeds in eliminating the tension raised by the DFF, open theists conclude that it is impossible for God to know any true propositions concerning future contingents (hereafter PCFC). Hence, open theists reject (2) – that is, they deny that God believes at $t1$ that $S$ will do $A$ at $t3$.[5]

---

[1]	Some maintain that libertarianism is merely the conjunction of incompatibilism and free will, which doesn't necessarily entail alternative possibilities. I won't discuss this view, seeing as how no open theists defend this view of libertarianism.

[2]	This has sometimes been called counterfactual power over the past and is associated with Ockhamism. There exists a significant amount of literature on the subject, but a few pieces that stand out are William Hasker's *God, Time, and Knowledge* (Ithaca, NY: Cornell University Press, 1989), pp. 96–115 and Alvin Plantinga's 'On Ockham's Way Out' in *Faith and Philosophy* 3/3 (1986), pp. 235–69. See also George Mavrodes, 'Is the Past Unpreventable?' in *Faith and Philosophy* 1/2 (1984), pp. 131–46; and William Ockham, *Predestination, God's Foreknowledge and Future Contingents*, trans. Marilyn McCord Adams and Norman Kretzmann (Hackett, IN: Hackett, 1969).

[3]	Of course, this is contentious. Counterfactual power over the past does not necessarily require the ability to causally influence the past. Causation is one kind of counterfactual power, but not all counterfactual power amounts to causation. Ockhamists fail to persuade open theists of this as it concerns the DFF.

[4]	This is often mistakenly identified as Ockhamism, and open theists maintain that Ockhamism requires the possibility of 'changing the past'.

[5]	This does not necessarily entail that God is in time. Even if God is timeless, it would be true at $t1$ that God believes (timelessly) that I will do $S$ at $t3$. Cf. Peter van Inwagen, 'What Does an Omniscient Being Know About the Future?' in *Oxford Studies in Philosophy of Religion* 1 (2008), pp. 216–30, specifically pp. 218–20. Much debate exists as to whether divine timelessness presents a genuine solution to the DFF, but I won't engage that literature

Nonetheless, open theists maintain both (1) and (3) – that God's knowledge is infallible, and that humans enjoy LFW, at least sometimes.

To ensure that I am not mischaracterizing the open theist's argument, let us consider exactly what is meant by LFW. Offering a definition of LFW that I believe is representative of all open theists, Hasker writes,

> (FW)  N is free at $T$ with respect to performing $A =_{df}$ It is in N's power at $T$ to perform $A$, and it is in N's power at $T$ to refrain from performing $A$.[6]

With this understanding of LFW, and believing that humans do possess this kind of freedom, Hasker offers two arguments for open theism. The first argument:

> (A1)  Necessarily, God has always believed that Clarence will have a cheese omelette tomorrow morning. (Premise: the necessity of the past)
> (A2)  Necessarily, if God has always believed that a certain thing will happen, then that thing will happen. (Premise: divine infallibility)
> (A3)  Therefore, necessarily, Clarence will have a cheese omelette tomorrow.[7]

But most open theists carefully distinguish between different concepts of necessity that operate in the arguments they use to argue for the incompatibility between freedom and foreknowledge, so it won't do to critique the equivocation between modal necessity (broadly logical necessity) and accidental necessity. After all, it is clearly false that in every possible world in which God is infallibly omniscient God believes that Clarence will have a cheese omelette tomorrow morning. As but one example, consider a world in which Clarence does not exist, which is certainly a possible world. If God believes all and only true propositions, God obviously does not believe that Clarence will have a cheese omelette tomorrow morning in

---

here for the simple reason that I am presupposing open theism for the sake of argument. To date, all open theists affirm divine temporality. Hasker at one time thought that divine timelessness, if it were true, offers a solution to the DFF, but he later changed his mind. For the first view, see Hasker, *God, Time, and Knowledge*, pp. 144–85. For the second, see 'The Absence of a Timeless God' in Gregory E. Ganssle and David M. Woodruff (eds), *God and Time* (New York, NY: Oxford University Press, 2002), pp. 182–219.

[6]  Hasker, *God, Time, and Knowledge*, p. 66. I use the capital $T$ here to preserve Hasker's exact text.

[7]  Ibid., p. 68. Open theists divide into two camps when debating the ontological status of PCFC (limited foreknowledge open theists like Hasker, Swinburne, and van Inwagen on the one hand; open future open theists such as Rhoda, Tuggy and Zimmerman on the other), but they agree that open theism is the proper response to the DFF. Hence, taking Hasker's arguments as representative of all open theists does not misrepresent open future open theists, for their arguments against the compatibility of foreknowledge and LFW do not differ from those articulated by Hasker, regardless of any metaphysical differences between these groups on other matters.

a world in which Clarence does not exist. Hence, (A1) is false as it stands, and it needs to be rewritten as something akin to

(A1*)   If Clarence has a cheese omelette tomorrow morning, then it is necessarily the case that God has always believed that Clarence would do so. (Premise: the necessity of the past and divine knowledge of the future)

It is also worth mentioning that articulations of the DFF which rely on the transfer of accidental necessity face technical problems. When the medievals introduced the notion of accidental necessity, they did so in order to denote the necessity of the past. Therefore, given an A-theory of time, by definition, no aspect of the future can be accidentally necessary, for accidental necessity, by definition, refers only to the fixity of the past.[8] Rather, what open theists likely mean is something akin to what William Alston called 'S-logical necessity' – that, given some situation, it is logically necessary that something follow from that situation.[9] I will employ the term 'consequential necessity' to refer to this same idea (symbolized by (CN)).

Aware of the difficulties that his first argument faces, Hasker offers a second argument which many find to be a strong argument for the incompatibility of freedom and foreknowledge:

(B1)   It is now true that Clarence will have a cheese omelette for breakfast tomorrow. (Premise)
(B2)   It is impossible that God should at any time believe what is false, or fail to believe anything that is true. (Premise: divine omniscience)
(B3)   Therefore, God has always believed that Clarence will have a cheese omelette for breakfast tomorrow. (From 1, 2)
(B4)   If God has always believed a certain thing, it is not in anyone's power to bring it about that God has not always believed that thing. (Premise: the unalterability of the past)
(B5)   Therefore, it is not in Clarence's power to bring it about that God has not always believed that he would have a cheese omelette for breakfast. (From 3, 4)

---

[8]   Cf. Thomas P. Flint, 'The Varieties of Accidental Necessity' in Kelly James Clark and Michael Rea (eds), *Reason, Metaphysics, and Mind: New Essays on the Philosophy of Alvin Plantinga* (New York, NY: Oxford University Press, 2012), pp. 38–54; Linda Zagzebski, *The Dilemma of Freedom and Foreknowledge* (New York: Oxford University Press, 1991), pp. 15–24; and Alfred Freddoso's helpful introduction to his translation of Luis de Molina's *On Divine Foreknowledge: Part IV of the Concordia* (Ithaca, NY: Cornell University Press, 1988), pp. 1–81.

[9]   Cf. William Alston, 'Divine Foreknowledge and Alternative Conceptions of Human Freedom' in *Divine Nature and Human Language* (Ithaca, NY: Cornell University Press, 1989), pp. 162–77.

(B6)   It is not possible for it to be true both that God has always believed that Clarence would have a cheese omelette for breakfast, and that he does not in fact have one. (From 2)

(B7)   Therefore, it is not in Clarence's power to refrain from having a cheese omelette for breakfast tomorrow. (From 5, 6) So Clarence's eating the omelette tomorrow is not an act of free choice.[10]

Call this argument the consequentialist argument against divine foreknowledge. To restate their position, open theists conclude that divine foreknowledge is incompatible with LFW. Believing that we possess LFW, open theists therefore reject divine foreknowledge in the face of the DFF.[11] Much more can and should be said about Hasker's argumentation, but space precludes a more detailed investigation. For our present purposes, let us concede that it follows that LFW is eliminated as a consequence of divine foreknowledge. That is, Clarence's eating of the omelette for breakfast tomorrow is consequentially necessary given divine foreknowledge of such. For open theists, this conclusion follows logically from the valid argument above for two reasons: 1) the transfer of necessity principle, and 2) divine infallibility.

*Transfer of Necessity Principle*

$$\Box_w \Phi$$
$$\Box (\Phi \leftrightarrow \Psi)$$
Therefore, $\Box_w \Psi$[12]

*Divine Infallibility*

$A$ is *essentially omniscient* $\leftrightarrow$ It is impossible that $A$ exist and fail to know the truth-value of any proposition.[13]

---

[10]   Ibid., p. 69.

[11]   Although LFW serves as a premise in *God, Time, and Knowledge*, Hasker has defended LFW in numerous articles, and also in *The Emergent Self* (Ithaca, NY: Cornell University Press, 1999), pp. 81–109.

[12]   Zagzebski identifies this as *TNP 2* in *The Dilemma of Freedom and Foreknowledge*, p. 7. In clarifying the nature of the transfer of necessity principles, Zagzebski immediately continues, '*W*-necessity may be any sort of necessity, but accidental necessity (the necessity of the past) is the sort of necessity relevant to our dilemma. The idea behind these two principles is that a necessity weaker than logical necessity can be transferred by strict implication (or strict equivalence) from the antecedent to the consequent of the conditional'.

[13]   Zagzebski, *The Dilemma of Freedom and Foreknowledge*, p. 5.

## A New Argument: The Freedom/Knowledge Dilemma

In light of the definitions offered above, I want to suggest that open theists shouldn't merely see an incompatibility between freedom and *fore*knowledge. Rather, the arguments which serve to motivate openness theology actually show that there is a fundamental incompatibility between contingency and *anything* that God knows.

In light of the transfer of necessity principle and divine infallibility, the freedom/knowledge dilemma runs as follows:

(6)    Necessarily, if God knows $p$, then $p$. (Premise: divine infallibility)
(7)    No one has the ability to bring it about that God is wrong. (From (6))
(8)    God knows $p$. (Premise)
(9)    It is not possible that $p$ be false. (From 6, 7, and 8)
(10)    Thus, it is necessary that $p$.

In a sentence, whatever God knows cannot fail to obtain. Some open theists are careful to distinguish between different concepts of necessity that operate in the arguments they use to show the incompatibility between freedom and foreknowledge, so it won't do to critique the equivocation between modal necessity (broadly logical necessity) and accidental necessity. So, instead of getting hung up on those issues, allow me to offer an argument as to why, given open theism's unwavering commitment to LFW, God does not know the present:

(B1*)    It is now true that Clarence is presently eating a cheese omelette for breakfast, and Clarence does so freely. (Premise)
(B2*)    It is impossible that God should at any time, including the present, believe what is false, or fail to believe anything that is true. (Premise: divine omniscience)
(B3*)    Therefore, God presently believes that Clarence is presently eating a cheese omelette (freely) for breakfast. (From 1, 2)
(B4*)    If God believes a certain thing, it is not in anyone's power to bring it about that God does not believe that thing. (Premise: the inalterability of the present, for surely the present lies on the side of the past with respect to temporal asymmetry)
(B5*)    Therefore, it is not in Clarence's power to bring it about that God presently believes that Clarence is not presently eating a cheese omelette (freely) for breakfast. (From 3, 4)
(B6*)    It is not possible for it to be true both that God believes that Clarence is presently eating a cheese omelette for breakfast, and that Clarence is not, in fact, presently eating a cheese omelette (freely) for breakfast. (From 2)
(B7*)    Therefore, it is not in Clarence's power to refrain from presently eating a cheese omelette (freely) for breakfast. (From 5, 6) So Clarence's present act of eating the omelette for breakfast is not an act of free choice.

Allow me to explain why this argument against divine knowledge of the present ought be taken just as seriously as open theists expect philosophers to take the argument offered by Hasker concerning freedom and foreknowledge.

First, recall that the definition of LFW in play requires that someone is free with respect to some action at some time *t* IFF at *t*, a person can choose between multiple options. So, if Clarence has LFW at the present, then it must be the case that Clarence *in the present* can choose between eating the cheese omelette and refraining from eating it.[14] But contingent choices cannot be known by God, for divine infallible knowledge is sufficient to eliminate the principle of alternative possibilities, which is a necessary condition on the libertarian's understanding of free will.

If God knows that *p* in world *w* → (**CN**) *p* in world *w*

Hence, divine knowledge undermines LFW.


## Consequential Necessity

It is not exactly a radical idea to postulate that God knows the present. But, given that any standard definition of knowledge entails that knowledge is factive – that knowledge entails truth – whatever God knows about the present in this world cannot fail to obtain in this world, a point made all the more clear in virtue of divine infallibility. But this means that if God knows at $t_\alpha$ that some agent *S* is performing some action *A* at $t_\alpha$, then the action *A* done by agent *S* at $t_\alpha$ is consequentially necessary, and therefore not free. Besides this, once the present has arrived, it is fixed – accidentally necessary – and cannot be other than what it is, for surely the present lies on the side of the past with respect to the issue of temporal asymmetry.

Of course, open theists affirm that actions performed in the present need be done freely in order for moral responsibility to supervene on those actions, such as when we presently choose to do something – the present is the moment when the decision is made, presumably with the ability to choose differently (that is, LFW). But, since open theists insist that any type of necessity affixing to a choice is sufficient to eliminate LFW, they are forced to choose between one of two options: (a) God lacks knowledge of all present truths involving LFW, or (b) we lack LFW at the present.

Perhaps open theists would be inclined to opt for (b), arguing that we enjoy freedom in the present with respect to what will occur in the future.[15] This requires a modification of the definition of LFW:

---

[14]    I set to one side the more complicated issues involved in debates concerning the extent of free will as it concerns the formation and concretization of one's character because all the examples offered by open theists presuppose that we examine instances in which alternative possibilities are genuine.

[15]    Hasker modifies his definition of LFW to accommodate this move in his recent article, 'Theological Incompatibilism and the Necessity of the Present' in *Faith and*

> (FW*)   N is free at *t1* with respect to $A =_{df}$ It is in N's power at *t1* to perform *A* at *t2*, and it is in N's power at *t1* to refrain from performing *A* at *t2*.

As Michael Rota has recently pointed out, Hasker cannot gloss his definition of LFW to accommodate this concern, for if Hasker jettisons the fact that we possess LFW in the present, he defeats his own case for theological incompatibilism.[16] That is, denying that we have LFW at present offers another response to the DFF, namely, Augustinian compatibilism, or, if you prefer, theological determinism. But this road obviously eliminates any motivation for open theism. Besides this, Hasker is committed to the notion that this response raises serious concerns as to the problem of evil.[17]

Additionally, modifying the definition of free will such that a person is free only with respect to the future presents a new set of problems raised by presentism, the metaphysics of time championed by all open theists to date.[18] If the present is the only time that exists, it follows that the only time at which anyone is free is the present; furthermore, the only time at which anyone can choose or make a decision is the present. Defenders of agent causal accounts of LFW (which are the most popular theories of LFW among open theists) wherein the decisions of an agent causally determine a given outcome, face the problem of accounting for when a free decision is made to determine which of multiple future options becomes actual. Considering that the present is the only time that exists, and given the necessity of the present, if an agent's choice is what determines what occurs later, one wonders when such a choice is free. To see why this is tricky, recall again that the thesis of temporal asymmetry entails that the present, once it arrives, is necessary. But if open theists insist that alternative possibilities be genuinely available at the time that such freedom exists, it is difficult to say that one is free with respect to the present given that, once the present arrives, it is no

---

*Philosophy* 28/2 (2011), pp. 224–9.

[16]   Michael Rota defends Anselmian eternalism as a solution to the DFF in 'A Problem for Hasker: Freedom with Respect to the Present, Hard Facts, and Theological Incompatibilism' in *Faith and Philosophy* 27/3 (2010), pp. 287–305. Two things make the argument I offer here different than Rota's. First, I have not set out to defend Anselmian eternalism, which is Rota's primary motivation. Second, whereas Rota states that Hasker's denial of Anselmian eternalism requires that God lack knowledge of the present, I argue that Hasker's position requires this lack of divine knowledge *simpliciter*. Even if Anselmian eternalism provides a solution to the DFF, because Hasker denies divine timelessness, such a solution has no appeal to him.

[17]   For more on Hasker's take on open theism and the problem of evil, see *Providence, Evil, and the Openness of God* (London: Routledge, 2004), and *The Triumph of God over Evil* (Downers Grove, IL: InterVarsity Press Academic, 2008). For Hasker's concerns about theological determinism, see his exchange with Paul Helm, 'Does God Takes Risks in Governing the World?' in Michael L. Peterson and Raymond J. Vanarragon (eds), *Contemporary Debates in Philosophy of Religion* (Oxford: Blackwell, 2004), pp. 218–41.

[18]   To clarify, the dynamic view of time (the A-theory) actually creates the problem.

longer possible that the present be different than it, in fact, is. Said differently, the present, once it obtains, is accidentally necessary. Assuming both presentism and the accidental necessity of the present, it is difficult, it is difficult to see how LFW can exist at all. Hence, we are left to conclude in favour of (a) God lacks knowledge of all present truths involving LFW.

My argument against God's ability to know the present, given open theism, runs as follows:

$\Box$ (If God, at $t_\alpha$, knows $p \rightarrow$ (**CN**) $p$ at $t_\alpha$)

Divine omniscience entails that God knows all reality, such that in all worlds in which God exists, it cannot be the case that God fails to know all truths about the present. This is obviously true if we understand omniscience to entail knowledge of all truths, even for open future open theists who motivate their denial of divine foreknowledge on the basis of the metaphysics of time. Those subscribing to open future open theism cannot respond by saying that God does not know the present in the way that they might when it comes to denying that God knows the truth-values of PCFC. This is so because, while they might want to argue that presentism precludes the existence of truth-values for PCFC, presentism also ensures that the present exists, and therefore all actions that take place in the present certainly possess truth-values. If God is omniscient, then God knows those truth-values. Divine omniscience, coupled with presentism, allows us to see that there is something *necessary* about God's knowledge of the present – God cannot fail to possess knowledge of the present. And this is enough to generate an argument perfectly parallel to any argument for open theism that relies on accidental necessity. But again, whatever God knows is necessary, so if God knows the present, then we lack LFW at the present.

Open theists might attempt to escape this conundrum by asserting that God knows the present directly, and that the source of his knowledge is the event itself. So, if an action occurs at the present, then God at the present knows the present action. The logical priority means that God's knowledge at $t_\alpha$ of $p$ at $t_\alpha$ is dependent upon the action being performed such that if $p$ did not take place at $t_\alpha$, then God would not know $p$ at $t_\alpha$.

Presumably, this all saves the possibility of LFW in the present. But that God enjoys his knowledge directly in no way alleviates the issues raised by divine infallibility, so divine infallible knowledge of the present still renders the event known by God (or anyone else, so long as knowledge is taken to be factive) consequentially necessary. And, if an appeal to direct knowledge works to save LFW in the present, many advocates of Anselmian eternalism have pressed the point in asking why the same won't do to allow divine timelessness to serve as a solution to the DFF in the same way.[19] This is especially important since both

---

[19]  Besides Rota's 'A Problem for Hasker: Freedom with Respect to the Present, Hard Facts, and Theological Incompatibilism', here one also thinks especially of Katherin Rogers's work. See her articles 'Anselmian Eternalism: The Presence of a Timeless God'

Hasker and van Inwagen (and presumably other open theists) deny not only divine atemporality, but also that divine timelessness so much as offers a genuine solution to the DFF were it true.[20]

My intent is not to defend divine timelessness as an adequate response to the DFF. Rather, I mean only to show that, regardless of what one thinks about divine timelessness, open theism is an inadequate response unless a proponent of that view welcomes the fact that God lacks knowledge of all truths concerning the present that involve LFW.

## Simultaneous Causation

Open theism rules out many possible responses to such a dilemma because appealing to those solutions to this conundrum eliminates any motivation for open theism in the first place. But there is another response that hasn't been considered. Perhaps God knows the present instantaneously, such that any present action or event is the cause, simultaneously, of God's knowledge of the present. However, such a position comes at a tremendous cost: affirming simultaneous causation. A few remarks are in order to clarify why I don't believe this option is a viable path for open theism. I first summarize why affirming simultaneous causation is so problematic. I go on to show why the only escape left available for the open theist requires their affirming simultaneous causation. While discussing these issues, I cover the views concerning simultaneous causation of three significant open theists: Richard Swinburne, Peter van Inwagen, and William Hasker in order to show that open theism faces insurmountable problems with respect to simultaneous causation, the metaphysics of time, God's knowledge of the present, and LFW.

---

in *Faith and Philosophy* 24/1 (2007), pp. 3–27; 'The Necessity of the Present and Anselm's Eternalist Response to the Problem of Theological Fatalism' in *Religious Studies* 43/1 (2007), pp. 25–47; and 'Omniscience, Eternity, and Freedom' in *International Philosophical Quarterly* 36/4 (1996), pp. 399–412. See also the piece she co-authored with Jeffrey Green, 'Time, Foreknowledge, and Alternative Possibilities' in *Religious Studies* 48/2 (2012), pp. 151–64. Finally, consider Michael Rota, 'The Eternity Solution to the Problem of Human Freedom and Divine Foreknowledge' in *European Journal for Philosophy of Religion* 2/1 (2010), pp. 165–86.

[20]    Again, van Inwagen argues that the DFF poses the same problem even if divine timelessness is true in his 'What Does an Omniscient Being Know?'.

*Swinburne on Simultaneous Causation*

First, Richard Swinburne (himself an open theist) explicitly denies the possibility of simultaneous causation.[21] When discussing the metaphysics of time, Swinburne goes into great detail in describing what he calls the causal theory of time. He takes it to be beyond dispute that the future is contingent – that we can causally affect the future. But, Swinburne develops a proof that an effect cannot precede its cause, for such would be tantamount to circular causation, which he takes to be obviously false, especially given the account of causation he believes is necessary for Christian theism. In order to better understand the context of Swinburne's comments, I quote him at length:

> Causation in a circle is not logically possible. If A causes B, B cannot cause A (or cause anything which by a longer circle causes A). For what causes what is logically contingent – 'anything can produce anything', wrote Hume. Let us put the point in this way: a sufficiently powerful being could, it is logically possible, alter the laws of nature in such a way that some event had, instead of its normal effect at a certain time, one incompatible with that normal effect. So if causation in a circle were logically possible and A caused B and B caused A, a sufficiently powerful being at the moment of B's occurrence could have altered the laws of nature so that B caused not-A; in which case A would have (indirectly) caused A not to occur – which is absurd. So since manifestly the future is causally affectible, the past is not. It follows that backward causation is impossible – causes cannot be later than their effects. It follows too that simultaneous causation is impossible. For if simultaneous causation were possible and A caused B simultaneously, and B caused C simultaneously, then, by Hume's principle cited earlier, it would be logically possible that B could have had, instead of its normal effect, not-A. That logically impossible conjunction of causal sequences is, given Hume's principle, only rendered impossible if we suppose simultaneous causation itself to be impossible. Hence, given that causes and effects are events which last for periods of time,[22] any effect (which has a beginning) must begin at an instant later than its cause begins; and any effect (which has an end) must end at an instant later than its cause ends.[23]

So, Swinburne understands simultaneous causation to be logically equivalent to backward causation, which, if it were possible, would entail that counterfactual power over the past is coherent. Of course, if counterfactual power over the past

---

[21]    Swinburne defends limited foreknowledge open theism in *The Coherence of Theism* (New York, NY: Oxford University Press, 1993, rev. edn), pp. 167–83.

[22]    Swinburne defends this claim in *The Christian God* (New York, NY: Oxford University Press, 1994), pp. 51–71.

[23]    Swinburne, *The Christian God*, p. 82.

is coherent, then it might be possible. If possible, then Ockhamism presents a successful response to the DFF, and open theism would prove unnecessary.

In his *Critique of Pure Reason*, Kant offers the standard example still used today by many to support the possibility of simultaneous causation. In fact, Kant claims that 'the great majority of efficient natural causes are simultaneous with their effects'. He asks readers to consider a ball that falls and comes to lie on a cushion, thereby forming a hollow. Kant contends that the formation of the hollow is caused simultaneously by the impact of the ball with the cushion. Swinburne offers a compelling reason why one should reject Kant's articulation of the possibility of simultaneous causation, so I quote from Swinburne again at length:

> But Kant gives no argument in favour of the claim that these are simultaneous, let alone in favour of his wide general claim; and he seems to have casually supposed that where he was unable to observe a time interval between the ball beginning to exert its gravitational force (concentrated at the ball's centre of gravity) and the first depression of the cushion, there was in fact no interval. But Kant's casual supposition was mistaken; special relativity can now tell us the length of that very small interval. In the Middle Ages it was generally supposed that light had an infinite velocity, and Newton and his successors supposed the force of gravity to act with infinite velocity; and infinite velocity involves the simultaneity of cause and effect. The Special Theory of Relativity has the consequence that all causal action is propagated with finite velocity. But, if my arguments in the text [of my chapter on time] are correct, it did not need special relativity with its empirical foundation to show this; it follows from logical considerations alone. It did of course need empirical considerations to show that the velocity of light is the fastest signal. Hume, by contrast, had an argument to show the logical impossibility of simultaneous causation (*Treatise*, 1. 3. 2). He argues that cause and immediate effect must be as close as possible. (If an earlier event causes a later event separated from it by an interval of time, it can only do so via a chain of close events which connect the two.) And how close is close? If cause and effect could be simultaneous, argues Hume, they would be; and then all effects would be simultaneous with their causes and that would lead to 'the utter annihilation of time'. So cause and effect cannot be simultaneous, and the requirement of closeness will have to be satisfied by mere contiguity of time. But Hume gives no argument as to why if nature allows one effect to be simultaneous with its cause, it has to allow all so to be. My claim in the text is that the *Treatise* contains the resources for a much stronger argument.[24]

Before moving on, let us consider another problem regarding simultaneous causation. It is commonly accepted that change requires the passage of time. In fact, many open theists affirm divine temporality precisely because they deny

---

[24]   Swinburne, *The Christian God*, additional note 6, p. 245.

absolute divine immutability. But the type of causation necessary to preserve divine knowledge of the present on open theism requires a violation of the law of non-contradiction. Clearly, on open theism, God learns, which is obviously a change, and therefore requires the passage of time. The question we are seeking to answer is: *when* does God learn? Is it possible for an effect to obtain simultaneously to its cause when a change results? I think not, as an example will show.

Rather than considering Kant's ball and a cushion, consider the case of a baseball breaking a pane of glass. In this example, the effect is the broken glass, and the cause is the baseball striking an otherwise sound pane of glass. That the glass goes from being unbroken to broken constitutes an obvious change. Common sense shows that such a change renders impossible simultaneous causation such that the glass actually breaks (the effect) at a moment later than the moment when the ball strikes the glass (the cause). If simultaneous causation were possible, when a change results, in this example, we would have a broken pane of glass simultaneous to the ball causing the glass to break, which can only mean one of two things. Either the ball never comes into contact with a non-broken pane of glass because the effect is simultaneous to the cause (in which case it seems odd to say that the ball broke an otherwise sound pane of glass), or at one and the same moment the pane of glass exists in two mutually exclusive states, both broken and unbroken (an obvious violation of the law of non-contradiction). If open theists wish to make use of simultaneous causation to avoid the dilemma I raise against them, it will remove any motivation for open theism in the first place, for, as Swinburne rightly notes, such a move likely accommodates counterfactual power over the past, thereby allowing Ockhamism to settle the DFF.

But let us ignore for a moment that Ockhamism likely solves the DFF if simultaneous causation is metaphysically similar enough to backwards causation so as to allow for counterfactual power over the past (as Swinburne contends). Recall that open theism is working with a very precise definition of LFW:

(FW') N is free at $T$ with respect to performing $A =_{df}$ It is in N's power at $T$ to perform $A$ and it is possible at $T$ for N to exercise that power, and it is in N's power at $T$ to refrain from performing $A$, and it is also possible at $T$ for N to exercise *that* power.[25]

The precision of this definition proves to be quite problematic for the open theist, precisely because it *requires* the possibility of simultaneous causation. Let us suppose that God is somehow able to know in the very same present moment our present actions. After all, given divine omnipotence, and given even the possibility of divine timelessness, perhaps God has the ability to do what we cannot, and we should note that God's knowledge is not dependent on the passage of light, the firing of neurons or anything else of the temporal processes that ours is. That is, perhaps by some miraculous demonstration of perfect cognitive

---

[25] Hasker, *God, Time, and Knowledge*, p. 138.

power, our present actions are all that is necessary to cause (simultaneously) God's knowledge of the present. But even granting all this, we encounter yet another problem for those insisting on the above conception of LFW. And now we can see why.

Even if omnipotence renders simultaneous causation possible for God, yet impossible for metaphysically smaller beings such as humans,[26] this does not mean that we could, as free agents, be the determining cause of any simultaneous decisions, especially when we consider that decisions require deliberation, even if only the briefest moment thereof.[27] Recall that the present, once it obtains, is necessary. That is, with respect to any temporal asymmetry between past and future, the present lies on the side of the past; once it arrives, it cannot be changed into anything other than what it already is. But, in order for humans to possess the kind of LFW which open theists insist is necessary, we must be able to render what has become necessary (for example, the present), different than it is, which is, of course, absurd.

Suppose that an agent $S$ chooses to do some action $A$ at $t_\alpha$. That is, in the present moment, $S$ has chosen to do $A$. Now, in order for $S$ to be free at $t_\alpha$ with respect to $A$, then it must be possible – *at the exact same moment* – that $S$ refrain from choosing to do $A$ and that $S$ possess the power to exercise such a choice. But, this requires that the present – having arrived and thereby being accidentally necessary, so that it cannot change – can be different than it in fact is. This is different than saying that it *could* have been different, but has become accidentally necessary. No, in order for the definitions of LFW offered by open theists to succeed, it must be possible for an agent $S$ to be presently deciding to do $A$ and, while presently deciding to do $A$, an agent $S$ must in the same moment have the ability to simultaneously decide to refrain from doing $A$. But clearly this is impossible, for once the present arrives, it cannot be other than what it is. Furthermore, it violates the law of non-contradiction, for this amounts to an agent being in two mutually exclusive states, namely presently deciding to do $A$ while also presently deciding to refrain from doing $A$. Also, given an open theist's denial that God can know future contingents, the present must obtain prior to God's ability to know the event in question. Hence, an event's coming into being must somehow simultaneously cause divine knowledge of such. But so long as open theists argue against the possibility of simultaneous causation, they should abandon the working definition of LFW.

Some might maintain that it is possible for an agent $S$, in one and the same present moment, to decide to do $A$, and then deliberate and decide to refrain from doing $A$ in such a way that the latter decision is not simultaneous to the first. While this option would alleviate the tensions created by the impossibility of simultaneous causation, it rests upon a misunderstanding of what constitutes the

---

[26]    Thanks to Eleonore Stump for this helpful turn of phrase.

[27]    Agent-causal models of LFW exacerbate this problem, although the same problems likely obtain for event-causal libertarians.

present. For presentists, the present is the moment that divides the past from the future.[28] Since the present serves as the boundary between the past and the future, it is the very smallest time-slice that could possibly exist. Hence, to suggest that there would be time for choosing something other than that which one already chooses is to suggest that the smallest possible time-slice is actually larger than it is. For, one can easily conceive of a time-slice so small that it would not allow for movement from one decision to another, and surely this smaller time-slice must be what serves as the present boundary between the past and the future. Therefore, this method does not allow for open theists to escape the fact that simultaneous causation must not only be possible, but an incredibly common – nay, constant – reality, at least so long as one wishes to maintain that God possesses exhaustive knowledge of the present.

*Van Inwagen on Simultaneous Causation*

Peter van Inwagen offers a different account of causation from that of Swinburne. Van Inwagen denies that causation exists at all if causation is understood as a relation between events. Instead he believes that causal relations (such as pushing and pulling) hold between substances, not events.[29] Additionally, when discussing Alvin Plantinga's famous replacement argument concerning personal identity across time, van Inwagen writes,

> There cannot be two 'adjacent' intervals (two intervals such that a certain mathematical instant $t$ is the least upper bound of one them [sic] and the greatest lower bound of the other) such that $x$ is not a part of Alice at any instant that belongs to the earlier interval and is a part of Alice at every instant that belongs to the later one. Assimilation, whatever else it may be, is a causal process, and causal processes take time.[30]

Van Inwagen also insists that causal influence never moves faster than the speed of light.[31] Hence, even if God's knowledge is not dependent on the passage of light, no cause (for example, the obtaining of the present) could produce an effect (for example, divine knowledge of the present) at a rate faster than the speed of light. This is due to the fact that causation, according to van Inwagen, occurs as a process over time, and necessarily so, such that one

---

[28]   Swinburne, *The Christian God*, p. 81. Cf. Tom Crisp, 'Presentism' in Michael J. Loux and Dean W. Zimmerman (eds), *The Oxford Handbook of Metaphysics* (New York, NY: Oxford University Press, 2003), pp. 211–45.

[29]   Personal communication, 5 September 2011.

[30]   Peter van Inwagen, 'Plantinga's Replacement Argument' in Deane-Peter Baker (ed.), *Alvin Plantinga* (Contemporary Philosophy in Focus) (New York, NY: Cambridge University Press, 2007), pp. 188–201, 195.

[31]   Ibid., p. 200, n. 16.

substance cannot exert causal influence over another so as to produce an effect simultaneously.

*Hasker on Simultaneous Causation*

Hasker, in contrast to both Swinburne and van Inwagen, does not deny the possibility of simultaneous causation. He argues that Swinburne's account must proceed as follows:

> There are two objects, A and B. A is able to exert some sort of causal power on B, bringing about some unspecified change in B. A has two relevant states: *causing*, when it is exercising the causal power in question, and *not-causing*, when it is not. B also has two relevant states: *allowing*, the state in which it allows A to exercise power on B, and *preventing*, which prevents A from exercising such power.
>
> Now, suppose B is in *allowing*, and A goes into the state *causing*. Then all goes smoothly, and A produces the appropriate changes in B. On the other hand, if B is in *preventing*, A cannot go into *causing*, and A produces no change in B.
>
> Now, suppose causation is instantaneous. B is in *allowing*, and A goes into *causing* at t. But the instantaneous effect of this is that B goes into *preventing*, again at t, and A exerts no causal power on B. So A, by exerting causal power on B, causes it to be the case that A never exerts any causal power on B. Call this the *self-negating causation* sequence (hereafter SNC). SNC is obviously impossible. But the only way to forestall it, according to Swinburne, is to deny the possibility of instantaneous causation.
>
> I reply, SNC can be blocked without denying instantaneous causation. The problem with SNC is that B is said to go into *preventing at t*, the very time at which A's causal action begins. But this means that *there is no interval of time subsequent to t* during which A's causal action can occur. And since before t A is in *not-causing*, there is no interval at all during which A is in *causing*. But Swinburne would agree that there is no sense to the idea of a causal action which occurs at a single point in time but neither before nor after that point. So the description of SNC is incoherent: to restore coherence, we must suppose that B goes into *preventing* at some time *after* t, and the paradox disappears.
>
> SNC requires B to be in *allowing* at t, so as to enable A to be in *causing* at t. But it also requires B to be in *preventing* at t, so as to prevent A from causing B to change. But a scenario that requires B to be in two contradictory states simultaneously is obviously out of the question, and creates no problems for instantaneous causation as such.[32]

---

[32]   This quotation (and all other positions attributed to Hasker in what follows) comes from personal communication, 31 August 2011, and are offered with his permission.

Hasker believes simultaneous causation can escape the sort of paradox Swinburne raises by showing that SNC requires something (B) to be in two contradictory states at the same time. If this is a problem for the object being affected by a cause, then it must certainly be a problem also for a cause to be in two contradictory states at the same time. But this is precisely what is needed to preserve open theism given its definition of LFW. Let us carefully consider again why this is so.

Suppose the present has arrived such that God knows that some agent $S$ is presently choosing to do some action $A$. If $S$ is free with respect to $A$, it must be in $S$'s power to simultaneously refrain from choosing to do $A$, *even though the present has arrived so as to accidentally necessitate* $S$*'s presently choosing to do* $A$, *thereby guaranteeing that God knows that* S *is choosing to do* A. Of course, if $S$ has this power, then it is possible for $S$ to have – at one and the same moment – two contradictory states: choosing to do $A$ and refraining from choosing to do $A$. Hasker's recent reformulation of what constitutes free will perhaps allows him to navigate around this conundrum,[33] but such manoeuvring still requires him to affirm that change does not require the passage of time. He would have to maintain that God learns of the present once it obtains, and learns of it instantaneously in the present (thereby undergoing a change from ignorance to knowledge), yet without any passage of time. But this is clearly counterintuitive.

Additionally, if $S$ has the power described above, then $S$ has the power to bring it about that, at the present, God is not infallible.[34] Suppose again that the present has arrived such that, because God knows the present, God has knowledge that $S$ is choosing to do $A$. So, God believes that $S$ is choosing to do $A$, yet at the very time that $S$ is choosing to do $A$, $S$ is free to refrain from choosing to do $A$. It follows that $S$ has the power to bring it about that what God believes is not true, which is obviously untenable. Or, alternatively, $S$ has counterfactual power over God's beliefs, which is unacceptable for open theists, given their denial of Ockhamism. That $S$ could enjoy counterfactual power over divine beliefs is also likely to be incompatible with divine direct knowledge, which open theists need in order to allow for simultaneous causation to even potentially serve as a solution to the conundrum I raise here. So, Hasker's admission of the possibility of simultaneous causation does not allow him to avoid the dilemma of how God can know the present on the terms established by open theism.

## Conclusion

What possible explanation could be given for the fact that an omniscient being lacks knowledge of the present? Lacking any compelling answer to this question, we

---

[33]    Again, see Hasker's reply to Rota, 'Theological Incompatibilism and the Necessity of the Present' in *Faith and Philosophy* 28/2 (2011), pp. 224–9.

[34]    This is sufficiently analogous to counterfactual power over the past such that those who deny the possibility of such should also deny counterfactual power over the present.

should conclude against open theism's response to the DFF, recognizing that such a response entails far more serious consequences than originally intended. As it turns out, philosophically driven open theism requires not only redefining omniscience such that God lacks foreknowledge, but also God not knowing any truths about the present reality involving LFW. This is so because, as Hasker notes, open theists tend to be more willing to hedge against divine knowledge than significant freedom. That is, open theists are more comfortable denying that God knows certain things – things which they insist are logically unknowable – than they are willing to deny that humans enjoy significant freedom as understood by libertarians. Consider Hasker's explanation of this. 'Both [of my arguments] conclude to a denial of libertarian free will. In fact, however, relatively few incompatibilists accept this conclusion. Rather, incompatibilists tend to adopt modified conceptions of omniscience so as to avoid the deterministic outcome'.[35] On this point, Hasker is simply incorrect. Throughout Christian history, and theism in general for that matter, the vast majority of theological incompatibilists have denied LFW in order to preserve the most robust conception of divine omniscience rather than accommodate omniscience towards LFW. But, if Hasker thinks omniscience should accommodate LFW and not vice versa, and, if it is logically impossible for God to know aspects of the present reality involving LFW, as I have shown, then open theists (so long as they are consistent) will go on to conclude against the idea that God possesses exhaustive knowledge of the present.

Because openness advocates seek to preserve LFW at all costs (even by offering a highly attenuated conception of omniscience), it seems that they are stuck with denying that God knows the present. My argument, at minimum, puts the open theist on the horns of a dilemma: open theists can simply acknowledge that God lacks knowledge of any present truths involving LFW, but rather comes to learn of these truths as soon as knowledge of such is logically possible; or open theists can rethink the metaphysics of time in regards to the possibility of simultaneous causation (which likely undercuts the motivation for open theism as a response to the DFF in the first place). Taking both of these to be undesirable consequences of open theism, and because there might be still further consequences even more radical than those discussed here that remain thus far unforeseen, I suggest that philosophers and theologians alike close the door on open theism even if they remain unwilling to endorse some other response to the DFF.[36]

---

[35]    Hasker, *God, Time, and Knowledge*, p. 73.

[36]    Many friends offered me helpful feedback and comments on this essay. Special thanks are due to David Alexander, James Anderson, Doug Blount, Oliver Crisp, Bill Hasker, Paul Helm, Elijah Hess, Daniel Hill, Jay Howell, Katherin Rogers, Tom Senor, Eleonore Stump, Richard Swinburne, Kevin Timpe, Peter van Inwagen, Greg Trickett, Greg Welty and Jordan Wessling.

# Chapter 8

# Corcoran's Anthropological Constitutionalism and the Problem of Post-Mortem Survival

James K. Dew, Jr

Dualism, of some sort or another, has deep roots within the Christian tradition and had been the dominant anthropological position of Christians for most of church history. Recently, however, numerous theologians and Christian philosophers have abandoned this view in favour of a materialist view of human beings. Thinkers like Trenton Merricks, Peter van Inwagen, Nancey Murphy, Lynne Baker and Kevin J. Corcoran,[1] to name just a few, have suggested that a materialist view of man is compatible with the Christian faith.

For example, Kevin Corcoran's Constitutional View (CV) of human beings seeks a middle ground between dualism and animalism by arguing that persons are not identical to their bodies, even if they are wholly constituted by them. As such, Corcoran believes that his materialistic account of human persons is compatible with Christian thought. One of the more pressing issues for materialists like Corcoran, who is also a Christian, is accounting for post-mortem survival. In short, Christianity teaches that people live on after their physical death, which seems to be at odds with materialist accounts of human beings. Corcoran offers two ways that post-mortem survival might be possible from within a materialistic perspective: 'Gappy' existence and 'Non-Gappy' existence. After a brief account of his CV, in this chapter I will explore his two accounts of post-mortem survival and will argue that, without significant revisions, both approaches have significant problems and should be rejected.

---

[1]    For a quick sample, see Trenton Merricks, 'How to Live Forever without Saving Your Soul: Physicalism and Immortality' in Kevin Corcoran (ed.), *Soul, Body and Survival* (Ithaca: Cornell University Press, 2001), pp. 183–200; Peter van Inwagen, 'A Materialist Ontology of the Human Person' in Peter van Inwagen and Dean Zimmerman (eds), *Persons: Human and Divine* (Oxford: Oxford University Press, 2007), pp. 199–215; Nancey Murphy, *Bodies and Souls, or Spirited Bodies* (New York: Cambridge University Press, 2006); Lynne Rudder Baker, *Persons and Bodies* (New York: Cambridge University Press, 2000); Kevin Corcoran, *Rethinking Human Nature* (Grand Rapids: Baker Academic, 2006).

## Dualism and Constitutionalism

In chapter 1 of *Rethinking Human Nature*, Corcoran offers a brief assessment of three types of dualism: Substance Dualism, Compound Dualism and Emergent Dualism. After rejecting each of these for various reasons, Corcoran adopts and defends his own version of CV. As he sees it, this is a materialistic perspective that offers a middle path between dualism (which says we are distinct from our bodies) and animalism (which says that we are identical to our bodies). As he explains:

> According to CV, we human persons are constituted by our bodies without being identical with the bodies that constitute us. This is not an *ad hoc* claim. Many medium-sized physical objects stand in Constitution relations. For example, statues are often constituted by a piece of marble, copper, or bronze, but statues are not identical with pieces of marble, copper, or bronze that constitute them. Likewise, dollar bills, diplomas, and dust jackets are often constituted by pieces of paper, but none of those things is identical with the piece of paper that constitutes it.[2]

To explain why a person is not identical to his body, even if he is constituted by it, Corcoran argues that persons and physical organisms have different identity conditions. A physical organism, for example, has 'an individual biological process of a special sort, a sort that is remarkably stable, well individuated, self-directing, self-maintaining, and homeodynamic'.[3] Persons, by contrast, are something that Corcoran believes 'are, minimally, beings with a capacity for intentional states (e.g., believing, desiring, intending, etc.)'.[4] Additionally, Corcoran says, 'Persons are also the only sort of thing that has what Lynn Baker calls a first-person perspective'.[5]

Since persons and physical organisms have different identity conditions, Corcoran believes that the person is not identical to his body. He suggests:

> A conceptual impossibility is not involved in thinking about the physical organism that is my body existing while completely lacking a capacity for intentional states … That is why I believe that, while I'm constituted by my body, I am not, strictly speaking identical with it. Indeed, I believe that my body came into existence before I did, and it is conceivable that my body will outlive me.[6]

---

[2]   Corcoran, *Rethinking*, pp. 65–6.

[3]   Ibid., p. 69.

[4]   Ibid., p. 67.

[5]   Ibid., p. 68.

[6]   Ibid., p. 69.

## CV and the Problem of Post-mortem Survival

There are numerous places where one might critique Corcoran's CV. Philosophically speaking, one might consider certain ambiguities in his perspective: if in fact it is really different from animalism, if his account of personhood is sufficient or if there might be metaphysical problems with his perspective. Likewise, one might also consider various theological concerns with his perspective like his understanding of the image of God, treatment of biblical texts on the soul or his departure from church tradition on the issue. For now, however, I want to limit my assessment to considering whether or not his account offers an adequate basis for the possibility of post-mortem survival.

For all naturalists, and most materialists, this would not be that serious a problem, if it is a problem at all. They could simply deny the possibility of post-mortem survival. But, as a Christian, Corcoran must explain how his view can account for the Christian doctrine of the afterlife if he hopes to be consistent with the teachings of Christianity. He says, 'I do suppose that, at minimum, in order for an answer to be compatible with Christian theism it must be compatible with belief in the resurrection of the dead, with an afterlife or survival'.[7] As a materialist, Corcoran is committed to the idea that we cannot exist apart from our bodies. If, however, my body ceases to exist, then it would seem that Corcoran has no room for the afterlife.

Now on first appearances, one might simply suggest that God could bring our future existence about by giving us duplicate bodies. But, as Corcoran is well aware, this is not an available option for him. For his materialistic account of human persons to succeed in providing for post-mortem survival, he must offer a plausible account of how two bodies separated by a temporal gap can be numerically identical. If the body that exists at a later time is merely a phenomenological duplicate, then his account is unsuccessful since a duplicate body would be a different body, and thus constitute a different life. If this is the case, then there is no post-mortem survival for the human being.

Realizing the need for numerically identical bodies, Corcoran considers the possible persistence conditions for persons over time. And, in particular, Corcoran is especially concerned with finding persistence conditions that would allow two bodies at two distinct times to be numerically identical. He first considers spatiotemporal continuity as a possible account of these conditions, but he quickly rejects it, thinking that it is neither a necessary nor a sufficient condition for persistence through time. Instead, he suggests that Immanent Causal Condition (ICC) is a better account of persistence since it has one body being causally connected to a later body. He describes ICC as follows:

> A human body B that exists in the future is the same as a human body A that exists now if the temporal stages leading up to B are immanent-causally connected to the temporal stage of A now.[8]

---

7    Kevin Corcoran, 'Persons and Bodies' in *Faith and Philosophy* 15/3 (1998) p. 332.
8    Corcoran, *Rethinking*, p. 182.

In other words, Corcoran's account of persistence requires there to be a causal connection between the body A at an earlier time with body B at a later time. In this approach, the existence of B is causally and continuously related to the existence of A before it.

With a sufficient theoretical account of persistence in hand, Corcoran then considers two possible scenarios under which numerically identical human bodies might persist and achieve post-mortem survival: (1) Gappy or Intermittent Existence, and (2) Non-Gappy (Body Fission) existence. In what follows, I will show how neither of these two proposals establishes an adequate basis for reconciling his materialist account of human persons with the Christian notion of post-mortem survival.


## Gappy Survival

What the Gappy theory suggests is that the human person can experience a gap in his existence caused by death. So, for example, it suggests that a person A can exist at $t_1$, completely cease to exist at $t_2$, and then come back into existence at $t_3$. In Corcoran's version, he not only suggests that it is possible for A to exist at both $t_1$ and $t_3$, he also suggests that A's bodily existence at $t_3$ is numerically identical to his existence at $t_1$. How exactly this is possible is not completely clear. Corcoran simply asks the reader to consider the following argument:

(1)   Bodies cease to exist.
(2)   The Scriptures teach that my body is going to be raised.
(3)   The Immanent Causal Condition for the persistence of bodies is true.
(4)   Therefore, causal relations can cross temporal gaps.[9]

In Corcoran's mind, this argument establishes the ICC as the persistent condition for bodies across temporal gaps, such that the body at $t_1$ is numerically identical to the body at $t_3$. But, there seems to be a problem with this account. While there may be some other logically possible way for humans to have Gappy existence with numerically identical bodies across temporal gaps, it does not look like Corcoran's argument is successful in establishing ICC as the means by which this can happen.

Christians should not dispute premises (1)–(2). Premise (1) is obviously true to anyone who has ever considered what happens to a corpse after being in the ground for hundreds of years, or in cases of cremation. Premise (2) is also affirmed by Christians without hesitation since the Bible does claim such things (1 Cor. 15, 1 Thess. 4 and so on). At first look, premise (3) – ICC is true – appears to be acceptable as well since it suggests a common-sense notion of persistence from one point in time $(t_1)$ to a subsequent point immediately following $(t_2)$. Yet, the conclusion –

---

9   Kevin Corcoran, 'Dualism, Materialism, and the Problem of Postmortem Survival' in *Philosophia Christi* 4/2 (2001), p. 423.

that ICC can cross temporal gaps – is rather odd and surprising. Thus, despite first appearances, the problem with Corcoran's argument seems to be with premise (3).

In short, it appears that Corcoran's affirmation of ICC goes too far by suggesting that it is even true in cases of Gappy existence. Yet, this does not seem possible given his general definition of ICC. Again, he describes ICC in the following way: 'A human body B that exists in the future is the same as a human body A that exists now if the temporal stages leading up to B are immanent-causally connected to the temporal stage of A now'.[10]

In general, this appears to be a perfectly acceptable account of the persistence conditions of a particular body from one moment $(t_1)$ to another subsequent moment $(t_2)$ in a continuous series of moments that are connected to each other. In other words, this really does seem to explain what causes A to persist over a given amount of time when A's existence is continuous. But, according to ICC, what is required for persistence is an actual causal chain which connects two distinct moments – $t_1$ and $t_3$. But, given premise (1) of Corcoran's argument – that bodies cease to exist – it looks like ICC could not possibly allow for the Gappy existence of a particular body across temporal gaps. For example, if, as he explains, the object before me at 10:00 AM $(t_3)$ must be causally connected to the object that was before me at 9:58 AM $(t_1)$, then how is persistence possible if at 9:59 AM $(t_2)$ the object ceases to exist? If the body does not exist between death and resurrection, then the person does not exist either. Corcoran says, 'I would argue that a necessary condition for the persistence of a person is that his or her constituting physical organism persists. If your body does not persist, then you do not persist. Not because you are your body but because the existence of your body is necessary for your own persistence'.[11] And so, if the body ceases to exist at 9:59 AM $(t_2)$, then the causal link is broken and future existence at 10:00 AM $(t_3)$ would be impossible.

It is one thing not to know how something works. It is another thing to affirm something in the face of what appears to be an impossibility. In light of this puzzling scenario, Corcoran simply says, 'I think there are aesthetic reasons for preferring a view of the resurrection that involves God on the front end of the gap ... bestowing on the parts that compose the bodies a capacity for passing on causal "umph" across temporal gaps'.[12] This is hardly satisfying. If Corcoran's first premise is true – that bodies cease to exist – then nothing exists to connect A before and after death. In other words, nothing exists that can span the gap, cause later existence and allow for Gappy existence. We might state the problem as follows:

(5)   According to Corcoran's ICC, for A to persist from $t_1$ to $t_3$, there must be a causal link to A at $t_1$.

(6)   A ceases to exist at $t_2$.

---

[10]   Corcoran, *Rethinking*, p. 182.

[11]   Corcoran, *Rethinking*, p. 73.

[12]   Ibid., p. 129.

(7)   Since A no longer exists at $t_2$, there is no causal link between A at $t_3$ and A at $t_1$.

(8)   Therefore, ICC cannot bridge the gap of A's existence from $t_1$ to $t_3$.

Again, perhaps there is some other way to account for the Gappy existence of a numerically identical body at $t_1$ and $t_3$, but it does not look like Corcoran's particular account of how this might happen is successful. But, since this is only one of the possible ways that he thinks post-mortem survival is possible, we must also consider his non-Gappy proposal.

## Non-gappy Survival – Body Fission

In addition to his Gappy account of post-mortem survival, Corcoran also offers the possibility of body fission as a means to post-mortem survival. In this case, at the instant just prior to death, a person experiences a fission event wherein two sets of 'bodily simples' – two bodies – emerge. The life of the person is passed onto one of these sets, while the other experiences death. We might illustrate his notion with the following drawing:

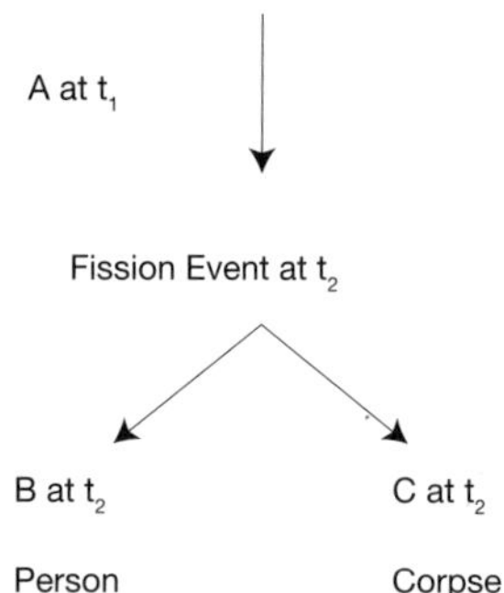


At this point, a very important question arises about Corcoran's understanding of the bodies after the fission event. What exactly is the physical relationship between B and C at $t_2$? It appears that there are really only two options. They are either physically identical, or they are not physically identical. If they are physically identical, then that would mean that B and C would be physically indistinguishable from each other. Phenomenologically, one would not be able to tell them apart. What is physically true of one would have to be physically true of the other. If, on the other hand, they are not identical, then they could appear very different from each other. Phenomenologically, they would be easy to distinguish from each other since what is physically true of one would not be physically true of the other. So which way does Corcoran understand it? Does he see B and C at $t_2$ as being physically identical or non-identical? In short, there is an ambiguity in his writings about this question. In some places, he appears to envision physically identical bodies, and in other places he seems to think of them as not being physically identical. In either case, I suggest that however we interpret Corcoran, his approach will collapse back into some form of dualism. Let's consider each approach in turn.

Suppose that Corcoran sees the bodies B and C as being physically identical to each other at $t_2$. This may be what he has in mind, since in one place he says:

> Suppose the simples composing my body just before my death are made by God to undergo fission such that the simples composing my body then are causally related to two different, spatially segregated sets of simples. Let us suppose both are configured just as their common spatiotemporal ancestor. Suppose now that milliseconds after the fission one of the two sets of simples ceases to constitute a life and comes instead to compose a corpse, while the other either continues on in heaven or continues on in some intermediate state.[13]

The key sentence here is 'Let us suppose both are configured just as their common spatiotemporal ancestor'. This seems to suggest that Corcoran sees these bodies as being physically and phenomenologically identical, even though they are numerically distinct. They are physically identical in that each is 'configured just as their common spatiotemporal ancestor', but numerically distinct because one body is alive and continues the life of the given person, while the other body suffers death. As he explains, 'The set of simples along one of the branching paths at the instant after fission fails to perpetuate a life while the other set of simples along the other branch does continue to perpetuate a life'.[14] We might illustrate this as follows:

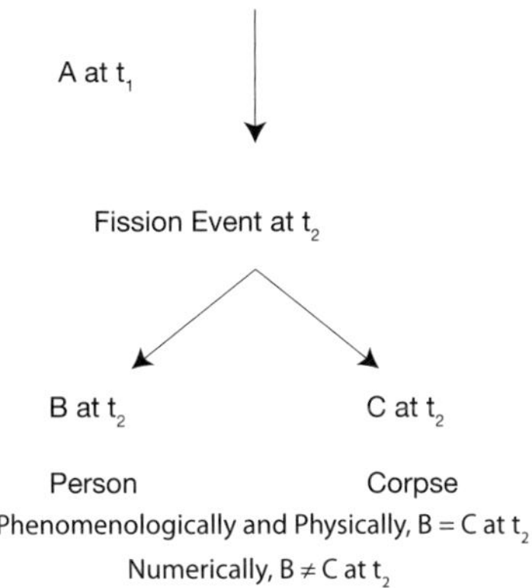


---


13    Corcoran, 'Persons', p. 335.
14    Corcoran, 'Dualism', p. 424.

For Corcoran, this account of body fission offers a plausible account of how post-mortem survival is possible. If it works, the person A persists though death in a numerically identical body that is immanent-causally connected to A's previous body. Corcoran says, 'It looks to me like the defender of Constitution has got all she needs in order to make a case for my continued existence, *post mortem*'.[15]

Nevertheless, it is not clear that this account of post-mortem survival succeeds for materialists like Corcoran. In short, it seems to betray materialism by strongly implying the existence of something over and above the physical in cases of persons. As such, the fission account of post-mortem survival would be an available option for dualists, but not for materialists like Corcoran.

Here is why. At $t_1$, A exists as a person prior to death and the fission event. At $t_2$, just prior to her death, A experiences a fission event wherein two sets of physical simples, B and C, arise that are phenomenologically identical to A at $t_1$, and to each other at $t_2$. Now since B and C at $t_2$ are phenomenologically identical to each other at $t_2$, then they are also physically identical to each other at $t_2$. As such, neither has anything physically unique from the other at $t_2$. Thus, B and C at $t_2$ are phenomenologically and physically identical to each other at $t_2$. They have identical physical sets of bodily simples.

Interestingly, however, B and C are not numerically identical at $t_2$. To preserve the life of A at $t_1$ through death, Corcoran suggests that A's life at $t_1$ is transferred to B at $t_2$. As such, B at $t_2$ comes to compose the life and person of A at $t_1$, whereas C comes to compose a dead corpse at $t_2$. Thus, even if B at $t_2$ is physically identical to C at $t_2$, there is a radical distinction between them at $t_2$ such that they are not numerically identical at $t_2$. So what is it that causes this radical distinction between B and C at $t_2$? According to Corcoran, B has life and is thus a person. As he explains, the life and personhood of A at $t_1$ is preserved by being passed on to B at $t_2$. As such, B at $t_2$ has personhood, whereas C at $t_2$ (though physically identical) is just a corpse. B at $t_2$, then, can be said to possess a physical body, and the non-physical attribute of personhood.

The concern for Corcoran is this. If body fission is what is used to account for post-mortem survival, then it seems that he is really a dualist after all. We must remember that both B and C at $t_2$ are phenomenologically and physically identical to each other at $t_2$. And yet, there is something radically different about them. One is alive and counts as a person, the other is a corpse. But since B and C have exactly the same physical properties, there should be no such distinctions between them if, as Corcoran argues, persons are wholly physical. Yet, as he explains, B at $t_2$ is numerically distinct from C at $t_2$ precisely because B is a person, and C is not. Thus, it looks like B has something over and above the physical.[16] If this is right, then it

---

[15]   Corcoran, 'Persons', p. 335.

[16]   The argument might be expressed like this:
    1. Phenomenologically and physically, B is equal to C at $t_2$.
    2. B at $t_2$ is unique from C at $t_2$ since B is a person.
    3. Numerically, B and C are not identical at $t_2$.

looks like the possibility of body fission for post-mortem survival points towards dualism as opposed to materialism. If so, then Corcoran's body fission approach offers an untenable account of post-mortem survival in a materialistic perspective.

But what if we interpret Corcoran differently with regard to the physical relationship of B and C at $t_2$? If we understand him as saying that B and C are neither numerically nor physically identical at $t_2$, would this keep his account from collapsing back into dualism? Later I will suggest that such a construction might work for materialists like Peter van Inwagen. But, for now, I suggest that it will not work for Corcoran. To show why, let's consider how Corcoran's approach might work.

If we understand Corcoran as denying that B and C are physically identical, then we could say that A experiences a fission event at $t_2$ where two bodies (B and C) emerge that are physically and numerically distinct from each other. They are numerically distinct because B comes to compose the person and C comes to compose the corpse. As such, one is a person and the other is not. What makes this approach different from the last account, however, is that B and C are not even physically identical. We could illustrate this with the following drawing:

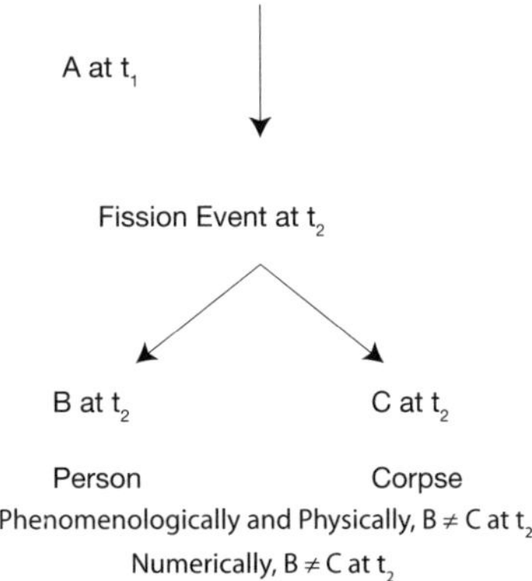


On the surface, this interpretation of Corcoran seems to dodge the objection I raised above regarding two fission bodies that are physically identical to each other. There we saw that having two physically identical bodies that are numerically distinct seems to require some form of dualism to successfully account for one body being a person while the other composes the corpse. But, if we interpret Corcoran as saying B and C are physically distinct, then my objection would lose

---

4. Given (1) and (2), at $t_2$, B possesses an attribute distinct from all the physical attributes of C at $t_2$.

5. B possesses something distinct from its physical body.

its force. In this case, what is physically true of B is not also physically true of C, and it is now easy to see how one can have life and the other cannot.

Despite the success this revision might have against my last objection, it seems that even this interpretation of Corcoran would require some form of dualism to work. The reason for this comes from the way in which Corcoran envisions life and personhood passing from one body to another. In other words, in this approach, Corcoran seems to say the life and person A transfers out of the original body and into a different body that comes into existence at the fission event. He illustrates this as follows:

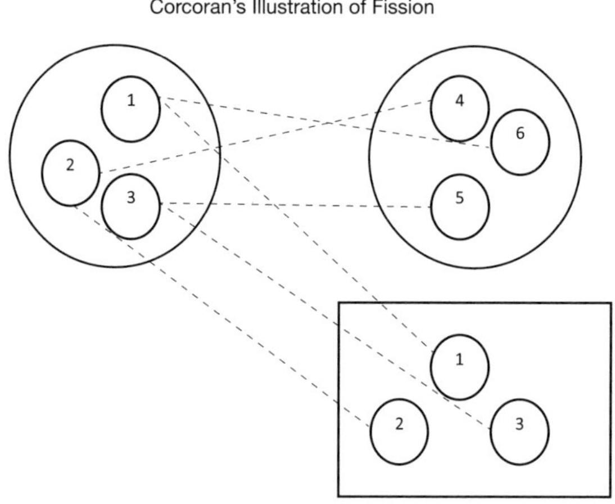



He explains the illustration: 'Let the smaller circles … represent the physical simples propertied and related in such a way that they are caught up in the life of my body. But the larger circles represent the life into which the physical simples are caught up. But the box represents a corpse. Broken lines will represent causal paths'.[17] What is important to note about this construction is the way life transfers from one physical body to another. He says:

> Notice on this view that the stuff left behind in the corpse at death really is the
> stuff that at one time did constitute me and is no simulacrum. True, none of the
> simples that survives in the living body is identical with any of the ones left
> behind, but the life now associated with the simples that survive in the living
> body is identical to the life once associated with the simples left behind in the

---

[17]    Kevin Corcoran, 'Physical Persons and Postmortem Survival without Temporal Gaps' in Kevin Corcoran (ed.), *Soul, Body and Survival* (Ithaca: Cornell University Press, 2001), pp. 210–211.

corpse – that is, they are immanent-causally connected with them in the relevant, life preserving way.[18]

In other words, at the fission event, Corcoran envisions a body splitting where the body that once constituted the person now constitutes a dead corpse. The life of the person is transferred from the original body into the new body that came about from the fission event.

If this interpretation of Corcoran is correct, then there is a problem for his materialistic perspective. In short, it looks like this interpretation relies on the possibility of body transfer in order to work. Corcoran suggests that the person persists since the new life constituting the body at $t_2$ is immanent-causally connected to the old life constituting the body at $t_1$. While the causal connection might be granted, some metaphysical problems remain. Despite the causal link between the original body and the new body, he admits that these are in fact distinct bodies. Again, he says, 'the stuff left behind in the corpse at death really is the stuff that at one time did constitute me and is no simulacrum. True, none of the simples that survives in the living body is identical with any of the ones left behind'.[19] As such, Corcoran's account relies on a transfer from one body to another to accomplish post-mortem survival. But if this is true, it looks like his approach again collapses back into a form of dualism. On this account, the person is something different from the body, such that it can move from one body to another.

## Possible Revisions to Corcoran's Gappy and Non-gappy Accounts

Before we dismiss Corcoran's accounts of post-mortem survival, it is important to consider possible ways that he might revise his Gappy and non-Gappy approaches in order to meet the objections raised here. There are possibilities for both accounts which must be explored and evaluated.

For Corcoran's Gappy account of post-mortem survival, he might modify it in such a way that he can fill the temporal gap at $t_2$ with something physical. If this is possible, then his Gappy account of post-mortem survival via ICC might be plausible. He might do this by employing a partial reassembly in combination with some notion of psychological continuity. Corcoran rejects traditional reassembly accounts of resurrection for at least two reasons. First, he notes the difficulties relating to thought experiments about cannibals and the cannibalized. For example, what if a person is eaten by a cannibal and his molecules come to compose the body of the cannibal just before he dies himself. If we survive in the resurrection via reassembly, then it looks like God cannot use the same molecules to reassemble two numerically and physically different human beings. Second, Corcoran also notes the difficulty of identifying exactly which set of

---

18   Ibid., p. 211.
19   Ibid.

molecules from a person's embodied life should be thought of as 'his' or 'hers' in the resurrection. Since our bodies constantly shed old molecules and take on new ones, such that every seven years our bodies are composed of totally new molecules, it is hard to say exactly which particular set should compose our bodies in the resurrection body. And, given the logical possibility that several different complete sets of molecules from the person's previous body might be reassembled, it seems problematic to think of one having greater claim to 'being the person' than any of the others. So, for such reasons, Corcoran rejects traditional reassembly accounts of resurrection.

In the revision suggested here, however, a total reassembly is not required. All that is necessary to meet the criticisms I have raised is that some physical part from the person at $t_1$ exists at $t_2$ which would fill the temporal gap and allow for ICC to cross from $t_1$ to $t_3$. As such, Corcoran might revise his approach to say that at death the body is destroyed and the atoms and molecules of the person's body are dispersed throughout the earth, but continue to exist nonetheless. He could also suggest that the memories, characteristics and beliefs of the person are stored by God, in the mind of God during the gap at $t_2$. With this, he might suggest that in the resurrection God creates a virtual duplicate body and then locates at least one (or several molecules) of the person's previous body and then reassigns the memories, characteristics and beliefs of the person prior to death. So, in short, this revision would entail a partial reassembly plus some kind of psychological continuity.

On first appearances, it looks like this approach could meet the concerns I have raised in this chapter about Corcoran's Gappy account of post-mortem survival. For example, this account maintains that something physical of the person at $t_1$ persists through $t_2$ to $t_3$. As such, the objection I have raised about ICC not being able to cross temporal gaps, since nothing exists in the gap, has been met. And, Corcoran's original concerns with the reassembly view would not apply here. In the case of the cannibal, God could simply take one molecule from him and leave all the others in place.

Despite these first appearances of success, there are good reasons to reject even this modified version of Corcoran's Gappy account of post-mortem survival. To begin with, this revision would be completely ad hoc, offering no other reason for accepting it than that it fixes a problem with his particular approach. And, this revision further complicates an account that is already conceptually inefficient and unnecessarily complex, by positing partial reassembly and some kind of psychological continuity. But there are bigger concerns even still.

First, this revised account reduces the human person to a few microscopic particles. In this case, the persistence of human persons through death is literally dangling by a molecular thread. It looks like this account is on very weak and fragile physical and conceptual ground. After all, we constantly shed molecules from our bodies and would never think that this is somehow significant for the persistence of our personhood. Why would we now be inclined to think that our personhood does significantly depend on a particular molecule surviving and persisting through death?

Second, and finally, while the survival of a molecule might bridge the gap at $t_2$ from $t_1$ to $t_3$, making it appear that ICC is really possible, it is not at all clear that it is actually ICC which gives rise to the resurrected person in this account. In this case, the person has post-mortem survival, not because the molecule at $t_2$ actually causes his existence at $t_3$. Rather, he has post-mortem survival because God constructs a virtual duplicate body, reinserts the molecule into this body, and then reassigns the old memories, characteristics and beliefs to the person in the resurrection. In short, post-mortem survival is caused not by ICC, but by God. This might not seem like a problem for many Christians. Yet, given Corcoran's commitments to ICC and materialism, this approach to post-mortem survival would violate his persistence conditions. In other words, the person at $t_3$ would not be numerically identical to the person at $t_1$, and thus the person at $t_1$ would not actually survive death.

Third, and finally, it seems like this approach would not qualify as an actual Gappy approach to post-mortem survival since some physical part of the person would persist from $t_1$ to $t_3$. In other words, since some part still exists at $t_2$ that connects $t_1$ to $t_3$, there is no actual gap in the existence of the person after all. Something like this might work for a non-Gappy approach to post-mortem survival, which I will discuss in a moment, but it would not work for a Gappy approach. As such, it looks like there are no viable options for revising Corcoran's Gappy account of post-mortem survival.

But what about Corcoran's non-Gappy account of post-mortem survival? Can it be revised in such a way that it defeats the objections raised in this chapter? I suggest there is at least one possible way to revise it that has some degree of promise for materialists like Corcoran. As I have argued in this chapter, the problem for Corcoran's non-Gappy body fission account is that, no matter how we interpret it, it seems to collapse back into some form of dualism. If we take the two bodies produced by the fission event to be physically and phenomenologically identical, then it looks like personhood must be something over and above the physical body. Yet, if we interpret Corcoran differently, as saying the two bodies produced by the fission event are physically distinct from each other, his account does not seem to fare much better. This is because Corcoran's account depends on a kind of body transfer from one physical organism to another. Yet, if body transfer is possible, then the person must be a distinct entity from the body, such that it is capable of being either in or out of a particular body.

Despite the problems I have highlighted, a materialist like Corcoran might still revise his approach in such a way that it avoids these philosophical problems. For example, the fission event described and endorsed by Peter van Inwagen and Dean Zimmerman might do much better against the concerns I have raised in this paper. Van Inwagen has famously suggested something like the following:

> Perhaps at the moment of each man's death, God removes his corpse and replaces it with a simulacrum which is what is burned or rots. Or perhaps God is not quite so wholesale as this: perhaps he removes for 'safekeeping' only the

'core person' – the brain and central nervous system – or even some special part of it. These are details.[20]

Like Corcoran's account, van Inwagen's approach relies on some kind of fission event at the moment of death. But unlike Corcoran's approach, van Inwagen's fission event does not require physically identical bodies nor does it rely on body transfer. Instead, it preserves the life of a person in the parts that are taken by God at the moment of death and leaves the body to be destroyed by cremation or natural decay. Because of these key differences, van Inwagen's approach does not collapse back into dualism.

This revised approach does come with an interesting theological price tag. If this is what really happens, why does God go to such great lengths to make it look like something completely different happens at death? If this scenario is true, then God regularly deceives us about important matters of our existence. Theologically speaking, this paints a disturbing picture of God. But philosophically speaking, I suggest that van Inwagen's approach is much more tenable than either of the two proposals Corcoran has given so far. Many Christian theologians and philosophers, like myself, will still reject van Inwagen's account for theological or biblical reasons, but his approach is at least logically plausible.

## Conclusion

This chapter has considered Corcoran's CV as it relates to the possibility of post-mortem survival. In particular, it has examined his two accounts of how post-mortem survival might be possible in a materialistic account of human persons. Corcoran recognizes the need for numerically identical bodies in order to account for this survival. His first account (non-Gappy survival) fails because it does not demonstrate how ICC can cross temporal gaps and allow for intermittent existence. His second account (Gappy survival) seems to betray his materialistic perspective in favour of dualism. Yet, I have suggested that Corcoran's account might be modified to posit something like what van Inwagen has endorsed to satisfy these concerns. This revised approach might still have some significant theological concerns, but would do much better on philosophical grounds than Corcoran's current proposals.

---

[20]   Peter van Inwagen, 'The Possibility of Resurrection' in *Philosophy of Religion* 9/2 (1978), p. 121.

Chapter 9

# The Paradox of Eden
# and Black-and-White Mary

Yujin Nagasawa

## 1 Introduction

God created Adam and Eve, placed them in the Garden of Eden and commanded them not to eat fruit from the tree of knowledge of good and evil. However, Adam and Eve disobeyed God's command and ate the forbidden fruit. Accordingly, God punished them for their disobedience. This is the famous story of Eden in Genesis 2–3.

This story is likely the best known account of the origin of sin. It has been overlooked, however, that the story contains a puzzle, if not a flaw. Richard R. La Croix makes this point by deriving what he calls the 'paradox of Eden' from the story and argues that it entails, contrary to what Judaeo-Christian theists believe, that justice is not one of God's essential properties.[1] The aim of this chapter is to formulate the strongest possible formulation of the paradox and argue that it nevertheless fails. In order to develop a novel solution to the paradox I try to show that we can appeal to a hitherto unnoticed structural similarity between the story of Eden and the black-and-white Mary scenario which is used in the philosophy of mind to construct arguments against physicalism.

This chapter has the following structure. In section 2, I introduce La Croix's paradox of Eden. In section 3, I offer objections to the paradox. In section 4, I develop a new form of the paradox that is not vulnerable to the objections. In section 5, I introduce the Mary scenario and existing responses to it. In section 6 I provide a solution to the paradox, which appeals to a structural similarity between the story of Eden and the black-and-white Mary scenario. Section 7 concludes.

## 2 The Paradox of Eden

According to La Croix, the story of Eden shows that justice is not one of God's essential properties because God's act in the story is unjust. La Croix presents his point by formulating a paradox or a dilemma that Judaeo-Christian theists face.

---

[1]   Richard La Croix, 'The Paradox of Eden' in *International Journal for Philosophy of Religion* 15 (1984), p. 171.

Before eating the forbidden fruit, either Adam and Eve knew that obeying God is good and disobeying God is evil, or they did not. Suppose that they knew, that is, they already possessed knowledge of good and evil. Since God is omniscient, He must have known this. He must have known, moreover, that Adam and Eve would not very likely be tempted to eat the forbidden fruit because they would have nothing to gain by doing so, their already being in possession of the very knowledge that would be gained by eating the fruit. Hence it is unjust for God to have set such a test for Adam and Eve. Suppose, on the other hand, that Adam and Eve did not know, before eating the fruit, that obeying God is good and disobeying God is evil. In this case Adam and Eve did not possess knowledge of good and evil in advance and so they could not possibly have understood that it is good to obey and evil to disobey God's command. Thus God's punishing Adam and Eve for eating the forbidden fruit is unjust. Hence, in either case God's act in the story is unjust. Therefore, La Croix concludes, the story of Eden entails that justice is not one of God's essential properties. This is a devastating conclusion. For theists who believe that God is essentially just, the paradox of Eden is effectively an argument against the existence of God.

The paradox can be summarised as follows:

*The Paradox of Eden*

(1)   Before eating the forbidden fruit, either Adam and Eve knew that obeying God is good and disobeying God is evil, or they did not.

(2)   If, before eating the forbidden fruit, they knew that obeying God is good and disobeying God is evil, then it is unjust for God to have set the test for Adam and Eve.

(3)   If, before eating the forbidden fruit, they did not know that obeying God is good and disobeying God is evil, then it is unjust for God to have set the test for Adam and Eve.

Therefore,

(4)   It is unjust for God to have set the test for Adam and Eve.

Therefore,

(5)   Justice is not an essential property of God.


## 3   Objections to the Paradox

Let us focus on premises (2) and (3) as premise (1) is uncontroversially true. Premise (3) says that if, before eating the forbidden fruit, Adam and Eve did not know that obeying God is good and disobeying God is evil, then it is unjust for God to have set the test for Adam and Eve. This premise assumes implicitly that Adam and Eve had to know good and evil in order to follow God's command not to eat the fruit. One might reject this assumption. One might point out, for example, that, in order for Adam and Eve to follow God's command, they needed only an interest in self-preservation or a pragmatic reason to follow what God says.[2] However, if we interpret the story of Eden charitably as a story about morality, Adam and Eve do seem to have needed knowledge of good and evil in order to understand the command in a morally significant way. Hence, it does seem unjust for God to have set the moral test for Adam and Eve if they really did not know that obeying God is good and disobeying God is evil. Premise (3), therefore, seems reasonable.

Premise (2) says that if, before eating the forbidden fruit, Adam and Eve knew that obeying God is good and disobeying God is evil, then it is unjust for God to have set the test for them. This premise is problematic. La Croix says that if Adam and Eve knew that obeying God is good and disobeying God is evil, then God's setting the test is unjust because it would be unlikely for Adam and Eve to choose to eat the fruit and God must have known it in advance with his foreknowledge. However, it is far from clear that the mere fact that Adam and Eve knew that eating the forbidden fruit is evil entails that they were unlikely to eat it. Consider a parallel case. The fact that one knows that it is morally wrong to steal does not immediately entail that one is unlikely to steal. We know that there are many situations in which one is fully aware that it is morally wrong to steal but one does steal. In response to this, La Croix might emphasise that it is unlikely for Adam and Eve to eat the fruit because, given that they already knew what is good and evil, they would gain nothing by eating the fruit. Eating the fruit while already possessing knowledge of good and evil is comparable to stealing something that one does not need. However, whether or not Adam and Eve knew what good and evil are in advance, the story of Eden tells us that they did eat the forbidden fruit!

Second, even if La Croix is correct in saying that Adam and Eve would very likely *not* be tempted to eat the forbidden fruit, it does not follow that God is unjust. On the contrary, it seems perfectly just for God to forbid people who do have knowledge of good and evil to perform a morally wrong action. God's act could be deemed unjust if, for example, He tricked Adam and Eve into eating the fruit. However, that is not what the story of Eden tells us. On the contrary, it tells us that they freely chose to eat the forbidden fruit.

Third, even if God had complete foreknowledge and He had known in advance what Adam and Eve would do, it is far from clear that God's test is unjust. Many Judaeo-Christian theists hold that human freedom and God's foreknowledge are compatible. If they are right, it might have been the case that, on the one hand, God knew in advance what Adam and Eve would do but, on the other hand, they made the decision to eat the forbidden fruit freely. If so, God's setting the test does not seem to be unjust.

---

[2]  I am indebted to Campbell Brown and Klaas Kraay on this point.

The paradox of Eden, therefore, fails at premise (2).


## 4   The New Paradox of Eden

We have seen that while premise (3) of the paradox of Eden is reasonable, premise (2) is untenable. Is it possible to reformulate the paradox by using premise (3)? As premise (3) says, if, before eating the forbidden fruit, Adam and Eve did not know that obeying God is good and disobeying God is evil, then it is unjust for God to have set the test for them. This means that in order for God's command for Adam and Eve to make sense it has to be the case that Adam and Eve did know, before eating the fruit, that obeying God is good and disobeying God is evil. In fact, that seems consistent with what the Bible says. At the beginning of the story of Eden God commanded Eve, 'You must not eat fruit from the tree that is in the middle of the garden, and you must not touch it, or you will die' (Gen. 2:16–17). This command implies that Adam and Eve did know, before eating the forbidden fruit, what good and evil are. In sum, in order for God's command to make sense the following must be true:

> (6)   Before eating the forbidden fruit Adam and Eve had knowledge of good and evil.

However, at the end of the story of Eden, according to the Bible, God also said 'The man has now become like one of us, knowing good and evil' (Gen. 3:22). Note the phrase 'has now become'. This suggests that Adam and Eve *acquired* knowledge of good and evil as a consequence of eating the forbidden fruit. That is, the following must be true:

> (7)   After eating the forbidden fruit, Adam and Eve acquired knowledge of good and evil for the first time.

Now the real puzzle in the story of Eden is clear. On the one hand, in order for God's command to Adam and Eve to make sense, it must be the case that Adam and Eve knew what good and evil are in advance. That is, (6) must be true. On the other hand, however, in order for the ending of the story to follow it must be the case that Adam and Eve acquired knowledge of good and evil only after they ate the forbidden fruit. That is, (7) must be true. But the problem is that (6) and (7) seem mutually inconsistent because (7) seems to imply the negation of (6):

> (¬6)   It is not the case that, before eating the forbidden fruit, Adam and Eve had knowledge of good and evil.

We can now formulate the following 'new paradox of Eden':

*The New Paradox of Eden*

(8)  If the story of Eden is coherent, then Adam and Eve had knowledge of good and evil before eating the forbidden fruit (otherwise God's command does not make sense).

(9)  If the story of Eden is coherent, it is not the case that before eating the forbidden fruit Adam and Eve did not have knowledge of good and evil (otherwise the ending of the story does not follow).

(10)  If the story of Eden is coherent it is both true and false that Adam and Eve had knowledge of good and evil.

Therefore,

(11)  The story of Eden is not coherent.

Unlike the original paradox, the new paradox does not entail that God is unjust. Yet the conclusion of the new paradox is also devastating for Judaeo-Christian theists as it undermines the coherence of the story of Eden, which is regarded as one of the most important stories in the Old Testament.

## 5   The Mary Scenario in the Philosophy of Mind

How can we respond to the new paradox? In the rest of this chapter I demonstrate that the inconsistency that the new paradox tries to reveal is illusory. I argue that the apparent inconsistency arises due to an equivocation on the notion of knowledge in premises (8) and (9). In order to show this, I set aside the story of Eden for the moment and introduce the black-and-white Mary scenario that has been adduced against physicalism in the philosophy of mind.

The black-and-white Mary scenario was introduced by Frank Jackson as part of his so-called knowledge argument against physicalism.[3] Imagine Mary, a brilliant scientist who is confined to a black-and-white room. Although she has never been outside her room in her entire life, she has learned *everything* there is to know about the physical world from black-and-white books and lectures on a black-and-white television. Mary's complete physical knowledge subsumes everything about the physical facts and laws of physics, which includes causal and relational facts and functional roles; this is the beginning of the Mary scenario. Physicalism is the metaphysical thesis that, in the relevant sense, everything is physical, or as contemporary physicalists often put it, in the relevant sense, everything logically or metaphysically supervenes on the physical. Thus, if physicalism is true, Mary,

---

[3]   Frank Jackson, 'Epiphenomenal Qualia' in *Philosophical Quarterly* 32 (1982), pp. 127–36; Frank Jackson, 'What Mary Didn't Know' in *Journal of Philosophy* 83 (1986), pp. 291–5.

who has complete knowledge about the physical, must have complete knowledge *simpliciter*. What will happen, Jackson continues, when Mary leaves her room and looks at, say, a ripe tomato for the first time? According to physicalism, she should not come to know anything new because she already knows everything physical there is to know. It appears obvious, however, that she will discover something new upon her release; namely, 'what it is like to see red', a phenomenal feature of her colour experience. This contradicts the physicalist assumption that Mary, prior to her release, has complete knowledge *simpliciter*. Therefore, Jackson concludes, physicalism is false.

A challenge for physicalists that Jackson poses here is this: on the one hand, physicalists must affirm that Mary knows, before her release, everything there is to know because she already has complete physical knowledge. On the other hand, however, it seems obvious that she will learn something new upon her release.

Physicalists have introduced a number of responses to Jackson's argument but the ones that are relevant to us here are responses according to which the knowledge argument equivocates on the notion of knowledge.[4] There are at least three such responses:

*Response 1    Know-how Response*

Gilbert Ryle defends the distinction between knowledge-that and knowledge-how.[5] Knowledge-that consists of propositions that one knows such as the proposition that one plus one is two. Knowledge-how is, on the other hand, tacit knowledge that arguably cannot be reduced to knowledge-that. Consider the knowledge of how to ride a bicycle. One can in principle have complete knowledge of a bicycle and a human body by reading extremely detailed books about them; yet one can never know how to ride a bicycle unless one actually acquires the know-how by riding a bicycle. According to the know-how response to the knowledge argument, the Mary scenario equivocates on knowledge-that and knowledge-how.[6] It says that Mary knows, before her release, everything physical there is to know in the form of knowledge-that. However, upon her release, she acquires new knowledge-how, such as knowledge of how to identify red, how to distinguish red from blue and so on. This does not mean that there is a non-physical proposition that escapes

---

[4]    For a comprehensive survey of responses to the knowledge argument see Daniel Stoljar and Yujin Nagasawa, 'Introduction' in Peter Ludlow, Yujin Nagasawa and Daniel Stoljar (eds), *There is Something About Mary: Essays on Phenomenal Consciousness and Frank Jackson's Knowledge Argument* (Cambridge, MA: MIT Press, 2004), pp. 1–36.

[5]    Gilbert Ryle, *The Concept of Mind* (Chicago: University of Chicago Press, 1949).

[6]    David Lewis, 'What Experience Teaches' in *Proceedings of the Russellian Society* 13 (1988), pp. 29–57, reprinted in William G. Lycan (ed.), *Mind and Cognition: An Anthology* (Oxford: Blackwell, 1999), pp. 447–61; Lawrence Nemirow, 'Physicalism and the Cognitive Role of Acquaintance' in William G. Lycan (ed.), *Mind and Cognition: A Reader* (Oxford: Blackwell, 1990), pp. 490–499.

Mary's complete physical knowledge prior to her release. Therefore, it concludes, the knowledge argument fails to undermine physicalism.

*Response 2    Indexicality Response*

The second response to the Mary scenario appeals to the distinction between non-indexical knowledge and indexical knowledge. Indexicals are such expressions as 'I', 'this' and 'now', whose references depend on a context of utterance. For example, my utterance of 'I' refers to Yujin Nagasawa, but Plato's utterance of 'I' refers to a different person, namely, Plato. According to the indexicality response to the knowledge argument, the Mary scenario equivocates on non-indexical knowledge and indexical knowledge.[7] It says that Mary knows, before her release, everything physical there is to know in the form of non-indexical knowledge. However, upon her release, she acquires new indexical knowledge expressed as '*this* is what it is like to see red'. This does not mean that there is a non-physical proposition that escapes Mary's complete physical knowledge prior to her release. Therefore, it concludes, the knowledge argument fails to undermine physicalism.

*Response 3    Acquaintance Response*

Bertrand Russell famously contends that there are two kinds of knowledge; knowledge by description and knowledge by acquaintance.[8] Knowledge by description is indirect knowledge of objects, knowledge that is mediated by other objects and truths. So we have knowledge by description 'when we know that it is "the so-and-so"'.[9] Knowledge by acquaintance is, on the other hand, knowledge of objects by means of direct awareness of them. So we have knowledge by acquaintance when 'we are directly aware [of a thing], without the intermediary of any process of inference or any knowledge of truths'.[10] According to the acquaintance response to the knowledge argument, the Mary scenario equivocates on knowledge by description and knowledge by acquaintance.[11] It says that Mary knows, before her release, everything physical there is to know in the form of knowledge by description. However, upon her release, she acquires new knowledge by acquaintance of her colour experience. This does not mean that there is a non-physical proposition that escapes Mary's complete physical

---

[7]    John Bigelow and Robert Pargetter, 'Acquaintance with Qualia' in *Theoria* 61 (1990), pp. 129–47; John Perry, *Knowledge, Possibility, and Consciousness* (Cambridge MA: MIT Press, 2001).

[8]    Bertrand Russell, *Problems of Philosophy* (Oxford: Oxford University Press, 1967, originally 1912).

[9]    Ibid., p. 29.

[10]    Ibid., p. 25.

[11]    Earl Conee, 'Phenomenal Knowledge' in *Australasian Journal of Philosophy* 72 (1994), pp. 136–50.

knowledge prior to her release. Therefore, it concludes, the knowledge argument fails to undermine physicalism.

In the next section, I show that the Mary scenario is structurally parallel to the story of Eden. I show, moreover, that we can construct a successful solution to the paradox of Eden by appealing to the indexicality response and the acquaintance response.


## 6   Responding to the New Paradox of Eden

Again, a challenge that the Mary scenario poses for physicalists is this: on the one hand, they must hold, given that Mary has complete physical knowledge, that she knows, before her release from her black-and-white environment, everything there is to know. On the other hand, however, they cannot deny the obvious fact that she acquires something new upon her release. Interestingly enough, this is structurally parallel to the challenge that the new paradox of Eden poses for Judaeo-Christian theists. On the one hand, in order to maintain the validity of God's command, they must hold that Adam and Eve had, before they ate the forbidden fruit, knowledge of good and evil. On the other hand, however, in order to maintain the ending of the story, they cannot deny that Adam and Eve acquired knowledge of good and evil by eating the fruit. The parallel structure motivates us to respond to the new paradox of Eden by adopting the above-mentioned responses to the Mary scenario.

Apply, first, the know-how response. We have seen that in order for premise (8) of the paradox of Eden to be true, that is, in order for God's command to make sense, Adam and Eve must have known, before eating the forbidden fruit, what good and evil are. Suppose that at that time they knew what good and evil are only in the form of knowledge-that. That is, they knew what good and evil are through propositional understanding of them. Nevertheless, it was perfectly possible for them to understand, in a morally significant way, God's command not to eat the fruit. We have also seen that in order for premise (9) to be true, that is, in order for the ending of the story of Eden to follow, Adam and Eve must have come to know, after eating the forbidden fruit, what good and evil are. We might suppose that at that time they came to know it in the form of knowledge-how. That is, they learned how to identify good and evil, how to distinguish good from evil and so on. Unfortunately, this solution does not succeed because Adam and Eve had to be able to identify good and evil and distinguish good from evil *before* eating the forbidden fruit. Without these know-hows they would not have understood God's command. The know-how response, therefore, is not applicable to the new paradox of Eden.

I submit, however, that the other two responses – the indexicality response and the acquaintance response – succeed in refuting the new paradox of Eden. Again, in order for premise (8) of the new paradox to be true, that is, in order for God's command to make sense, Adam and Eve must have known, before eating the forbidden fruit, what good and evil are. Suppose that at that time they knew what good and evil are only in the form of non-indexical knowledge or knowledge by proposition. Nevertheless, it was perfectly possible for them to understand, in a morally significant way, God's command not to eat the fruit. Now, again, in order for premise (9) to be true, that is, in order for the ending of the story of Eden to follow, Adam and Eve must have come to know, after eating the forbidden fruit, what good and evil are. We can suppose at this time that they came to know it in the form of indexical knowledge or knowledge by acquaintance. That is, they came to know that *this* is what good and evil are and they became *acquainted* with the experience of being good and evil. This means that the new paradox equivocates on the notion of knowledge: while premise (8) is based on non-indexical knowledge or knowledge by description, premise (9) is based on indexical knowledge or knowledge by acquaintance. Thus the story of Eden is not incoherent. The interpretation of the story of Eden that the above responses entail is faithful to the moral of the story. Adam and Eve perfectly understood God's command as they had already known what good and evil are in a morally significant way. However, by breaking God's command themselves they had a first-hand experience of committing a morally wrong act and thereby learned what good and evil are very vividly.

## 7 Conclusion

I began by arguing that La Croix's original paradox of Eden fails because its second premise is vulnerable to several objections. I then introduced the new paradox of Eden which is not vulnerable to these objections. I tried to develop a novel solution to the new paradox of Eden, a solution which appeals to a structural similarity between the Mary scenario against physicalism and the story of Eden. I showed that while the know-how response to the Mary scenario is not applicable to the new paradox of Eden, the indexicality response and the acquaintance response successfully refute the paradox.

The above discussion hints at an interesting point about the story of Eden. Perhaps Adam and Eve became acquainted with good and evil, not because the fruit had an unseen property that makes people understand what good and evil are, but simply because they had a first-hand experience of committing an evil act of disobeying God's command. So the fruit of the tree of the knowledge of good and evil is not essential to the story; God's command could have been concerned with some other object.

# PART III
# The Status of God

# Chapter 10
# Theology as Metaphor

Anthony Kenny

In this chapter I will pose two questions. First, is it possible to say anything that is literally true about the nature of God? I shall propose that the answer is negative. I shall then pose a second question: how is theological language to be understood?

The predicates that religious people apply to God can be divided into two classes. There are bodily predicates, and these seem to be almost universally agreed to be metaphorical. There are mentalistic predicates, and these would be claimed by at least some theologians to be literally true of God.

Mentalistic predicates are used primarily of human beings, and they are ascribed to human beings on the basis of their behaviour. It is not only to human beings, however, that we ascribe mentalistic properties and mental acts: we ascribe them also to animals who behave in ways similar to human beings. We also ascribe mental acts and processes to human institutions and artefacts – to governments, say, to texts and to computers. This is not because governments and texts and computers behave like individual human beings, but because of the relationships they have to the humans who constitute them, create them or make use of them. If we try to ascribe mentality to God we cannot do so in any of these ways. God has no behaviour to resemble human behaviour in the way that animal behaviour does; nor, if he really is God, is he a human creation like a government, a text or a computer.

It is perhaps possible to conceive of a disembodied spirit which is individuated not by having a body, but by having an individual locus or viewpoint on the world. By this I mean that we imagine it as possessing information which, in the case of a normal embodied mind, would be available only from a particular point in space and time. Such a being would be something like a poltergeist or tinkerbell: along this route the intelligibility of the notion of pure spirit seems to be in direct proportion to its triviality.

Even if such a spirit is conceivable it will not help us in giving content to the notion of a God who is a non-embodied mind. For it was precisely the limitations in space and time that we imagined for such a being which make it possible to individuate it without a body. That is of no assistance towards conceiving of a personal God who is immaterial, ubiquitous and eternal. It is not just that we cannot know what thoughts are God's thoughts, but that there does not seem to be anything which would count as ascribing a thought to God in the way that we can ascribe thoughts to individual human thinkers.

A divine mind would be a mind without a history. In the concept of mind that we apply to human beings time enters in various ways; but with God there is no variation or shadow of change. God does not change his mind, nor learn, nor forget, nor imagine nor desire. With us, time enters into both the acquisition and exercise of knowledge, and the onset and satisfaction of wanting. The exercise of knowledge and the execution of wants involve a course of conduct (external or internal) spread over time, which could not be attributed to a being outside time.

The notions of time and change enter into our very concept of intelligence. Intelligence entails speed of acquisition of information, and versatility in adaptation to altered and unforeseen circumstances. In an all-knowing unchanging being there is no scope for intelligence thus understood: no new information is ever acquired, and no circumstances are ever unforeseen.

Philosophical understanding is not related to time and change in the same intimate way as the acquisition and exploitation of information. No doubt this is why, in the tradition going back to Aristotle, it has been taken as a paradigm for divine thought. But the timeless contemplation that Aristotle holds out as ideal for the philosopher is difficult to make sense of even at the human level.

Reflection on what is involved in the attribution of mentalistic predicates to human beings, and to other finite creatures that resemble them, brings out for us the enormous difficulty in applying such predicates in any literal sense to a being that is infinite and unchanging, and whose field of operation is the entire universe.

But does it follow that we can only speak of God in metaphor? Are we using metaphor when we say that God is omnipotent? There is clearly a difference between saying 'God is a tower' and 'God is omnipotent'. We know what towers are, and when we say that God is one we know we are using metaphor. But it is not as if we were acquainted with omnipotent things, in the way that we are acquainted with towers, and then wonder whether God is sufficiently like the omnipotent things we know to deserve the name.

But 'omnipotent' quantifies over powers; and it is in the attribution of power to God that metaphor enters in. For one thing, the notion of power is in its natural place when we wish to make a contrast between activity and potentiality; a distinction which is not supposed to be applicable to God who is pure actuality. The distinction between potentiality and actuality also seems bound up with the time of before and after. Power cannot really be in God any more than change can. Secondly, if we specify the powers which God has (intellect, will and so on) then, as we have seen, these powers themselves can only be expressed metaphorically.

Philosophy in this area leads to the same conclusion as that of those theologians who have said that when we speak of God we do not know what we are talking about. God, in the time-honoured expression, is ineffable. If God is that of which we cannot speak, must we therefore keep silent about him? Woe to those who are silent about thee, said St Augustine: *Vae tacentibus de te.* There is, however, a third way between nonsense and silence. If we cannot say anything literally true of God, perhaps we can nonetheless speak of him in metaphor.

If religious language is metaphorical, there cannot be any science of theology. I have argued in *The God of the Philosophers* that the God of rational theology is an *Unding*.[1] Taken literally, the propositions of natural theology lead to contradiction. Even in talking about God we must not contradict ourselves. Once we find ourselves committed to contradictory propositions, we must draw back. We may seek to show that the contradiction is only apparent; we can trace back the steps that led to each of the conclusions, in the hope that minor modification to one of the steps will remove the clash. If this is not the case, the best way out of the impasse is to claim that the contradiction arises, because metaphorical language has mistakenly been taken literally.

To say that we cannot speak literally of God is to say that the word 'God' does not belong in a language-game. Literal truth is truth within a language-game. Some philosophers believe that there is a special religious language-game, and it is in that game that the concept of God is located. I believe, on the contrary, that there is no specifically religious language-game, and that we speak of God in metaphor. And to use metaphor is to use a word in a language-game which is not its home. Metaphor is, in the standard case, taking a word which has a role in one language-game and moving it to another. The predicates which we apply to God – predicates, for instance, concerning knowledge and love – are taken from other language-games, and used in the absence of the criteria which give them their meanings in the language-games in which they have their home.

I have suggested that theology speaks in metaphor. Some theologians have preferred to say that theological language is analogical, and analogical discourse is not necessarily metaphorical. 'Good', for instance, is an analogical term. A good knife is a knife that is handy and sharp; a good strawberry is a strawberry that is soft and tasty. Clearly, goodness in knives is something different from goodness in strawberries; yet one does not seem to be using a metaphor drawn from knives when one calls a particular batch of strawberries good.

The explanation of this kind of analogy, the scholastics explained, was a kind of proportion, thus

goodness of x:: essence of x =
goodness of y:: essence of y

It is because we know the essence or nature of knives and strawberries that we can understand what 'good' means when applied to them, without having to learn a separate lesson in each case.

The difficulty in applying this pattern of analogy in the case of God is that it is hard to make out that we know what his nature or essence is. St Thomas Aquinas often says that we have no idea what his essence is; if so, we have equally no idea what 'good' means when applied to him. Sometimes it looks as if St Thomas thinks we do know what his essence is, namely Being with a capital B. I have

---

[1]     Anthony Kenny, *The God of the Philosophers* (Oxford: Clarendon Press, 1979).

argued in *Aquinas on Being* that this thesis cannot be exempted from the charge of sophistry and illusion.[2] So the analogous predicates which, according to the theory, function as 'good' does cannot be applied to God in any meaningful way if we insist on literal meaning.

Among analogous notions there is a special class that is relevant when we are discussing the predicates that apply to God. Consider the notion of cause. The way in which I cause an uproar is different from the way in which a match causes a fire, and both of these cases differ from the way in which gravity causes heavy bodies to fall to earth. Moreover, the notion of cause is an open-ended one; we do not have a closed set of types of causation, and science long ago abandoned the Cartesian idea that in the material world collision was the only form of agency. The notion of cause is not only an analogous one, but a heuristic one – that is to say, a notion used to draw attention to a question to be asked. Similar notions are 'explanation' and 'solution'. We can speak of the cause of cancer, of the value of an equation or the solution of the problems of Palestine without knowing what is the cause, the value or the solution. We can do so sensibly even without knowing how to set about acquiring the relevant knowledge. So it is no objection against holding that God is the cause of the world to say that we have not the faintest idea what the mode of God's causation is.

I accept, therefore, that we can talk about God in heuristic terms. But I maintain that it is possible to make reference by a heuristic description only if it is in principle possible to find some other description of it, even if we do not yet know what it is (as the cure for cancer might be a drug of a particular molecular structure, and the solution to the problems of Palestine some as-yet-unthought-of constitutional arrangements). But given the other things that theologians say about God, it seems that He can be described by no predicates other than heuristic ones. It is not that we do not know the answers to the questions 'What kind of thing is God?' or 'What is the mode of divine causality?' It is that no answers are possible in principle. I conclude that one must give up the attempt to use the theory of analogy to give an account of how theological language can be used literally.

However, there is an important contrast to be drawn between analogy and metaphor, and the distinction between the two is not a matter of a fuzzy borderline. Analogy belongs in the realm of sense. A mastery of the language is enough to convey understanding of the analogous terms it contains (such as 'good' and 'real'). Indeed a person who did not understand that certain terms were analogous would not understand their meaning in the language at all. Being analogical does not prevent a predicate from being literally true of things. Consider the analogical nature of a verb like 'love'; loving chocolates involves wanting to eat them, loving my mother-in-law does not involve wanting to eat her, and so on.

Metaphor, unlike analogy, is not a matter of sense. To introduce a metaphor is not to introduce a new sense into the dictionary. Metaphor is the use of an expression outside the language-game that is its home. Understanding a metaphor

---

[2]    Anthony Kenny, *Aquinas on Being* (Oxford: Clarendon Press, 2002).

is not a matter of mastering a new language-game. To be sure, a metaphor may become dead. It becomes dead when it does enter a new language-game – when it is used, not as a creative act, nor as an allusion to a famous creative use, but as part of an independent language-game. Then a new sense is added to the word. The test of when this has happened is this: could you learn the new sense – the new language-game – independently of the old one. The use of 'high' and 'low' in respect of notes on the scale is an example of a dead metaphor of this kind.

If metaphor is not a matter of language-game or sense, nor is it a particular kind of speech act, in the sense in which stating and commanding are two different speech acts. You can command, no less than describe, in metaphor ('Don't be such a dog in a manger!').

My claim is that theological metaphor – the use of metaphor to speak about God – is irreducible. It can never become dead metaphor, and it can never be replaced by literal language. Consider the sentence 'God wrote his law in the hearts of men'. In this sentence we have three levels of metaphor. The word 'heart' is now a dead metaphor. Any dictionary will have some such entry as 'a person's capacity for feeling love and compassion'. 'Write' is not in the same case. Literal writing in the heart is, no doubt, possible for a surgeon. Metaphorically, to write something in someone's heart is to bring it about that they are emotionally attached to it. One might say, for instance, that St Francis wrote his rule in the hearts of his first disciples. This would not be an irreducible metaphor. One could describe literally what St Francis did. By his instruction, encouragement, example, he brought it about that his disciples grasped the way of life that he wanted them to lead, and followed it with enthusiasm. But when God wrote his law in the hearts of men, what did God do? There is nothing that can be assigned as the way in which he brought it about that the children of Israel loved his law.

I describe my own religious position as agnostic. You may ask whether this is compatible with claiming that religious language is irreducibly metaphorical. As A.J. Ayer pointed out long ago, the agnostic is committed, no less than the theist and the atheist, to the claim that religious statements have a truth-value, even if we do not know it. If religious language has no literal meaning, then there is nothing to be agnostic about.

The objection assumes that because a statement is metaphorical it cannot have a truth-value. But this is an erroneous claim. It is correct that it may be much more difficult to determine the truth-value of a metaphorical statement than it is of a literal statement. Nonetheless, the response to a metaphor may quite appropriately be 'very true!' On the other hand, while I have some reservations about our present prime minister, I would unhesitatingly qualify as false the statement 'David Cameron is a fascist hyena'.

Though they can have truth-values, metaphorical statements are not straightforwardly subject to the principle of non-contradiction. That is to say, two propositions that would rule each other out taken literally may both be true if taken metaphorically. If they are metaphorical, theological propositions cannot contradict each other in the straightforward way in which empirical propositions do. This provides a reason for toleration in religious matters: there is not that head-on clash between different theologies, and different religions, which has been used to justify the persecution and killing of one religious group by others.

It may be objected that a truth which is not subject to the principle of non-contradiction is not really a truth-value at all. In reply one might appeal to the distinction between information and understanding. Empirical statements and philosophical statements can both be called true, yet philosophy is a matter of understanding rather than of information. Those who wish to preserve 'true' for items of information might prefer the word 'sound' for matters of understanding. The question can then be put: is religious language – metaphorically understood – a valid part of understanding the world we live in. Agnosticism, in these terms, is a query whether theism is or is not sound.

To say that religious language is not literal, and to say that different religious creeds need not contradict each other is not to say that all religions are of equal worth. The mode of utterance of Shakespeare and of William McGonagall is poetic in each case; that does not mean that the writings of each of them display an equal insight into human nature. Equally, the fact that Christianity and Hinduism each speak in metaphor does not necessitate that each of them has an equally valuable insight into divine nature, or the nature of the universe as a whole.

Thus far, I have been summarizing points that I have made more than once in writings elsewhere. What I want to do next is to illustrate, in the case of a particular theologian and a particular theological text, how closely my account fits to the actual practice of believers. The theologian I shall consider is St Thomas Aquinas, and the theological text I shall take is the first clause of the Lord's Prayer: 'Our Father, who art in Heaven'.

In the Lord's Prayer, as prayed by a twentieth-century believer, neither 'Father' nor 'Heaven' is understood literally. With regard to 'Father', St Thomas Aquinas, rather surprisingly, is in agreement. When we say the Our Father, he says, we are praying to the whole Trinity (the prayer, after all, is not Jesus' own prayer to his heavenly Father, but the one he taught the likes of us to pray). And the Trinity is not a literal father, because fatherhood involves the origination of another being of the same nature as oneself; and we are not, by nature, in any way consubstantial with the Trinity.

What, then, does St Thomas make of the passage of Ephesians – 'I bow my knee to the Father of our Lord Jesus Christ, from whom all fatherhood in heaven and in earth is named' (Eph. 3:14–15)? His answer, as you might expect, is subtle. First of all, he does believe that the relationship of Father and Son within the Trinity itself is not a matter of metaphor, because the Son is not only of the same nature as the Father but that nature is itself numerically identical in both the begetter and the begotten. Secondly, he thinks that our word 'Father' as a matter of reference applies to God the Father primarily and to creatures secondly, but as a matter of sense applies first within the creaturely realm.[3]

---

[3]    Thomas Aquinas, *Summa Theologiae*, Ia. 33, 2. 4 and ad 4; 3. 1 and ad 1.

If we, following this hint, accept that the word 'Father' acquires its sense from within the world of human generation, then we cannot help but admit that its application to God in relation to creatures can be no more than a metaphor. God has no body and belongs to no species; he cannot therefore literally be described by a word which derives its sense from the material propagation of an animal species. St Thomas cannot, in consistency, have any quarrel with the feminist theologians who wish to describe God as our mother. No doubt when it was believed that only the male was the agent of generation, with the female no more than a seed-bed to nurture the offspring, fatherhood was the more appropriate metaphor for the divine influence on human development. But since we have learnt that each sex has an equal part in the generation of offspring, there is no reason, other than cultural and liturgical tradition, to object to anyone praying to 'Our Mother' above.

But where above? Can we take 'Heaven' literally? St Thomas was willing to do so. Of course, he believed that God was everywhere, and that meant that if anything was a place, God was there. But was heaven a place? Many contemporary theologians would deny this, and offer some unhelpful paraphrase such as 'an alternative mode of being'. St Thomas, too, was willing to allow that 'heaven' could be used metaphorically. He gave as an example from the Old Testament Isaiah 14:13 where Lucifer says 'I will ascend into heaven' – this, he explains, means equality with God. From the New Testament he gives a passage from the Sermon on the Mount, where Jesus tells those who are persecuted, 'Rejoice and be exceeding glad: for great is your reward in heaven' (Matt. 5:12). Since the reward is enjoyed in this life, 'heaven' must mean 'spiritual benefits'.

But for St Thomas heaven was undoubtedly a real place, and this belief was based both on philosophy and revelation. He accepted the Aristotelian cosmos according to which the earth was in the centre of the universe: around it a succession of concentric crystalline spheres carried the moon, the sun and the planets in their journeys around the visible sky. The heavenly bodies were not compounds of the four terrestrial elements, but were made of a superior fifth element or quintessence. They had souls as well as bodies: living supernatural intellects, guiding their travels through the cosmos. These intellects were movers which were themselves in motion, and behind them, Aristotle argued, there must be a source of movement not itself in motion. The only way in which an unchanging, eternal mover could cause motion in other beings was by attracting them as an object of love, an attraction which they express by their perfect circular motion. It is thus that Dante, in the final lines of his *Paradiso*, finds his own will, like a smoothly rotating wheel, caught up in the love that moves the sun and all the other stars.

Aquinas devotes several pages of dense argument in commentary on the verse of Genesis 'God called the firmament heaven' (Gen. 1:8) and he took it as a matter of scientific inquiry to determine what place, or places, were designated by this name. He compared the Genesis account with the theories of Empedocles (the firmament is made up of four elements), of Plato (it consists of fire) and Aristotle (it is not any of the four elements but a quintessence). He devotes great effort to reconciling together the Genesis narrative, the Patristic commentators and the

Greek cosmologists. His final conclusion is that by the word 'heaven' the Bible means a sublime, luminous and naturally incorruptible body. He goes on to say that there are, in fact, three heavens as thus defined. The first is totally shining, and is called the empyrean heaven; the second is entirely diaphanous, and is called crystalline; the third is called the *caelum sidereum*, or starry sky, and it consists of eight spheres, the outermost carrying the fixed stars and the seven interior ones carrying each a planet.

The heavens in which St Thomas believed could not survive within the Newtonian system in which the sun, the earth, the planets and the stars all cavort in empty space. Historians of science make much of the difference between the Ptolemaic and the Copernican universe. To me it seems that as long as one believes that the members of the solar system are carried around on concentric crystalline spheres, like jewels on an engagement ring, it is of comparatively little philosophical importance whether the sun is carried round the earth on a sphere, or whether the earth is carried round the sun. At least for the interpretation of the notion of heaven in religious discourse, the crucial change – the abandonment of the idea of crystalline spheres – was brought about not by Copernicus but by Tycho Brahe.

In 1577 Brahe observed a bright comet which he proved could not be travelling between the earth and the moon, but must travel among the planets themselves, actually crossing their orbits. This destroyed the notion of crystalline spheres, since the comet moved right through the places where the spheres were supposed to be. Though it took some while for the consequences to be fully spelt out, this was tantamount to the idea that planets moved through empty space. The heavenly bodies were no longer in heaven.

The abandonment of the Aristotelian heavens had no disastrous implications for the interpretation of the Lord's Prayer. God was and always had been in every place, and if heaven was not a place, then 'heaven' must be taken metaphorically, just as 'Father' was. But there were disturbing implications for the article of the Creed: 'he ascended into heaven and sitteth at the right hand of the Father'. The second clause of that article had always been taken metaphorically. The old penny catechism taught children to say 'When I say sitteth at the right hand of the Father, I do not mean that God the Father has hands, for He is a spirit'. But what of the first clause?

If the body of Jesus is still in existence, it must surely be in some place. For St Thomas, it could be a matter of scientific inquiry to determine which of the heavens is the one in which the body of the ascended Jesus now inhabits. (Sadly, I have been unable to discover his answer to the question.) So, too, there could be a quest for the location of the heaven in which the body of Mary resides, if she was assumed into heaven. But in a Newtonian world any such quest must surely seem absurd. If so, then 'ascended into heaven' and 'assumed into heaven' must be no less metaphorical than 'sitteth at the right hand of God'. Hell, too, as a sub-terrestrial region, went the same way as the Aristotelian heaven – even though the great Galileo began his academic career with a dissertation on the location and dimensions of Dante's *Inferno*.

It would take too long to show how other articles of the Creed make sense only if taken metaphorically. There remain some, however, that retain a literal sense, and indeed are literally true: notably 'suffered under Pontius Pilate, was crucified, dead and buried'. But what of 'the third day he rose again from the dead?' The semantic difficulties that stand in the way of our ascribing literal sense to statements about an omnipotent, omniscient, benevolent creator do not present the same difficulty for the doctrine of the resurrection. Whether or not 'he rose from the dead' is true there is no difficulty in understanding what it means – it is a proposition that could be waived through by even a rigid verification principle. On this point agnostic semantics reaches the same conclusion as religious devotion: the doctrine of the resurrection of Jesus occupies a unique position in the structure of Christian belief.

# Chapter 11

# Projecting God

Robin Le Poidevin

**Two Projectivist Projects**

From Hume's *The Natural History of Religion* to Freud's *The Future of an Illusion* to Daniel Dennett's *Breaking the Spell* there is a tradition of seeing religion as a natural phenomenon: something that arises from human nature itself, both individual nature and the nature of human society. The most radical expression of this idea is the proposal that God is a *projection* of aspects of our nature, fears, hopes, desires and so on.

Hume represents religion as a psychological strategy in response to uncertainty:

> We are placed in this world, as in a great theatre, where the true springs and causes of every event, are entirely unknown to us ... could men anatomize nature ... they would find, that these causes are nothing but the particular fabric and structure of the minute parts of their own bodies and of external objects ... But this philosophy exceeds the comprehension of the ignorant multitude ... and, however unwilling, they must at last have abandoned so arduous an attempt, were it not for a propensity in human nature, which leads into a system, that gives them some seeming satisfaction.

> There is an universal tendency amongst mankind to conceive all beings like themselves, and to transfer to every object those qualities, with which they are familiarly acquainted, and of which they are intimately conscious. We find human faces in the moon, armies in the clouds; and by a natural propensity, if not corrected by experience and reflection, ascribe malice and good-will to every thing, that hurts or pleases us.[1]

> By degrees, the active imagination of men, uneasy in this abstract conception [of the unknown causes of things] begins to render them more particular, and to clothe them in shapes more suitable to its natural comprehension. It represents them to be sensible, intelligent beings, like mankind, actuated by love and

---

[1]   David Hume, *The Natural History of Religion*, ed. A. Wayne Cover (Oxford: Clarendon Press, 1976), pp. 33–4.

hatred, and flexible by gifts and entreaties, by prayers and sacrifices. Hence the origin of religion: And hence the origin of idolatry or polytheism.[2]

Thus the world is made intelligible, if not more predictable. Only when cool reason has a say in the matter do people move from an anthropomorphic polytheism to a genuinely explanatory and rational monotheism.

Something very similar to Hume's account of the origin of religious thought can be found in Freud, though here the emotional springs of such thought are emphasised:

> Nothing can be made of impersonal forces and fates; they remain eternally remote. But if the elements have passions that rage like those in our own souls, if death itself is not spontaneous, but the violent act of an evil Will, if everywhere in nature we have about us beings who resemble those of our own environment, then indeed we can breathe feely, we can feel at home in face of the supernatural, and we can deal psychically with our frantic anxiety. We are perhaps still defenceless, but no longer helplessly paralysed; we can at least react; perhaps indeed we are not even defenceless, we can have recourse to the same methods against these violent supermen of the beyond that we make use of in our own community; we can try to exorcise them, to bribe them, and so rob them of part of their power by thus influencing them. Such a substitution of psychology for natural science provides not merely immediate relief, it also points the way to a further mastery of the situation.[3]

However, whereas Hume thought (or at least said) that the shift from a multitude of regrettably human-like gods to a more unified conception of a single, all-powerful and wise God was the result of reason, Freud still sees the operation of desire:

> The race that first succeeded in … concentrating the divine qualities was not a little proud of this advance. It had revealed the father nucleus which had always lain hidden behind every father figure … Now that God was a single person, man's relations to him could recover the intimacy and intensity of the child's relation to the father.[4]

Whatever the details, the basic idea is that, urged by our hopes, doubts and anxieties, we take our awareness of our own mental lives, and of our understanding of human interactions and behaviour, and project that onto the world itself in the form of an all-powerful being (or somewhat less than all-powerful, but still very powerful, beings). Within this basic schema we can discern two projectivist projects, one

---

[2]    Ibid., p. 57.

[3]    Sigmund Freud, *The Future of an Illusion*, trans. W.D. Robson-Scott (London: Hogarth, 1928), pp. 28–9.

[4]    Ibid., pp. 33–4.

concerning belief systems, and the other concerning phenomenology. *Projectivism about theistic belief* says that the origin of our belief in God lies in our desire to make the world intelligible and less alien, and what we project onto the world are the personal attributes that we use to explain human behaviour. Theism as a belief system has its origin in human nature: it is an expression of our hopes, desires and fears, a story we tell because we need to find our world intelligible, and so on. *Projectivism about theistic experience* says that religious experience, and more specifically experience as-of a divine being, has its origin in our own emotional states, which we project onto the world (feelings of love, in particular) and so do not merely interpret what we perceive as signs of a divine being, but have what appears to be a non-inferential perceptual experience of a divine being. What appears to be *perception* is, in fact, *projection*. The remarks of Hume and Freud quoted above have to do mainly with projectivism about belief. My concern in this chapter is with projectivism concerning experience. Clearly, however, the two projects are intimately related.

*Is* God a projection? That's an interesting, indeed a vital question, but it is not the one I want to ask. Instead, I want to ask, if we – for the sake of argument – grant that experience as-of God does indeed involve projection of our feelings, what follows?

I want to examine three suggestions concerning the possible threat that projectivism might be thought to pose to realism about God – the view that is, that there does, entirely independently of human thought and language, exist a transcendent divine being:

*First*, that the projectivist account is inconsistent with realism;

*Second*, that, if it is not actually inconsistent with realism, projectivism nevertheless renders theism redundant as an explanation of our religious experience;

And *third*, that, even if it does not render theism redundant, projectivism nevertheless undermines a vital part of the realist view (at least, as traditionally understood): that we can engage in singular thought about God.

We will look at each of these in turn.

## The Threat of Inconsistency

First, then, the suggestion that a projectivist account of religious experience is inconsistent with realism. It is certainly true that when a projectivist account is proposed for a certain property, it is often put forward in opposition to realism. Projectivist accounts have been proposed concerning a very wide range of properties: moral values, aesthetic values, secondary properties, causal necessity relations, the 'tensed' properties of pastness, presentness and futurity and so on. What is almost invariably the point of such projectivist accounts is to offer an alternative view of the world to the one proposed by the realist about such properties. Take, for example, the case of moral values. Realism takes it to be an objective, mind-independent matter that such-and-such an act is wrong, or good, and that these are properties we are able to perceive (in perhaps an extended sense of 'perceive'). Projectivism about moral value, as it is often presented, says that acts in themselves, considered independently of our perspective on them, have no moral properties, only natural ones, but perceiving these natural properties evokes certain emotions in us – emotions of approval, admiration or disgust – and the evaluations these feelings prompt are then projected onto the acts.[5] Projectivists may boost their case by drawing attention to the peculiar nature of objective moral values – how would we come to be aware of them? By some special faculty of moral intuition? This kind of objection is known as 'the argument from queerness'.[6]

If, however, we take realism and projectivism to be at odds with each other, then our view of the world will be a rather austere one, given how widespread projection seems to be. Consider projectivism about secondary qualities. Locke reflected a long tradition in philosophy when he distinguished between the primary qualities of things (shape, size, number, motion) and the secondary qualities (colour, taste, sound, heat and cold). Primary qualities are in the objects, and they resemble the ideas we have of them. Secondary qualities, says Locke, are nothing in things themselves but powers to affect us in certain ways. The effects objects have on us (the sensation of colour, taste or heat) are, he seems to be suggesting, projected onto objects: whatever in the objects is causing those sensations does not resemble our ideas of them. If this is, effectively, a rejection of realism over secondary qualities, then the world is a purely geometric place. As Arthur Eddington puts it in what is presumably intended as ironic terms:

> … bodies are perceived as with qualities which in reality do not belong to them, qualities which are in fact purely the offspring of the mind. Thus nature gets the credit for what should in truth be reserved for ourselves: the rose for its scent: the nightingale for its song: and the sun for its radiance. The poets are entirely mistaken. They should address their lyrics to themselves and turn them into odes of self-congratulation on the excellency of the human mind. Nature is a dull affair, soundless, scentless, colourless; merely the hurrying of material, endlessly, meaninglessly.[7]

---

[5]    See, for example, Simon Blackburn, *Spreading the Word: Groundings in the Philosophy of Language* (Oxford: Clarendon Press, 1984), chapters 5 and 6.

[6]    J.L. Mackie, *Ethics: Inventing Right and Wrong* (Harmondsworth: Penguin, 1977), chapter 1.

[7]    Arthur Eddington, *Science and the Modern World* (Cambridge: Cambridge University Press, 1926), chapter 3.

But projectivist accounts need not be inconsistent with realism. Consider depth. Variation in two dimensions can be represented by an exactly corresponding variation across the retina. The third dimension cannot be represented directly like this. We therefore have to rely on indirect methods: binocular vision, in which depth is indicated by small discrepancies between the retinal images; perspective, in which depth is indicated by diminishing apparent size; and other cues, such as shading, together with background assumptions about the likely shapes of things. Depth, it seems, is not something that is given directly in experience, but is a result of active interpretation by the mind of the various cues the two-dimensional retinal images offer. Depth, in other words, is projected. But accepting the psychological explanation of depth perception does not make us non-realists about depth. Why? Because a real third dimension explains aspects of the phenomenal third dimension. It would even explain certain observations if our experience were restricted to two dimensions. Consider this vignette from E.A. Abbot's 'romance of many dimensions' *Flatland* (Flatland, of course, is a country of two-dimensional shapes moving about on a flat region): A stranger arrives in Flatland. He appears to the inhabitants as a circle, but has a strange story to tell of being what he calls 'a solid'. To demonstrate this, he proposes to 'rise' through Flatland. The circle gets smaller, gradually diminishes until it becomes a dot, and then disappears. A little later, he reappears, and the circle expands to its former size. What explains this strange phenomenon? The stranger is, of course, a sphere which has passed through Flatland vertically! This is a simpler explanation than the one which takes him to be a two-dimensional shape because, although it involves the third dimension, it allows greater real stability in the object observed. Realism about the third dimension can explain experience in two.

There is, then, no formal inconsistency between the projectivist story and realism. That much is allowed by both Hume and Freud. As Freud remarks, improbable things can happen. The young girl dreams of being carried off by the handsome prince. And, once in a blue moon, it happens. Freud describes religions as illusions, not because they are false, but because their causal origins in our own nature float free of the conditions under which they would be true. They are a form of wish fulfilment, though that may not be all they are.

The projectivist stories we have encountered so far tend to fall into three types, associated with different attitudes towards realism, illustrated by the following cases:

*Depth*: depth perception involves projection, but it is also sensitivity to real depth in the world.

*Colour*: colour perception involves both projection and sensitivity to a genuine feature of the world, but that feature is not colour.

*Value*: the natural properties of acts (giving to charity, the deliberate taking of human life) invoke feelings in us, giving rise to evaluations which are projected onto the acts and described in moral terms (good, wrong).

The more of ourselves goes into the awareness of the property in question, the more, reflecting on this, we want to depart from realism. So is the projectivist story concerning theistic experience more like that concerning value (and so distinctly non-realist), or more like that concerning depth? It depends on what explanatory function is left for a transcendent being to fill. If the causal story concerning religious experiences does not include their veracity – their sensitivity to objective reality – then their truth is redundant: it is not required to explain the experience itself. That takes us to the second projectivist challenge to realism, to which we now turn.

## The Threat of Redundancy

Perhaps there are independent reasons for theological realism, ones which have nothing directly to do with experience, but we might ask whether there is a gap in the projectivist account, an anomaly that might make us look beyond it. What I want to suggest is that religious experiences are, in one respect, anomalous: they exhibit a feature not found in other putative cases of projection, and so should make the projectivist wonder whether there might be something outside the mind that is making a contribution.

How should we characterise a religious experience? Let's content ourselves with conditions which would be sufficient for such a label, rather than necessary and sufficient, because we might think of 'religious experience' as a family resemblance concept. Well, then, suppose we imagine a state of strong emotion, of intense joy or deep peacefulness, that intimates, or at least seems to intimate, something beyond our concrete situation. It might come about as a result of contemplating something in that situation (a particularly beautiful landscape, a piece of music), but its object is something beyond that situation, something personal in nature. I think that would count as a religious experience (and here we are not requiring that such an experience be wholly veridical in order to deserve the label 'religious'). It will help, I think, if we have before us some reports of religious experiences. What follows are three reports. The first two are quoted in William James's *Varieties of Religious Experience,* and the third appears in a more recent study, Timothy Beardsworth's *A Sense of Presence.* All three are cited in William Alston's *Perceiving God* as representative of the phenomenon of religious experience.

> All at once I ... felt the presence of God ... as if his goodness and his power were penetrating me altogether ... I think it well to add that in this ecstasy of mind God had neither form, colour, odour, nor taste; moreover that the feeling of his presence was accompanied by no determinate localization.[8]

---

[8]   William James, *The Varieties of Religious Experience: A Study in Human Nature* (London: Longmans, Green and Co., 1904), pp. 67–8.

> ... the Holy Spirit descended upon me in a manner that seemed to go through me, body and soul. I could feel the impression, like a wave of electricity, going through and through me. Indeed, it seemed to come in waves and waves of liquid love.[9]

> I was seized with a violent trembling, but had no fear. I knew that what I felt was great awe. This was followed by a sense of overwhelming love coming to me, and going out from me.[10]

What features do these reports exhibit? First, they are perceptual, or quasi-perceptual: they appear to be direct presentations of some external state of affairs. Second, they are emotional, quite markedly so. Third (and this is the curious feature), the emotional state is experienced as a perceptual, or quasi-perceptual state: the feeling of love is at one and the same time an awareness of an external love. What will the projectivist make of this? At first sight, there seems no difficulty in formulating a projectivist account: the emotional states of the subjects are projected onto something external (the something in question not being already given in perception, but posited by the subject) in such a way as to give rise to the quasi-perceptual impression of a corresponding external emotional state. Just how complete this is as an explanation will become apparent when we come to look at the features of other cases of projection.

The first case concerns what Locke called the secondary qualities, for example of colour, taste, warmth and cold. Locke suggests that secondary qualities are really powers in objects to produce certain sensations in us, but that, as we ordinarily conceive of them, colour and taste, and the like are not in the objects, for what is really responsible for their effects are the primary qualities: that is, the geometrical properties of size, shape, arrangement and motion of the minute parts of the objects. To persuade us of this, he draws the following comparison:

> ... he, that will consider, that *the same Fire*, that at one distance produces in us the Sensation of *Warmth*, does at a nearer approach, produce in us the far different Sensation of *Pain*, ought to bethink himself, what Reason he has to say, That his *Idea of Warmth*, which was produced in him by the Fire, is actually *in the Fire*; and his *Idea of Pain*, which the same Fire produced in him the same way, is *not* in the Fire. Why is Whiteness and Coldness in Snow, and Pain not, when it produces the one and the other *Idea* in us; and can do neither, but by the Bulk, Figure, Number and Motion of its solid Parts?[11]

---

[9]   Ibid., p. 250.

[10]   Timothy Beardsworth, *A Sense of Presence* (The Religious Experience Research Unit, 1977), p. 30.

[11]   John Locke, *An Essay Concerning Human Understanding*, ed. Peter H. Nidditch (Oxford: Clarendon Press, 1975), II. viii. 16.

Another example:

> A piece of *Manna* of a sensible Bulk, is able to produce in us the *Idea* of a round or square Figure; and, by being removed from one place to another, the *Idea* of Motion ... And this, both *Motion and Figure are really in the Manna*, whether we take notice of them or no: This every Body is ready to agree to. Besides, *Manna* by the Bulk, Figure, Texture, and Motion of its Parts, has a Power to produce the Sensations of Sickness, and sometimes of acute Pains, or Gripings in us. That these *Ideas of Sickness and Pain are not in the* Manna, but Effects of its Operations on us, and are no where when we feel them not: This also every one readily agrees to. And yet Men are hardly to be brought to think, that *Sweetness and Whiteness are not really in the Manna*; which are but the effects of the operations of the *Manna*, by the motion, size, and figure of its Particles on the Eyes and Palate ...[12]

We should therefore concede the point, and confess that whereas we do have good reason to ascribe size and motion to the object, we do not have any more good reason to ascribe colour, warmth and taste to it than we would pain and sickness. That is the conclusion, but we are still left with a psychological problem of explaining our natural tendency before reason (or science) gets hold of us. Locke is aware of this puzzle:

> ... why the Pain and Sickness, *Ideas* that are the effects of *Manna*, should be thought to be no-where, when they are not felt; and yet the Sweetness and Whiteness, effects of the same *Manna* on other parts of the Body, by ways equally as unknown, should be thought to exist in the *Manna*, when they are not seen nor tasted, would need some reason to explain.[13]

But he does not offer an explanation. To put the puzzle in a nutshell: we project colour, warmth, cold and taste; we do not project pain and sickness. We say 'the fire is hot'; we don't say 'the fire is in pain'. Why? We might say that we can't make sense of the idea of the pain being in the fire, or sickness in the food, because these are purely qualitative states; they are non-intentional: that is, they are not object-directed, they aren't *about* anything. We don't say 'I have a pain *of* this fire'. Colour sensation, however, is intentional: one sees a coloured object. But this doesn't look so much an explanation as another way of noting the asymmetry that Locke is drawing attention to.

Why, then, do we project when we do? The most appropriate explanation here is a teleological one: we project precisely when there is a point to our doing so. Projecting the heat onto the fire will help us avoid it; projecting the pain onto the fire would have no such purpose. Similarly, projecting colours onto external

---

12	Ibid., II. viii. 18.
13	Ibid.

objects assists us in spatial orientation, since colours provide a ready means of recognising different objects. But projecting pain onto external objects would not assist us in spatial orientation. However, we *do* project pain onto parts of the body. Although pain is plausibly identified with a brain state, the pains are experienced as occurring in the part of the body which is injured or affected. Again, there is a teleological explanation for this: projecting the pain onto the relevant part of the body directs our attention to the part that needs to be attended to.

We can, perhaps, imagine circumstances in which there was a systematic connection between pain and spatial orientation. Anthony Quinton considers such a case, and what might be the result:

> ... suppose ... that everyone whose body is in a certain region of space during a certain period of time feels a pain of much the same sort, that the intensity of this pain uniformly diminishes as they move away from a determinable point in the region, and that it disappears altogether when they are at a certain distance, roughly agreed upon by all, beyond this central point ... we might well cease to think of pains, as we do now, as being private and might come to accord them much the same status as we now give to material things. 'Look out', we might say to a man walking in a certain direction, 'there's a pain there'.[14]

But of course, this is *not* how things actually are.

Reflecting on these considerations, and the difference between secondary qualities on the one hand and pain and nausea on the other, we might suppose emotions to be like pains: that is, as something not usefully projected onto the external world. But are there cases of such projection? Consider again the projection of moral values. Here, emotions are an integral part of the story, but it is not the emotions themselves, the feelings of disgust or admiration, that are projected, but rather the evaluations that those emotions evoke, so that the act contemplated is perceived as either good or bad. Perhaps, then, the projection of aesthetic values would provide a more promising model. In aesthetic experience, we see, or hear or otherwise perceive some external object or event. That then evokes a certain qualitative state in us, of pleasure, for instance. As a result of that qualitative state, we are led to value the object or event, and that evaluation (that it is good, or bad), is then projected onto the external object.

Similarly, in religious experience, the world evokes a certain emotional response in us that then leads to a certain image of a divine presence, which is then projected onto the external situation. Why are we led to do this? For the reasons that Hume and Freud (and cognitive scientists of religion) give: that we have a tendency to clothe the unknown with the familiar.

---

[14]   Anthony Quinton, 'Spaces and Times' in *Philosophy* 37 (1962), pp. 130–47; reprinted in Robin Le Poidevin and Murray MacBeath, *The Philosophy of Time* (Oxford: Oxford University Press, 1993, pp. 203–30), p. 213.

But that doesn't quite capture the phenomenon I'm trying to articulate. Perhaps we can approach it by looking at the disanalogies between aesthetic and religious experience, considered as projections. In the account just given of aesthetic experience, we perceive an external object (the sunset, the waterfall, the painting), it evokes a certain feeling in us, and the evaluation that feeling prompts is then projected as a property of the object perceived. In religious experience, the object of that experience (the divine) is not perceived, but is itself projected. And part of the projection is the projection of the feeling that we have – the sense of joy, as it might be. The feeling itself is projected. We have the sense of joy, and that is presented as a perception of a corresponding joy – a divine joy – outside us.

We can perhaps close the gap between the aesthetic and the religious experience by thinking of the divine not as an object, but as a way of experiencing the world, so then the projection is onto something already given in perceptual experience. But that still leaves the projection of the feeling itself, a qualitative state that is not the kind of thing that is ordinarily projected, anymore than pain is ordinarily projected onto the external world. We have, in other worlds, an anomaly. As we might put it, it's the *wrong kind of projection*.

Are there any other cases in which emotional states are projected onto the world? There is, of course, poetic exploitation of the pathetic fallacy, as in this passage from Shelley:

> ... Thou
> For whose path the Atlantic's level powers
> Cleave themselves into chasms, while far below
> The sea-blooms and the oozy woods which wear
> The sapless foliage of the ocean, know
> Thy voice, and suddenly grow grey with fear,
> And tremble and despoil themselves: O hear![15]

But here the projection of emotion is intended as purely metaphorical. It is not as if one feels fear, and then projects that very fear onto the ocean flora.

A case whose structure seems rather closer to the one we discern in religious experience is provided by what is known as Freudian projection. Unable to tolerate the idea of being in a certain frame of mind, I project my state of mind onto someone else: love, loathing, distrust. Here there is the correspondence we are looking for between one's own emotional state and the one that is externally projected. But still, this is less the direct perception of another's emotion than an inferential belief in it, which then affects one's experience. The projectivist account of the belief will therefore have explanatory priority over the projectivist account of experience.

---

[15]	Percy Bysshe Shelley, 'Ode to the West Wind'.

Religious experience, then, does not seem precisely to match the other cases of projection we have considered. What inferences might be drawn from that? One is simply that religious experience is *sui generis*. It is different from other kinds of projection, but then we should not expect all forms of projection to follow precisely the same structure, as the disanalogies between pain and secondary quality perception illustrate. However, in those cases, we could discern a teleological explanation for the difference. When we come to a teleological explanation for the anomalous nature of religious experience, it is hard to find one that does not make reference, at some point, to a mind-independent being. There is, at least, then reason to resist the suggestion that projectivism makes theism completely redundant as an explanation of religious experience.

## The Problem of Singular Thought

Let me turn finally, and rather more briefly, to the third possible consequence of projectivism. Even if, as I have just suggested, projectivism and realism can sit side by side, there is the worry that projectivism undermines a key element in the realist conception of God: that we are able to have thoughts about him. And here we do not simply mean thoughts about divinity in general, but thoughts about *God himself*. 'Singular thought', as philosophers call it.

Baby Bear looks at his porridge bowl, and says '*Someone* has been eating my porridge'. He does not yet know who it is, so as yet he can only frame the general thought 'there exists someone, possibly with an accomplice, who, in the last hour, has consumed my porridge'. He then goes upstairs, and finds Goldilocks upstairs in his bed. He then thinks '*this individual here* consumed my porridge, in all probability'. His thought has shifted from a general one about 'someone', to a singular thought about *this* person.

What enables us to have singular thoughts about objects? One of two conditions has to be met. The first condition is that we have in mind a uniquely identifying description of the object: 'The person who, at 4.31pm on the 1st March, 1885, entered the lodgings of Mr T. Edgar Sneedwell, and, pausing only to adjust his bow-tie in the mirror in the hallway, removed the third volume of Gibbon's *Decline and Fall* from Mr Sneedwell's library'. That, if it identifies anyone, is likely to be a uniquely identifying description, one that applies to just one person. By holding that description in your mind, you can have thoughts about that particular individual, and only them.

But, as Saul Kripke pointed out in *Naming and Necessity*,[16] this is not the situation we are in for many, if not most, historical characters that we nevertheless succeed in referring to. We may have heard of the Anglo-Saxon King Edgar, for instance. But have we a uniquely identifying description in our minds? When did he reign, exactly? What did he do? And was there only one of them, or two? Our

---

16    Saul Kripke, *Naming and Necessity* (Oxford: Blackwell, 1981).

ability to say much about any given character from the past may be very limited indeed. What we rely on in these cases is a causal link between our use of a name and that historical character.

It is this causal chain which is the basis of one kind of singular thought: perception. What it is to see that very tree is for my visual system to be affected by it, rather than something else.

But a causal chain is not sufficient to guarantee singular thought. It has to be of the right kind. Consider the following rather improbable story, due to Christopher Peacocke:

> Consider … a man who, with his eyes open but under the influence of a hallucinogen, is surrounded by redwood trees that produce a scent that causes him to have a vivid visual image of redwood trees which happens precisely to match his surroundings.[17]

This is an example of what is known in the trade as a *deviant causal chain*. Although the man in Peacocke's example is having a visual image, the image is of redwood trees, *and* that image is caused by the presence of redwood trees in the vicinity, he does not perceive those very trees. The causal chain is not of the right kind: it has a 'kink' in it. We can construct less *outré* examples. Let's say that sometime in your childhood you met the Duke of Windsor. You subsequently forgot all about the occasion, but are told about it repeatedly by your parents. You know from their testimony that you met the Duke, and by some strange mental alchemy this propositional knowledge is transmuted into what appears exactly like an episodic memory: it now seems to you not only that you met the Duke of Windsor, but that you remember meeting him. Here again we have a causal connection between event and current memory-like state, but it is not a genuine episodic memory, and the false memory does not count as a singular thought about that very occasion.

Now, on a combined projectivist/realist account of religious experience (that images of the divine are projected, but there is also a divine reality that has some causal role to play in our propensity to project), the causal chain that links us to God is similarly deviant. So although we may be able to think thoughts about an individual who has certain divine properties, we cannot think singular thoughts about God. The alternative method for guaranteeing singular thought, that we have a uniquely identifying description in our minds, is not one the projectivist is in a good position to appeal to. The image that we project says more about us than about the reality it is intended to grasp. (And the enormous gap between our ways of thinking about God and the reality of God is, of course, a traditional feature of realist thought.)

---

[17]    Christopher Peacocke, *Holistic Explanation: Action, Space, Interpretation* (Oxford: Clarendon Press, 1979), p. 55.

How damaging is this to theistic realism? It may be thought that if we cannot even have singular thought about God, we cannot enter into the kind of relationship with him that the realist wants to make room for.

However, our capacity to engage in genuinely singular thought in everyday life may be much exaggerated. If we cannot form singular thoughts about God, are we in any better position with regard to the familiar objects or our immediate vicinity? Consider this chair. I seem to see it, to be able to point to it, to refer to it and think about it. But what is it, really? A cloud of atoms, or rather sub-atomic particles, all whizzing around, and some of which, on the boundaries of the chair, are swapping places with the air around. 'This chair', apparently the paradigm of singular reference, doesn't actually pick out a single object: the boundaries of the chair are vague. What we have is a series of overlapping clouds of particles, none of which is determinately the reference of 'This chair', and that series is constantly changing, so even if we were to pick out a determinate cloud at one time, it would have to be quite different cloud being picked out at another. *The chair*, as a single, determinate stable object that remains in existence for a significant period of time is a projection. But that doesn't stop me engaging with it in the ways I need to, for example by sitting on it.

If we cannot have singular thoughts about the real objects in our environment, is it such a disaster for realism that we cannot have singular thoughts about God? Just as our thoughts about 'the chair' are made true, or approximately true, by the behaviour of certain clouds of sub-atomic particles, even though our thoughts are not *about* those particles, so our thoughts about God could be made true, or approximately true, by the ineffable nature of some transcendent being.

**Conclusion**

There is, I think, room for a combination of projectivism and realism when it comes to religious experience. Instead of thinking of the projectivist story as all there is to say, we can incorporate it into a larger picture, one that contains realist elements. Just this combination of realism and projectivism can be found in Locke's representative realist account of perception: the immediate objects of our perceptions are our ideas, but there is a world beyond that these ideas represent. In the case of secondary qualities, we project properties onto objects. But these projections are causally related to real properties in the objects – it's just that those real properties are rather different from our representations.

Similarly, in the case of religious experience, the world is a screen onto which we project divine images. But it is a translucent screen, so that our projected images are, to borrow a phrase from C.S. Lewis's words from his autobiographical *Surprised by Joy*, 'lit by a light beyond the world'.[18]

---

[18]   C.S. Lewis, *Surprised by Joy: The Shape of My Early Life* (London: G. Bles, 1955), p. 189.

That representative realist account of religious experience is not merely a consistent story. If we are struck by what I have suggested is the anomalous nature of religious experience, its failure to be subsumed within the already available projectivist models, then we will see a point to it. There is a piece missing in the pure projectivist account, one which realism can provide. Undoubtedly, representative realism puts something of a gap between perception and reality. But what we know about the psychology of perception and the nature of the physical world should already incline us to concede the existence of that gap. In suggesting that we do not have singular thought about the objects of the world – including, perhaps, a transcendent being – I am simply proposing that that gap is a little wider than we ordinarily, even in our more philosophical moments, suppose.

# Chapter 12

# God, Reason and Extraterrestrials

Stephen R. L. Clark

## Alone in the Universe

One recurrent modern myth, alongside such perennials as that medieval peoples thought the earth was flat, and had views about how many angels could dance on the point of a pin, is that our ancestors lived in an enclosed and cosy universe, conformable to the human scale.[1] The gradual progress of astronomy revealed – it is supposed – that we lived amid immensities beyond our imagination, that the earth was a tiny dot with no distinguishable features in a cosmos vaster and older than we imagined. Old-style religion, it is routinely argued, is now incredible: how could we be of any interest to a cosmic engineer (even if there were one)? How could we imagine that stars and galaxies far away existed for any good that they might do for us? How could this planet be the moral or metaphysical centre of the universe, when it was so far from being physically central, or this age of the world be special when it is no more than a moment? 'Can the Earth be thus the centre of the moral and religious universe, when it has been shewn to have no claim to be the centre of the physical universe?'[2]

In fact, of course, this story is almost entirely mythical. Amongst the most influential texts of medieval Europe was the *Dream of Scipio* (first century BC), in which the eponymous hero learns his place. On his ascent through the planetary spheres, 'stars were visible which we never see from this region, and all were of a magnitude far greater than we had imagined ... From here the earth appeared so small that I was ashamed of our empire which is, so to speak, but a point on its surface'.[3] So also Boethius (fifth century AD):

> It is well known, and you have seen it demonstrated by astronomers, that beside the extent of the heavens, the circumference of the earth has the size of a point;

---

[1]    On these and other myths, see Ronald L. Numbers (ed.), *Galileo Goes to Jail and Other Myths About Science and Religion* (Cambridge, MA: Harvard University Press, 2009).

[2]    William Whewell, *Of the Plurality of Worlds*, ed. Michael Ruse (Chicago: University of Chicago Press, 2001; first published as *Of the Plurality of Worlds: An essay* (John W. Parker: London, 1853), p. 19. Whewell is here summarizing the problem, not endorsing the conclusion.

[3]    Macrobius, *Commentary on the Dream of Scipio*, ed. William H. Stahl (New York: Columbia University Press, 1952), p. 72 (Cicero Republic 6.3).

that is to say, compared with the magnitude of the celestial sphere, it may be thought as having no extent at all.[4]

And God, being infinite and eternal, transcends even the largest universe (which is why, to Him, a sparrow is no smaller than a supercluster, and quasars no more powerful than a single quark). Similarly, all the ages of the created universe are no more significant, in God, than a passing second: however long we, our civilization, our species or our cosmos lasts it is no more than an instant in the eyes of God; and however small and transient a moment, God is present there. Or rather, God is the Place where all things are present.[5]

Nor did our ancestors find it difficult to imagine that there were other peoples who seemed far away from us, but no further away from God, and with as good a claim on God as we. Indeed, this seems to have been as popular a theme in the medieval world as the modern. The land outside our city walls was populated by wild men, dwarves and dragons, and men whose heads do grow beneath their shoulders (which is perhaps to say, Antipodeans). As late as the nineteenth century Richard Owen, the palaeontologist who identified the class of dinosaurs, was convinced that there must be thinking beings on Jupiter so that the sight of the Jovian moons could be enjoyed. Whewell argued against the thesis, remarking that we had no reason to think that God required His work to be admired, close up, by finite, mortal intelligence, and that we did not know what other purposes He might have in scattering the stars and rocks so widely.[6]

Whewell was not alone in doubting a plurality of inhabited worlds. Augustine had similarly questioned the earlier belief in Antipodeans.[7] Like Whewell, he observed that we had no direct empirical evidence that there were human inhabitants, or even land, on the other side of the globe, and must find it incredible that anyone from this side had ever taken ship to populate whatever lands there were. He also insisted that even the most monstrous seeming births, as well as any tribes which all had the same apparent oddities as were occasionally attested (fewer fingers or two heads), must be descended from Adam, and our kin: all humanity was of one lineage – a doctrine that was also of use rather later, in rejecting racist attempts to portray 'Hottentots' or other 'Native Peoples' as aliens.[8] The motive was a good one, but we may by now be rather less insistent that only our biological kin deserve respect.

---

[4]	*Boethius Consolation of Philosophy*, trans. V.E. Watts (Harmondsworth: Penguin, 1969), p. 73 (Book 2, chapter 7).

[5]	'Why is God called "the Place" (hamaqom)? Because the universe is located in Him, not He in the universe': [Midrash] Genesis R.68, cited by Hyam Maccoby, *The Philosophy of the Talmud* (London: Routledge, 2002), p. 24.

[6]	Whewell, *Of the Plurality of Worlds*, pp. 183–4.

[7]	Augustine, *City of God*, trans. Henry Bettenson (Harmondsworth: Penguin, 2003), p. 664 (16.9).

[8]	See Philip Almond 'Adam, Pre-Adamites, and Extra-Terrestrial Beings in Early Modern Europe', in *Journal of Religious History*, 30/2 (2006), pp. 163–74: 'Thus, for

## The Neglected Experiment

Owen's reasoning was not ridiculous – or at any rate it was not unfamiliar. If the world is made to be enjoyed and contemplated by such beings as we think ourselves, and if it stretches immensely further than we ourselves can ever hope to see, it must be that there are other beings Out There, of different ancestries and physiologies, who are still thinking beings like us: *hnau*, in C.S.Lewis's imagined language.[9] If we understand the physical world, so can those distant *hnau*. In Alexander Winchell's words (in 1883):

> We have neighbours; they live beyond impassable barriers, but they gaze on the same galaxy, and we know they are endowed with certain faculties which establish a community between them and us. However conformed bodily, whatever their modes and means of organic activity, we know that they reason as we reason, and interpret the universe on the same principles of logic and mathematics as ourselves. The orbits which their planetary homes describe are ellipses; they have studied the same celestial geometry as ourselves; they have written their treatises on celestial mechanics; they have felt the impact of the luminous weave of ether; they have speculated on the nature of matter and energy; they have interpreted the order of the cosmical mechanism as the expression of thought and purpose; they have placed themselves in communion with the Supreme Thinker who is so near to all of us that his voice is audible alike to the ear of reason in all the worlds.[10]

Even atheistical naturalists nowadays often expect the same – though they may doubt that those other creatures will be theists, or share our merely 'moral' values. My own suspicion is that if they have never been theists they will also not, as it were, be *rationalists* either: they will have no reason to suppose – no logical reason and no natural impulse – that the little effusion of their brains or quasi-brains that they call 'thought' could be a model for the universe! Nor need they feel any moral obligation to find out the truth of things, beyond whatever seems immediately useful. Intelligence, as an evolutionary adaptation, is never likely – on naturalistic terms – to be more than a guide to getting food, and mates, and

---

example, in 1625, the philosopher Nathanael Carpenter in his Geography maintained that Moses' motivation, in writing his genealogical lists was so that all people would understand themselves to be descended from the same original "than which there is no greater meanes to conciliate and ioyne mens affections for mutuall amitie and conversation." (Nathanael Carpenter, *Geography Delineated Forth in Two Books* (Oxford, 1625), 2:207)' (pp. 168f).

   [9]   The term is taken from his interplanetary trilogy, beginning with *Out of the Silent Planet* (London: Bodley Head, 1938).

   [10]  Alexander Winchell, *World Life or Comparative Geology* (Chicago, 1883), pp. 507–8, quoted by Karl S. Guthke, *The Last Frontier: Imagining Other Worlds from the Copernican Revolution to Modern Science Fiction*, trans. Helen Atkins (Ithaca: Cornell University Press, 1990), p. 344.

avoiding being food for long enough to reproduce! Each sort of creature has its own *Umwelt*, constructed from a range of markers that may be invisible to any other kind.[11] These, for any social species, will include social markers, and much of our activity will be directed, in the first place, to keeping a place in our social group – but this is to say that our intelligence, where it is more than 'practical', is concerned with gossip and make-believe![12] This may make us curious, but nothing in nature suggests that our curiosity will be satisfied. On the contrary, our curiosity may kill us! What the Real World beyond all little worlds may be we have no good reason to expect to know – unless we have good reason to believe that we also carry something of the divine in us, that Real Reason is at least an image of the one creative intelligence that makes and sustains the world. It is because we still believe or half believe that human beings are 'special' by comparison with more limited living things, and that there is some overriding reason for our existence, that we can so easily imagine that there will be other sort-of-human beings elsewhere: human in the sense defined by Winchell.

I have in the past suggested, therefore, that if we ever do have empirical reason to believe that there are *hnau* Out There, we shall have an extra reason to believe that more is going on in us than evolutionary theory can explain. Without that gloss, we can no more expect to discover *hnau* (or other *hnau* – more probably – to discover us) than to find that the Great Galactics (so to speak) are native English speakers. If we found that they were, the obvious explanation would be that English speakers had already influenced the Galaxy (and perhaps Poul Anderson was more or less correct in imagining his High Crusade), not that God was an Englishman or that the English language was, somehow, the endpoint of linguistic evolution.[13] Most biologists – though there are exceptions such as Simon Conway Morris[14] – would suspect a similar influence if we found that the Galactics were *physically* like us. Maybe the Great Galactics – the first and only naturally occurring *hnau* to emerge on a wider scene – have seeded their spores everywhere, both to begin the

---

[11]    J. von Uexkuell, *Theoretical Biology*, trans. D.L. Mackinnon (London: Kegan Paul, 1926); and 'A stroll through the worlds of animals and men' in C.H. Schiller (ed.), *Instinctive Behavior* (New York: International University Press, 1957), pp. 5–80·

[12]    See Robin Dunbar, *Grooming, Gossip and the Evolution of Language* (London: Faber, 1996).

[13]    Poul Anderson, *The High Crusade* (New York: Doubleday 1960): a medieval English village is kidnapped by an alien scout ship, and almost accidentally takes over from the decadent rulers of the Galactic Empire. Centuries later terrestrial explorers are disconcerted to discover that the Galaxy is ruled – rather well - by the heirs of a feudal baron, and the Roman Church.

[14]    Simon Conway Morris, *Life's Solution: Inevitable Humans in a Lonely Universe* (Cambridge: Cambridge University Press, 2003). Morris' arguments for the convenience of the human form are good ones, but perhaps not fully convincing. Even in terrestrial history there are many life-forms built on entirely different templates which we would be rash to underestimate.

processes of evolution on any available world, and to guide it towards their goal (to have talkative companions, maybe, or convenient slaves). If *we* are the very first *hnau* we might someday do this ourselves. But given the enormous difficulty of this interstellar project – far harder even than Augustine thought the trip to the antipodes – it would be likelier that there was some *metaphysical* reason rather than an historical for a mental or spiritual identity. The First Cause, we should say, is not a distant, accidental agent, but one present at all times and places. There may come a moment in any evolutionary story when creatures of whatever lineage begin to get messages, as it were, from the Real World, from God – who can, we are assured, raise children up from stones.[15]

Modernists usually insist that there is a radical division between Reason and Inspiration. My own suspicion is that there really isn't: what seems suddenly obvious may be reckoned rational insight or prophetic inspiration. In either case it needs to be checked against other revelations of whatever sort. That the universe is *rational* at all – or anything that we would describe as rational – is as much a matter of faith or spiritual vision as that it rests on God. But that is not my present topic. And neither do I intend to make any further defence of my more usual theses (that is, that the discovery of alien intelligence – of a recognizably human sort – would support theism, and that the apparent success of scientific endeavour, even now, is also much more likely to be real on a theistic theory than on an atheistic).[16] Instead, I shall explore a different theme – that the creatures we find Out There may be as alien as the creatures we have already found on earth, and that 'humanity' has no more privileged status than the mind and form of any other creature. Is this bound to be atheistical in its effect?

What exactly it means to be made 'in the image of God'[17] (as the Hebrews held) or to belong to the same class of things as God or gods (as some Greek philosophers supposed) may be uncertain: perhaps the author of Genesis meant only that Adam would be God's viceroy in the world, and that everything in the end would be given into his hands. Or perhaps the claim was a larger one, and more like the pagan philosophical: that only human beings – or even only sensible or virtuous human beings – could hope to join God's fellowship. Even now we typically suppose that human beings are like God or the gods in being 'rational', in having a larger view of things than 'animals', in being able to talk about the causes of events and the reasons for their actions, in being capable of overriding their passions and weighing up advantages for themselves and others. We also suppose that human beings and gods are 'individuals', distinct from others of their kind but able to recognize themselves as individuals or 'persons' like their neighbours.

How likely is it, on either a naturalistic or a theistic basis, that we should expect that beings like that, like us, will have dominion elsewhere? How likely is

---

[15]   Matthew 3:9.

[16]   See my 'Extraterrestrial Intelligence, the Neglected Experiment', in *Foundation*, 61 (1994), pp. 50–65.

[17]   Genesis 1:26–7, 9:1–6.

it that all 'intelligent experience' will have that form? How is it, we might also ask, that *human* intelligence, of the sort I have just half sketched, has only evolved – as far as we can see – in the last few hundred thousand years of Earth's long history. If the world was waiting for 'us', why did it have to wait so long? If it is so easy to produce the – broadly – human sort that we could expect to find it Outside Over There, why haven't we found it also in the Long Ago?[18]

Adopt, for a moment, John C. Wright's definition of the human: 'any naturally self-aware self-defining entity capable of independent moral judgment is a human' (and any entities likely to become so fall in a 'special protected class' until they do).[19] There are then at least two questions. What conditions must obtain, physically and biologically and culturally, for there to be such entities, 'persons', *hnau*? And are such entities truly the central thrust of creation, the reason why God made the world (as some believers think) or even the likely outcome of the world's unguided changes?


## Thinking Beasts and Alien Moralities

The philosophical assault on anthropomorphism has a long history. So Xenophanes of Colophon (c. 570–c. 475 BC): 'If cattle and horses or lions had hands, or were able to draw with their hands and do the works that men do, horses would draw the forms of the gods like horses, and cattle like cattle'.[20] The point was never only the superficial one, that God or the gods would not *look* like human animals, but the much more radical thought that their ways, their thoughts, weren't ours. We should not make God or the gods in our image, according to our likeness. True piety is to prefer the truth to any of our easy idols.[21] This is likely to be uncomfortable: 'truth must of necessity be stranger than fiction, for fiction is the creation of the human mind, and therefore is congenial to it'.[22]

---

[18]  Strictly, of course, we don't *know* that there weren't such creatures Long Ago: maybe they surfaced many times in different geological ages, and were ground down by climate change, or meteor strike, or plague or genetic drift. But we have no *naturalistic* reason to expect this much, nor any empirical evidence.

[19]  John C. Wright, *The Phoenix Exultant* (New York: Tor Books, 2003), p.155. Wright's three-volume work, *The Golden Age*, of which this is the second part, is one of the very few SF works to offer explicit and clearly reasoned arguments about the nature of mind and morals.

[20]  G.S. Kirk, J. Raven and M. Schofield (eds), *The Presocratic_Philosophers* (Cambridge: Cambridge University Press 1983), p. 169; see also Sextus Empiricus, *Against the Mathematicians* 9.47, in A.A. Long and D.N. Sedley, *The Hellenistic Philosophers* (Cambridge: Cambridge University Press 1987), p. 143 (23F).

[21]  Aristotle, *Nicomachean Ethics* 1.1096a16, after Plato, *Republic* 10.595c.

[22]  G.K. Chesterton, *The Club of Queer Trades* (London: Darwen Finlayson Ltd, 1960; first published 1905), p. 82.

For that very reason, of course, it is rather difficult for us to imagine wholly alien intelligences Out There. Even those SF writers who don't imagine them as 'just like us' in whatever important respect must usually portray them only as different in ways already open to us. Alien empires too often turn out to be vulgar imitations of 'oriental despotisms' or feudal monarchies as they, in turn, have been imagined by Western writers. The triumphalist strand of twentieth century SF will usually suggest that 'human beings' turn out to be more versatile, more creative and more humane than the aliens, even when the latter have the longer history.[23] In either case, it is easy to imagine, SF writers are re-visioning what they take to be an Abrahamic theme: the angels must bow before Adam. Even less triumphalist writers – like Gregory Benford (writing, as he has remarked, from a perspective given by the fact that the Southern States are the only parts of the USA to have experienced absolute defeat) – conceive that humans will still have right on their side, despite being of no more weight with the rulers of the universe than commensal rodents. That image of our possible future is less vulgar than the triumphalists', but perhaps it is still too anthropic to be entirely just.

One further gloss: both Classical and Hebrew writers used to mock Egyptians for the respect they gave to 'animals', and their habit of depicting gods in animal form. Even Plutarch of Chaeronea, one of those Classical writers who was most sympathetic both to Egyptian thought and to the lives of animals, thought that Egyptian practice must lead 'the weak and innocent into "superstition" (*deisidaimonia*), and the cynical and bold into "atheistic and bestial reasoning" (*atheos kai theriodes logismos*)'.[24] Imagining gods as animals might seem to suggest that we should imitate them; imagining animals as gods might make it harder to exploit them. Mainstream Classical and Hebrew thought preferred to elevate *humanity* as our ideal. We should aim to be good *people* and might use whatever animals we pleased in this pursuit. Moderns who have abandoned, as they think, traditional religion almost always share this doctrine. Traditional moralists like Chesterton at least had metaphysical reasons for their claim: 'cruelty to animals is cruelty and a vile thing; but cruelty to a man is not cruelty, it is treason. Tyranny over a man is not tyranny, it is rebellion, for man is royal'[25] – though in other moments he might recall that the duty of kings is to care about and for their subjects, not to claim the larger portion. But it is the very claim to royalty that should now be questioned.

The Egyptians did not actually seek to imitate the animals whose forms they gave to gods, but there have been philosophical and other sects that did. What 'animals' do has sometimes been taken to show, for good or ill, what *we* should:

---

[23]   So, for example, James Blish's juveniles: *The Star Dwellers* (London: Sphere, 1961) and *Mission to the Heart Stars* (London: Granada, 1965).

[24]   Ingvild Saelid Gilhus, *Animals, Gods and Humans: Changing Attitudes to Animals in Greek, Roman and Early Christian Ideas* (Routledge: London, 2006), p. 98, after Plutarch, *On Isis and Osiris*, chapter 71.

[25]   G.K. Chesterton, *Charles Dickens* (Methuen: London, 1906), p. 197.

Cynic philosophers openly sought to live as they imagined feral dogs would live; other philosophers proposed that we might model ourselves on bees. But let us accept that we – at any rate at this stage of our line's evolution – are social primates, strongly compelled and well-advised to live in couples, families and tribes, self-governing townships and professional guilds or craft associations. But it is not obvious either that other species, even social species, will feel just those emotions, or that no other sorts of species could ever dominate their worlds or seek to expand their influence. The issue here is what we might encounter Outside Over There: creatures with very different natures but as strong a claim to God's approval as His image or His agent. God, we must presume, hates nothing that He has made: why else would He have made it?[26]

What different moralities might be founded on different physiologies, even amongst creatures of our scale and type? Might some of them be so far from 'ethical' in any sense we recognize as to offer a real alternative to what Lewis called 'the Tao', the principles which all *hnau*, he supposed, must recognize?[27] Might Darwin have been right to suggest, in the first edition of *The Descent of Man*, that 'if men were reared under precisely the same condition as hive-bees, there can hardly be any doubt that our unmarried females would, like worker bees, think it a sacred duty to kill their brothers, and mothers would strike to kill their fertile daughters, and no one would think of interfering'?[28] Henry Sidgwick's mildly witty response (cited by Darwin in later editions) that 'a superior bee would aspire to a milder solution of the population problem'[29] testifies to a common faith that a humane ethic *must* prevail among the rationally intelligent. But are we sure?[30] SF writers have sometimes seemed to suppose it *obvious* that different animal species, sharing a sort of intelligence, must be irreconcilable rivals: kindness, they suppose, must be restricted to creatures 'of our kind', and every sort of creature will be loyal only to its seed. 'Selfish Genes', we are led to believe, require that we have no other real goal than the preservation of those genes, regardless of any

---

[26]   Wisdom of Solomon 11.24. Zoroastrians supposed that there were two rival creative powers at work, and that there were therefore creatures, 'vermin', that the 'good God' hated. This has not been the usual Abrahamic theory, though it may sometimes have been the practice.

[27]   C.S. Lewis, *The Abolition of Man* (London: Bles, 1947).

[28]   Charles Darwin, *The Descent of Man* (London: John Murray, 1871), vol. 1, p. 86.

[29]   Henry Sidgwick, The Academy 15th June 1872, p. 231: see Darwin, *Descent of Man*, vol.1, p. 99. Orson Scott Card imagines this outcome in *Speaker for the Dead* (New York: Tor Books, 1986). Card's main enterprise seems to be to imagine what would have to be true, biologically and historically, to vindicate what would otherwise seem outrageously wicked behaviour (killing and abusing children; torturing people to death; installing mind-control devices in whole human populations).

[30]   See my 'Psychopathology and Alien Ethics' in Edward James and Farah Mendlesohn (eds), *The Parliament of Dreams: conferring on Babylon 5* (Reading: Science Fiction Foundation, 1998), pp.153–62.

other interests.[31] A more sensible strategy, even for those genes, would probably be to cooperate with any agreeable partner, but we may not be able – on naturalistic grounds – to exclude the possibility that the race is to the swift and ruthless.

But the moral most of us prefer is probably that only a certain sort of social animal has any hope of being 'more than animal': if we are ever to be 'rational' we must first be 'moral'; if we are to be 'moral' we must be able to recognize ourselves as agents amongst other agents, capable of keeping and breaking promises, and treating others (or not) as we would wish to be treated. That vision should be enough even on its own to encourage us to treat even other species kindly. But perhaps we need rather more than 'natural morals': being properly human, being the sort of human that has some claim to be cosmic, requires that we be able to reconsider our moralities, to know what it is like to live under judgement, and not suppose that what comes 'naturally' is always 'right', or even that what we wish for ourselves or others is the sole thing to consider. Without that sense of a universal justice, by which we might be found wanting, we can do no more than follow our natural impulses – and it is not certain that those need be what we wish. Consider, for example, C.J. Cherryh's *kif* (in the *Chanur* sequence), who function as perfect egoists, eat their own kind, acknowledge no restraint save power and feel no guilt. Cherryh too imagines that their very innocence, in a way, may make them, in the appropriate circumstances, the most reliable members of an inter-species compact. By human standards they are psychopaths – but whereas such failings in us go along with other and even more obvious faults and logical confusions, and no *human* society could be founded entirely on psychopathic principle – not even Colin Turnbull's Ik[32] – the *kif* are as coherent and capable a species as any. Or must there have been some trauma in their past, some fall into perversion – as perhaps there has been with us? 'If it be true (as it certainly is) that a man can feel exquisite happiness in skinning a cat, then the religious philosopher can only draw one of two deductions. He must either deny the existence of God, as all atheists do; or he must deny the present union between God and man, as all Christians do'.[33]

If it is true that 'there is no God', no transcendent resolution of creation's many goals, our morals will be bounded by our biology – though it does not follow that we will only care for members of our own species (in fact, after all, we mostly care much more for our 'companion animals' than we do for human strangers – and why not?). If there are genuinely rival moral codes, incommensurably and irrevocably different, then only one of them, at best or worst, can be the final answer, and we may need to consider whether it won't be ours. Greg Bear is unusual amongst SF writers in imagining, in *Eon* and *Eternity*, that it is the genocidal enemies of

---

[31]   E.O. Wilson, *On Human Nature* (Cambridge, Mass: Harvard University Press, 1978), p. 167: 'Human behavior – like the deepest capacities for emotional response which drive and guide it – is the circuitous technique by which human genetic material has been and will be kept intact. Morality has no other demonstrable function'.

[32]   See Colin Turnbull, *The Mountain People* (Cape: London, 1973).

[33]   G.K. Chesterton, *Orthodoxy* (London: Fontana 1961; first published 1908), p. 15.

humanity who will bring everything together, so that every otherwise passing good is preserved, in a way, in glory – a glory defined by them, and not by us.[34] More realistically, there will be no final answer, any more than there will ever be only one sort of creature to survive and breed. And that is itself a sort of answer: that no one individual, no one species, no one form of life will ever be sole survivor, and that every intelligent creature must acknowledge that it has limits. Wanting everything for oneself or for one's kind or lineage is absurd, whether or not we acknowledge that God rules. Can we still reasonably expect that our kind has at any rate a place, and a possible future? What E.O. Wilson has called the hodge-podge of evolutionary adaptations, mostly formed in the Neolithic, don't necessarily have any coherent sense or standard.[35] We are almost bound to be at odds with ourselves as well as with each other, in ways that older lines, in far more stable settings, would find – at least – unusual (and a signal not to trust us much). Would creatures more like birds, for example, have an easier time reconciling interests and demands between the sexes and the ages? Do 'reason' and 'morality' depend on our being particular sorts of social mammal, required to depend on a wider circle than merely that to which our passions – erotic and parental – may attach us? If it takes a village to rear a human being we must somehow have adapted to a village life. If it takes a larger, urban and electronically connected world to raise children who can run that world, we must somehow, in the future, learn to live in it. Are we sure that our inheritance is versatile enough to cope? Might there not be other lines that have already achieved stability?

## More Alien Possibilities

Can we go beyond merely *moral* difference between creatures of roughly our own scale and sensibility, and imagine creatures of a radically other sort? William Whewell spoke with some disdain of the only creatures he could believe inhabited Jupiter: 'aqueous, gelatinous creatures; too sluggish, almost, to be deemed alive, floating in their ice-cold waters, shrouded for ever by their humid skies'.[36] It was a strange comment. Even the aqueous and other creatures who float in the ice-cold waters of *our* world are often beautiful beyond belief, and no more sluggish than we (though the sea-slug *Elysia chlorotica* has a very restful life once it has incorporated photosynthetic chloroplasts from intertidal algae and need no longer eat).

What if we find that *entirely* different creatures are really dominant in other worlds than ours, and just as likely to spread their influence? What if we find that

---

[34]   Greg Bear, *Eon* (London: Gollancz, 1986); *Eternity* (London: Gollancz, 1989).

[35]   Wilson, *On Human Nature*, p.196; see my *Philosophical Futures* (Frankfurt: Peter Lang, 2011), p. 151.

[36]   Whewell, *Of the Plurality of Worlds*, pp. 185–6.

such entirely different creatures have as good a claim as ours to 'understand' the world, and have hopes of heaven? What sort of creature might these be?

Suppose that there are creatures who can communicate with each other over great distances of space and time, and organize their creative life accordingly, but have no sentiments for anyone as individuals at all. They treat individuals even of their own lineage rather more as we treat our own limbs and organs, or even as we treat more disposable, replaceable tools. They acknowledge – perhaps they can acknowledge – no common interest with us, nor do they recognize the sounds or gestures that we make as anything like their 'language'. We can postulate that they have somehow – by the same strange talent as perhaps we have and whatever accidents of history – acquainted themselves with principles that allow them to manage the raw stuff of their worlds. They don't need to construct either social artefacts or physical tools: everything they need to cooperate and grow is built into their natures. Maybe they even have interstellar travel, and maintain connections, somehow, with all their scattered colonies – though there is no need to suppose that those colonies are planet-bound. Maybe they live in the Oort Clouds of any available star, and spread by shedding spores into the solar winds. One version of the story is Wellsian: these are the Lunarians, with a biological rather than a technological solution for the division of labour. In another version their origins, conversely, are technological, but they have long since abandoned or destroyed their biological creators.[37] These are amongst the commonest of alien forms in modern SF. I cannot offer you, of course, a real-life example – but if you doubt that any creature could communicate and build across continents without recourse to any *human* understanding of their world I refer you to the case of ants:

> Researchers in Japan and Spain led by Eiriki Sunamura of the University of Tokyo found that Argentine ants [*Linepithema humile*] living in Europe, Japan and California shared a strikingly similar chemical profile of hydrocarbons on their cuticles … Whenever ants from the main European and Californian super-colonies and those from the largest colony in Japan came into contact, they acted as if they were old friends. These ants rubbed antennae with one another and never became aggressive or tried to avoid one another. In short, they acted as if they all belonged to the same colony, despite living on different continents separated by vast oceans.[38]

---

[37]     See H.G. Wells, *The First Men in the Moon* (Newnes: London, 1901); Karel Capek was perhaps the first to envisage the technological take-over, but his 'robots' are likely to become more human as they mature (see his R.U.R. (trans. P. Selver) (Oxford: Oxford University Press, 1923)).

[38]     See http://news.bbc.co.uk/earth/hi/earth_news/newsid_8127000/8127519. stm (accessed 28th November 2011), citing E. Sunamura et al., 'Intercontinental union of Argentine ants: behavioral relationships among introduced populations in Europe, North America, and Asia', *Insectes Sociaux* 56 (2009), pp. 143–7 (doi: 10.1007/s00040-009-0001-9).

Different varieties of the ants' enormously successful ancient lineage can make and employ tools, domesticate useful allies and learn short-cuts through the world. They use each other's bodies cooperatively as tools, rafts and larders. What their future holds, who knows? Is it obvious that 'humanity' must triumph, or even that it should? What would it take for ants or other such 'eusocial' creatures to begin to record their histories, and to learn from them? We can at least acknowledge that the same biologists who would be startled by the discovery of even faintly humanoid life-forms Outside, would be much less startled by the discovery of eusocial ones: eusociality, after all, has evolved on many separate occasions in terrestrial history, as termites, ants, bees, wasps and even naked mole rats. May there not be whole worlds dominated by such forms, without prurient curiosity or any conflict between the interests of 'individuals' and 'hives'? How odd would it be to suggest that the singing masons building roofs of gold are at least as good an image of the divine as are we naked apes? How odd to suppose that it is they and their descendants who will dominate the worlds? Are we sure that it would be 'wrong' to breed a line of eusocial primates?

Or consider other imaginable creatures, a further step away from these, who do more than recognize each other biochemically, and do not trouble to collect in hives or nests or classes: information of all sorts is passed between them, including genetic instructions for how to build or behave. There are no species barriers there, despite there being innumerable shapes and manners. Indeed, there are hardly even individuals, but only ever-changing, ever-evolving fashions, fissioning and coalescing according to whatever needs arise: a sea of information. If we were to encounter 'them' or 'it' our own biochemical effluescence would, no doubt, be absorbed, decoded and transformed.

Their form of life, of course, would not be ours: would they have any reason, for example, to distinguish the world of their experience from the world that contains and sustains them? According to Lovejoy,

> The primary and most universal faith of man [is] his inexpugnable realism, his twofold belief that he is on the one hand in the midst of realities which are not himself nor mere obsequious shadows of himself, a world which transcends the narrow confines of his own transient being; and on the other hand that he can himself somehow read beyond those confines and bring those external existences within the compass of his own life yet without annulment of their transcendence.[39]

That indeed is one aspect of our claim to be special: we are creatures who can imagine that there is a world larger than their experience which they can still learn

---

[39]    A.O. Lovejoy, *The Revolt against Dualism* (La Salle, Illinois: Open Court, 1960; first published 1930), p. 14. Richard Rorty reckoned this faith absurd, but has no adequate reason for the claim: R.M. Rorty, *Philosophy and the Mirror of Nature* (Oxford: Blackwell, 1980), p. 52n.

about. Do my imagined creatures offer a sort of counter? On the one hand, they are involved far more directly and immediately than ourselves in whatever is going on. Whereas it can be suggested, a little confusedly, that we never see or sense anything 'directly', but only the echo or reflection or effect engendered in our brains, my imagined creatures are not walled off from 'nature' or each other, and their experience is exact and realistic. Or rather, there is for them no distinction between reality and dreams: the information they exchange is enough to change both their worlds and the world. 'Real are the dreams of gods and smoothly pass their pleasures in a long, immortal dream'.[40] These creatures, at least, are not merely 'animal'.

Am I imagining something that simply could not be? Perhaps – but consider the bacterial population of our present earth. Multicellular life of the sort that seems most natural to us is a latecomer in terrestrial history, and microbes still outnumber and outweigh us all. We can distinguish different bacterial types, for our convenience, but notions like 'individual' or even 'species' have no real significance for the bacterial world, which exists in a ceaseless interchange of genetic and other biochemical information. Even the deeper distinction between archaebacteria and eubacteria (taxa each as distinct and distant from each other as either is from the taxon of eukaryotes – trees, mushrooms, molluscs, worms – and us) is probably not fixed. It is the bacterial population that rules our world, and may have other ideas about what to do than we do.[41] This notion has been explored by authors such as Greg Bear, in *Blood Music*, who imagines the moment when bacteria realize that they are living inside and upon immensely larger organisms which do not understand them.[42] Exobiologists suspect, with reason, that any life we ever find Out There, on Mars, or in the ocean of Europa or on exoplanets far away, is far more likely to be bacterial than ordinarily multicellular (as it was here on Earth for most terrestrial history), and we are usually rather disappointed by the news. Surely, we can't help thinking, the universe must 'want' multicellular beings like us – not just the bacterial sea, or the stromatolites that populated the early earth. But maybe we are their dreams.

These cases are all non-human in fairly familiar ways: they do not need a concept of their individual selves distinct from the wider unity, either because they are clearly cells within a massively multi-organic somewhat, or because they are not even single cells. They may be able to imagine a world that goes on without them (if the hives should perish or the microbial population suffer some lethal mutation), but 'death' as the closing of an individual eye, the end of all its projects, will probably be unknown. The first are non-human, explicitly in having

---

40     John Keats, 'Lamia' 1.127–8.

41     See Lynn Margulis and Dorion Sagan, *Microcosmos: Four Billion Years of Microbial Evolution* (New York: Summit Books, 1986).

42     Greg Bear, *Blood Music* (Westminster, Maryland: Arbor House, 1985). Orson Scott Card has also imagined a bacterial civilization in *Xenocide* (New York: Tor Books, 1991) and *Children of the Mind* (New York: Tor Books, 1996).

no common interest with such ordinarily mammalian forms as us, and no need to feel compunction about the troubles of particular creatures. The second are not even animal or plant organisms of a familiar sort, but might perhaps share some curiosity about the lumbering giants they may inhabit and control. The second especially can show us that there are no privileged *scales* in the cosmos, any more than privileged dates or locations. Neither story entirely rebuts the claim that any intelligent creatures Out There are bound to have the 'same principles of logic and mathematics as ourselves', and come to the same conclusions about the natural world, but perhaps they do suggest that this claim is a matter of faith. The claims of 'reason', so understood, may be as parochial as the claims of etiquette. Bacterial intelligence at any rate is as unlikely to start from the operations of counting and calculating that seem natural to us as it is to have an interest in soap opera. Nor does it seem necessary to suppose even that the law of non-contradiction binds that intelligence, any more than it binds a quantum computer. The very claim at the heart of 'logic', that there is one incompatible *other* significant counter to any particular proposition such that one is bound to be false and the other true, is unprovable, and may be unintelligible to bacterial intelligence.[43]

Some commentators will insist that microbes can't have 'concepts' or any imagination of the past or future (and maybe even that eusocial insects can't). One response to this may simply be that the claim misses my point. We may 'have concepts', and be able so to organize our memories and projects by the use of tokens representing them. But that may only be to say that we respond to *figments*, rather than real events. What modes of consciousness are available to other sorts of creature we don't know. A second response is rather to question the claim, on several levels. First, my scenarios do not suggest that either individual eusocial entities or microbes 'have concepts': the concepts exist, if they do, in the larger interchange of information across the nests or hives, or the global bacterial population. Information is conveyed biochemically, especially in the latter case, and the only way that we could represent it to ourselves is conceptually (which is to say, by proxy). Some of that passing information can be 'tagged' – that is, identified as less reliable or as an occasion for a sub-creative fantasy rather than feeding directly into a current fashion. It can, as it were, be quarantined until it proves its worth. Those theorists who suppose that it is language itself that dictates the sentences we seem to utter may be right in the case of the bacterial society, though they are wrong to think this true of humans! Second, there is evidence at least in the eusocial case that such creatures may even have languages of a more familiar sort: the only non-human animals, in fact, who have been shown to possess a complex, symbolic language of their own and so to be able to describe absent realities, are bees. What other eusocial lines might be able to do by way of representing reality and even recording reality or creating new sub-realities we

---

[43]    This may also be the moral of Naomi Mitchison's *Memoirs of a Space-woman* (London: Gollancz, 1962), where she explores the thoughts of a creature without bilateral symmetry. See my 'Deconstructing the Laws of Logic', *Philosophy* (82) 2008, pp. 25–53.

don't know.[44] But my aim, remember, is not to transform these alien sorts into anything like the human, but to allow for their development into something that can dominate a world and even be poised to transcend it.


## The Incarnate Word

Even creatures of a more familiar type may not be what we think them. 'A turkey is more occult and awful', so Chesterton remarked, 'than all the angels and archangels'.[45] We do not, cannot, know what it is like to be one, nor can we tell what insights into reality creatures like that may have. He exaggerated, no doubt, the difficulty: all earthly life is of one blood with us. But he was right to emphasise the Otherness of living creatures not of our kind. We hardly even know why dogs or horses willingly cooperate with us, nor what they are getting out of it. So can we conceive at least of the thought that the Great Galactics, so to speak, will turn out thus to be entirely Other, more distant even than eusocial insects or bacteria? To us they will look like rocks, or trees or cattle: whatever overt shape is most convenient at that time and place. But – by hypothesis – they will also contain the worlds, each modelling not only the world, but its origin. If we only knew the code we could read the history of all worlds in how they live. Is that not true? And if it is, doesn't that qualify them also as the images of a Creator?

On this account, the principle that governs all things and from which all possibilities take their beginning is as close to rocks, or trees or cattle as to us. Somewhere there is something, 'God', that is the real and final goal of all endeavour, the real standard of right conduct. Notoriously, we aren't obedient – or at least we feel we aren't. And this is what most humanists insist must make us 'more than animal', that we have a choice in what to do and be. Being *human* is being the sort of creature that has to *decide* what it is right to do[46] – and may often make mistakes. The mistakes made by the 'merely animal' are merely practical: missing a kill, or falling from a branch. Our mistakes are *practical* in the stronger, Aristotelian sense (a *praxis* is something done for a reason, which we can assess as good or bad): we do the wrong thing, thinking it is right, or failing to live by what we have decided. But why should this susceptibility to error be reckoned a mark of our 'superior' nature? It seems, on the contrary, to be a failure: a proof that we are not, after all, divine. If other creatures do exactly and entirely what they are meant to do, are they inferior? May they not be a better image, exactly, of what is meant to be?

---

[44]   For further insight into the life of eusocial creatures, see Bert Hölldobler and E.O. Wilson *The Superorganism: the beauty, elegance, and strangeness of insect societies* (New York: W.W. Norton, 2009).

[45]   G.K. Chesterton, *All Things Considered* (Methuen: London, 1908), p. 220.

[46]   Aristotle, *Nicomachean Ethics* 1.1098a3–18.

Philosophy can take us only a little way to truth. Or at any rate, I cannot – as a philosopher – see much beyond this conclusion. We should not expect that the God of Gods be *human*, nor that it is our kind of creature, whether the literally human or the larger sort deserving the title *hnau*, that will ever encompass the universe in thought, or be cosmic co-creators of the later days. The God of Gods, or whatever principle it is that governs things and is the good of all, may allow for human personality or personhood, but It is not confined by that. God's ways are not our ways. This doctrine is not as subversive of a more traditional religion as some moderns have supposed: on the contrary, it establishes one ancient theme. Really to serve God it may be necessary to put aside our preconceptions – even our preconceptions about what to do, or what we can expect from the real world. The God of Gods is more uncanny than we like to think it, and may in the end prefer beetles.

But it is possible to take one further step, not as a philosopher but as a believing Christian. The doctrine of the Incarnation is not the easier and more comfortable thought that moderns have sometimes made it: it is not the old delusion that actual humanity is now divine, and that all other forms of life and being, by the same doctrine, are inferior or subordinate. It is rather that humanity, as a particular form of life, has been taken up into the Godhead: *adopted* into life eternal. God is no more 'human' than He was: humanity has been alchemically, as it were, transmuted, at least in the person of the Lord Jesus Christ. Whatever other creatures we meet Out There, or here on earth, may be gathered into the dance of immortal love – as the pagan philosophers put it – by whatever means. We have been gathered in by an exceptional act of God – but not because we deserved it! According to the Muslim Brethren of Purity, putting their case for the non-human creation sometime in the tenth century AD, 'no finite being can reach out beyond the limits of its temporality and constitute its own character, as if to create itself', and so none have any right to boast of their own given nature.[47] Nor can we insist that *only* we, whether our biological lineage or the class to which we belong, have been invited to the dance. On the contrary, we are probably latecomers.

---

[47]   Brethren of Purity, *The Case of the animals against Man before the King of the Jinn* (Lenn E. Goodman and Richard McGregor, eds), (New York: Oxford University Press, 2009), p. 25.

# Afterword

In choosing a title for each biennial conference, the Committee of the British Society for the Philosophy of Religion aims for a theme sufficiently wide so as not to restrict speakers unduly, but also one sufficiently suggestive to stimulate reflection and encourage common threads between papers. For the 2011 conference, the Committee chose a trinity of problematic concepts: God, mind and knowledge. Their juxtaposition immediately suggests a series of questions. The nature and bounds of human knowledge are hard to define in most contexts, but in a religious context they are particularly so. Conceptions of the mind's relation to the physical world may be proposed outside any theological concerns, but once those concerns are raised, physicalist/dualist debates cannot but be informed by them. And what of the relation between human and divine minds? Should we stress the analogies between these, or the disanalogies? What are the consequences for our understanding of theological language? Finally, to what extent is God a product or projection of the human mind? Vital questions all, but they do not exhaust the range of issues thrown up by the conference title, which not only brings together three abstract concepts, but also three different disciplines: epistemology, philosophy of mind and philosophy of religion. How do developments in the first two disciplines affect the third?

Judging by the chapters in this volume, and other papers given at the conference but not represented here, the title did just what it was intended to, and we see here not only variety of theme, but also common threads.

The volume also illustrates the wider role and value of philosophy of religion. First, although both epistemology and philosophy of mind are typically conducted in wholly secular terms, the interactions illustrated here between those disciplines and theological concerns should encourage those whose main interests lie outside philosophy of religion to regard religious belief as an important case study. Second, as Andrew Moore points out in his fine introductory chapter, if cognitive science has revealed our hard-wired propensity to form religious – and perhaps specifically theistic – beliefs, then philosophy of religion is vital to our refining and controlling this propensity. Third, as evidenced by the different backgrounds of the conference delegates, philosophy of religion brings together in a common purpose different communities, inside and outside recognized religious and educational institutions. The issues here are not simply puzzle cases for the professional philosopher or theologian, but urgent matters which no one anxious to live a reasonably reflective life can be indifferent to.

It is a source of considerable gladness that we have a permanent memento of the conference in this second volume of the Ashgate BSPR series. Grateful thanks are due to the volume editor, Andrew Moore, who has brought it all together and added his own reflections, to the series editor, Harriet Harris, who brought the series into being, and to Ashgate, the publishers, for making it possible, and for their support and encouragement.

Looking ahead, we have in the title of the 2013 conference an intriguing contrast to those that have gone before: 'Atheisms'. The significance of the plural, as my successor Stephen Clark intended, will no doubt be appreciated by all who take part.

*Robin Le Poidevin*
*President, British Society for the Philosophy of Religion, 2009–11*

# Index